VIRGINIA AND THE PANIC OF 1819:
THE FIRST GREAT DEPRESSION AND THE COMMONWEALTH

FINANCIAL HISTORY

Series Editor: Robert E. Wright

VIRGINIA AND THE PANIC OF 1819: THE FIRST GREAT DEPRESSION AND THE COMMONWEALTH

BY
Clyde A. Haulman

Routledge
Taylor & Francis Group

LONDON AND NEW YORK

First published 2008 by Pickering & Chatto (Publishers) Limited

Published 2016 by Routledge
2 Park Square, Milton Park, Abingdon, Oxfordshire OX14 4RN
711 Third Avenue, New York, NY 10017, USA

First issued in paperback 2015

Routledge is an imprint of the Taylor & Francis Group, an informa business

BRITISH LIBRARY CATALOGUING IN PUBLICATION DATA
Haulman, Clyde A.
Virginia and the Panic of 1819: the first great depression and the Commonwealth.
– (Financial history)
1. Financial crises – United States – History – 19th century 2. Virginia –
Economic conditions – 19th century
I. Title
338.5'42

ISBN-13: 978-1-138-66363-3 (pbk)
ISBN-13: 978-1-85196-939-5 (hbk)

Typeset by Pickering & Chatto (Publishers) Limited

CONTENTS

ACKNOWLEDGEMENTS

Years ago as I explored contemporary writings regarding the economy and banking in the early republic, the Panic of 1819 continually appeared as an event of great importance to those who experienced the economic turmoil of the time. Yet, not much could be found that dealt substantively with the economy of the period or the underpinnings of the Panic. Douglass C. North, Murray Rothbard, Walter B. Smith and others provided important analysis and insights to the macroeconomic events, the policy impacts and the banking issues, but little could be found of the microeconomic aspects of the time and those studies that did relied primarily on contemporary observations. This led me to begin an in depth study of the Panic using Virginia data as a basis for answering some of the interesting microeconomic questions.

With interruptions for administrative duties at various levels at the College of William and Mary, a Fulbright in Hong Kong and service to the City of Williamsburg, work progressed slowly. Along the way many have contributed valuable time, effort, ideas and support to help the work develop. I am particularly indebted to Ed Perkins who saw value in the early work and helped make it better. Support from the College of William and Mary, the Virginia Foundation for the Humanities and the Center for the Study of Early America ensured that large portions of the work were completed. Peter Onuf, Jim Watkinson, Will Hausman, George Boyer, Howard Bodenhorn, Chandos Brown and Daniel Dupre all contributed at various stages as did Joe Rainer, Wade Schafer and Bob Wright who directed me to various sources. Presentations at meetings of the Economic History Association, The Society of the History of the Early Republic, the Washington Economic History Roundtable and the William and Mary American Studies Brownbag helped refine the analysis. A version of the Richmond commodity price index appeared in the *Journal of the Early Republic*. Series editor Bob Wright and anonymous referees contributed importantly to refining the final manuscript.

Margaret Cook and Susan Riggs of Manuscripts and Rare Books and Alan Zoellner, Government Information Librarian, at William and Mary's Swem Library provided invaluable assistance as did the staffs of the Library of Virginia,

Manuscripts and Archives, the University of Virginia's Alderman Library and the Virginia Historical Society.

My greatest debt however is to Fredrika J. Tuete who has supported and encouraged me and my work over our time together.

LIST OF CHARTS AND TABLES

INTRODUCTION

Bank panics and financial crises have been a staple of the United States economy for much of the nation's history. However, for many Americans at the beginning of the twenty-first century such economic crises are known only from history classes or from stories dredged out of the fading memories of parents and grandparents. Yet, within the last decade, events in Asia have demonstrated that the world is not free of the spectre of economic crisis stemming from problems originating in the financial sector. In addition, the near collapse of Long-Term Capital Management in 1998 brought the possibility of financial turmoil much closer than was comfortable for government officials, the financial community, and many American investors. Finally, the bursting of the stock market bubble in the late 1990s, the run-up of asset prices in the mid-2000s, particularly in housing markets, and growing concerns with unsustainable levels of debt continue to erode confidence in the economy. The nineteenth century, with its seemingly endless series of periodic financial panics and resulting economic distress, led Walter Bagehot, the English journalist and economist, to observe, 'Much has been written about panics and manias ... but one thing is certain, that at particular times a great deal of stupid people have a great deal of stupid money'. This money, he further suggested, is at intervals 'particularly large and carving; it seeks for someone to devour it, and there is a "plethora"; it finds someone, and there is "speculation"; it is devoured, and there is "panic"'.[1]

A great deal has been written about 'speculations' and 'panics' as forerunners of economic crises in the United States, particularly the many downturns of the post-Civil War nineteenth century and the Great Depression of the nineteen-thirties.[2] However, relatively little attention has been paid to what is arguably this country's first modern business cycle – the depression following the Panic of 1819. As historian Cathy Matson indicates, 'The Panic of 1819 was the first truly national depression American experienced, the first long-term financial crisis to prompt Americans to examine deeply their ideological moorings and reassess their still-fragile economic institution'.[3]

The purpose of this work is threefold. The first objective is to bring the Panic of 1819 and subsequent depression to the fore by undertaking an analysis of this important and underappreciated economic crisis from the perspective of one state, Virginia. The second purpose is to provide a thorough analysis of the Virginia economy of the period. Although much attention has been paid to the political history of Virginia in the period following the War of 1812, relatively little analysis has focused on the Commonwealth's economy of the period.[4] Thus, a study of Virginia's economy in this time period is long overdue. The final goal is to analyze the economic, social and political impacts of the Panic both for Virginia and for the nation.

Any analysis of the Panic and the Virginia economy will require reviewing and evaluating existing analysis of the Panic as well as searching out whatever information and data exists for the period. More importantly, it will require creating new data sets that will enable a more detailed and comprehensive analysis of the Panic and ensuing depression. This task will be accomplished in two stages. The first will use existing studies and data sources to provide an overview of the period and to compare the economic upheaval of the Panic and the following depression with other economic crises the United States has faced from the antebellum period through the 1930s. The second, and more important, stage will view the Panic of 1819 from the perspective of Virginia. Such an analysis will enable the construction of new data sets, particularly with regard to the Commonwealth's merchants, commodity prices, land values and poor relief system, and these data sets will yield unique and heretofore unavailable insights into the impact of the economic hard times in the wake of the Panic of 1819. It will also enable a comparison of Virginia during the Panic and the ensuing depression with what is known of events in other states and regions to determine in what ways the Commonwealth's experience was similar to or different from theirs.

The lack of attention to the Panic of 1819 to date is the result, in part, of the paucity of micro and macro data available for the time period. As one pair of authors suggest, 'data limitations prevent a detailed empirical analysis of the earliest panics'.[5] The lack of data has been a long standing rationale for ignoring early-nineteenth-century business cycles. Arthur F. Burns and Wesley C. Mitchell, in their groundbreaking studies of business cycles, occasionally refer to the cycles of the 1830s and use some data series that begin in the 1850s to establish cyclical turning points. However, most of their analysis is restricted to the period after 1878, a time for which data for the most important time series are available.[6] This has begun to change lately, and Chapter 2 will discuss recent works in detail. However, with one exception, these studies continue to ignore early cycles, including the Panic of 1819.

The tendency to ignore the Panic of 1819 is also, I believe, in part the result of the ease with which historians and economists have been able to point their pens at the role of the newly chartered Second Bank of the United States and thereby ignore or underemphasize the complexities of a post-Napoleonic War Atlantic economy.[7] For example, Charles Sellers suggests that the sharp contraction of credit begun by the Second Bank in the summer and fall of 1818 'saved the national Bank by sacrificing not only its debtors but the state banks and their hordes of debtors as well, which is to say, most of the market economy'.[8] Echoing this sentiment, Murray Rothbard in his study of the Panic indicates 'the Bank precipitated the Panic of 1819 by a series of deflationary moves'.[9] And, Samuel Rezneck's study of the depression of 1819–22 sees trouble 'precipitated by a sharp crisis in the affairs of the Second Bank' but that 'the collapse of the financial façade was the signal for, rather than the entire cause of, the rapid spread of distress and the mental attitudes characteristic of depression'.[10]

Economic theory has a critical role here, particularly in more recent analysis of the Panic. Commencing with the classic study of Unites States monetary history by Milton Friedman and Anna Jacobson Schwartz, monetarists stressing the role of the money supply have focused on banking panics 'because they view them as a major source of contractions in the money supply which, in turn, had led to severe contractions in aggregate economic activity in the United States'.[11] While broadening the scope of the monetarists, asymmetric information theory has continued to keep banks and their role in financial crises in the forefront. By emphasizing the 'differences in information available to different parties in a financial contract', the theory focuses on the impacts of adverse selection [the difficulty of distinguishing between good and bad borrowers, leading to credit rationing] and the agency problem [the moral hazard of borrowers engaging in 'activities that may be personally beneficial but will increase the probability of default'] and the way in which these two factors affect the ability of banks to perform their financial intermediary role.[12] Thus, banking panics not only affect economic activity through the drop in the money supply, but also by 'reducing the quality of certain financial services, primarily credit intermediation'.[13]

The Panic of 1819

This work will argue that the Panic of 1819 was America's first experience with a modern boom-bust cycle, and most importantly, that it was much more than a banking panic resulting from the mismanagement of the newly created Second Bank of the United States and a number of state- chartered banks. It was a complicated modern economic event involving the financial sector, international economic and political circumstances, and policy of the federal government. As Gary Browne, writing about the city of Baltimore, suggests, 'the events surrounding the panic of 1819 symbolized the end of one age and the beginning of another'.[14] The role of the Panic of 1819 as a fulcrum in the economic, political and social transformation of the new republic, particularly as seen through the lens of one state, Virginia, is the focus of this work.

Economic crises in the 1780s and 1790s and stagnant years following the Embargo had brought hard times to the new nation. However, the decade following 1815, including economic recovery after the War of 1812 and depression in the wake of the Panic of 1819, was very different from these earlier periods of economic distress.[15] The earlier downturns each could be traced to a particular event or events, and were more limited in the scope of their impacts on the early national economy. For example, Douglass North suggests that the 'unparalleled prosperity' of the years 1793–1808 was interrupted in 1797–8 and again in 1801–3 'by the external forces which had created it' – international trade and shipping.[16] Further, during the downturn of 1797–8 while prices fell 7 per cent and exports fell 8 per cent, imports rose 20 per cent for the period. These are quite mild when compared with changes in 1819–21. (See Table 2.3 below for data and sources.)

As will be demonstrated, the depression associated with the Panic of 1819 was very different from these earlier downturns. It will be argued that the depression of 1819–21 was the result of a complex set of economic and political circumstances involving changes in financial institutions and the operation of financial markets, foreign sector changes including the markets for American commodity exports and the carrying trade, and the beginnings of structural changes in the production and distribution of goods. These factors combined, in an economy very different from those earlier periods, to create a deflationary downturn which was much more severe, more pervasive and had greater social impacts than any of the earlier periods of economic distress.

Events surrounding 1819 were further complicated by a wave of intensified American nationalism and optimism following reports of Andrew Jackson's victory at New Orleans and news of peace from Ghent.[17] As a result, financial panic and depression coming on the heels of an expansion fuelled by optimism and foreign demands for American staples served to concentrate the new republic's attention on the economy. The energies the Revolutionary generation had directed to political theory and to problems of governance were now to be directed, with the help of an emerging new generation of political leaders, to questions regarding the nature of economic institutions. This focus on the economy was further intensified because increasing segments of society were being subjected to seemingly impersonal market forces. In addition, a liberal free trade ideology was emerging triumphant in the Northeast and South, clashing with protectionist sentiments among workers and industrialists, particularly in the Mid-Atlantic region.[18]

The goal here is to understand the origins, events and impacts of the Panic of 1819 nationally and in Virginia. From a national perspective, there is no recent overview of the Panic that provides a comprehensive compilation of available data, analyzes the complex factors involved in the Panic and the depression of 1818–21 and integrates the international perspective.[19] This work helps to rectify the situation by building upon and adding to previous works and by not only looking at the panic from a national perspective, but also considering the experience of one state, Virginia, in significant detail. As suggested earlier, the focus on a particular state will enable the development of new data sets needed to provide critical analysis of specific aspects of the economic crisis and to compare the depression following the Panic of 1819 with economic crises of other time periods and places. Virginia is chosen for two reasons. Because of the lack of data with which to analyze this period, constructing an adequate data base has to begin somewhere, and the state level appears to be the appropriate place to begin. Further, to the extent there are studies of the Panic, most either have focused on Philadelphia, New York and New England, or have relied heavily on contemporary reports from these areas. As a result, little is known about the economic, political and social impacts of this early economic crisis outside of these more economically developed areas. In particular, Virginia and the South have been largely ignored as studies of the state and region have concentrated on the critical periods closer to the Civil War.[20]

Plan of Study

The work is divided into three parts. The first provides an overview of the Panic of 1819 from a national perspective and compares the depression following the Panic with other depressions in the United States. Chapter 1 analyzes the years leading up to the Panic and how they set the stage for the downturn while Chapter 2 gives an economic overview of the Panic of 1819. The second part of this work examines various aspects of economic events in Virginia during the years of economic crisis. These include banking and government finance in Chapter 3 and agriculture, exports and land in Chapter 4. Chapters 5 and 6 consider the impacts of the Panic of 1819 in Virginia including changes in the business community, Chapter 5, and changes in the Commonwealth's system of poor relief, Chapter 6. In the final part, Chapter 7 analyzes the aftermath of the Panic in the Commonwealth and the nation economically, politically and socially, and provides a summary and conclusions.

1 THE ECONOMIC ORIGINS OF THE PANIC OF 1819

The year 1815 marked 'a transitional period in the American economy' according to the economic historian Douglass C. North. In his pioneering study of the antebellum American economy, *The Economic Growth of the United States, 1790–1860*, North stated that by the midpoint of the second decade of the century, 'it was clear that the Atlantic economy and its components were very different from the western world of 1790'. For much of the period between 1790 and 1815 Europe had been at war, and rapid American economic development of the time 'reflected our ability to take advantage of this war'. In addition, the almost fifty years following the end of the second war with Britain were ones of peace dominated by the tremendous expansion of an Atlantic economy 'in which artificial national barriers to the free movement of goods, services, productive resources, and ideas were being relaxed', and in which 'the "anonymous" impersonal forces of the evolving international market were the basic influences'.[21]

To understand the American economy and the transitions it experienced during the first thirty-five years of the new republic's existence, and in particular to assess the role of the Panic of 1819 in these transitions, it will be helpful to review the nature and process of economic change, domestic and international, in the years between the establishment of the Constitution and the end of the War of 1812. With this background in place, it will be possible to see the economic fortunes of the nation from the view of those who celebrated the Treaty of Ghent in 1815, witnessed the establishment of the Second Bank of the United States in 1816, and experienced the calamity of the Panic of 1819 three years later. It will also enable us to comprehend the nature of the postwar economy and appreciate the complexities faced by the Bank as it attempted to stabilize the monetary system. Finally, this background will help us begin identifying the origins of the Panic of 1819 and evaluating the role of various factors in generating America's first great depression.

The American Economy, 1790–1815

Economic changes providing the framework for the crisis of 1819 began with economic expansion in the late eighteenth and early nineteenth centuries, continued as the impacts of the Embargo (1807) and Non-Intercourse Acts (1809) were felt across the economy, and culminated as the War of 1812 further transformed the emerging national economy.[22] Trade-based economic development of the period 1793–1807 began to give way when the Embargo of 1807 encouraged the first important wave of investment in manufacturing. The Non-Intercourse Acts provided an additional spark for this nascent structural change.[23] For example, business incorporations in the states of New York, New Jersey, Pennsylvania and Maryland, which had averaged twenty-six per year for the period 1800–6, jumped to fifty-four new firms per year in 1807–11 with a peak of eighty-three in 1811.[24] Cotton spindles which stood at 8,000 in 1807 rose to 87,000 by 1810 and to 130,000 in 1815, while the number of bales of cotton used in factories rose from an estimated 10,000 in 1810 to 90,000 in 1815.[25] In Philadelphia, the value of manufactured goods increased from approximately $10 million in 1809 to $16 million in 1811 and by the latter date the city had 273 looms, four woolen mills, seventeen carriage shops, twenty-eight soap and candle works, seven paper mills, ten sugar refineries, twenty naileries, twenty-four brush factories, and three glass works. Steam engines and cotton machinery were also manufactured in the city.[26] The employment and income resulting from such growth helped provide a domestic market to replace partially the loss of foreign markets for American agricultural goods.

Additional changes in the period's economy came as the result of Congress's failure, by one vote, to renew the charter of the First Bank of the United States in 1811. Following an initial surge in bank incorporations in the last decade of the eighteenth century and beginning of the nineteenth, the growth of state banking slowed, particularly from 1807 to 1811. During this period the number of banks increased 30 per cent, from seventy-eight to 101, and their aggregate capital grew from $43.4 million to $66.3 million, a 53 per cent increase. The First Bank exercised control over state banks by means of the rapid presentation of their notes for redemption in specie. With such a quasi-central bank no longer in the picture, the number of state-chartered banks almost doubled in the years 1811–15, rising to 181, an 79 per cent increase. Bank capital in the period jumped to $115.2 million, reflecting a 74 per cent increase.[27]

The War of 1812 further accelerated structural economic change in the young nation. As the British Navy closed American ports, foreign trade became the domain of neutral ships and the level of both imports and exports declined dramatically, falling to $20 million and $11 million respectively in 1814 from prewar highs of $110 million and $117 million and pre-Embargo highs of $167 million and $162 million, respectively. Given the fall in imports, the major source of government revenues, customs receipts, also dropped. For example, in Philadelphia customs receipts fell from an average of about $300,000 per month in 1811 to some $25,000 per month in 1813.[28] Table 1.1 provides foreign trade and customs receipts data for the period 1800–25. In addition, net American shipping earnings, which had peaked at $42.1 million in 1807 and had been as high as $39.5 million and $40.8 million in 1810 and 1811 respectively, fell precipitously during the war.[29] With foreign supplies curtailed, prices rose dramatically with one index jumping from 131 in 1812 to a level of 193 in December 1814, a 47 per cent increase.[30] And, inflation was not just an East Coast phenomenon. An index of Ohio Valley prices rose 58 per cent, from seventy-seven in 1812 to 122 in 1814, while prices of commodities identified with northern agriculture rose 60 per cent in the same period.[31]

Another aspect of war's impact on the economy was the problem of federal finance.[32] Congress made no provision for financing the war, expecting normal revenues and loans to suffice. As tariff revenues declined, the government turned to bond and Treasury note issues. Between 1812 and 1814 Congress authorized bond issues of $61 million but obtained only $45.2 million – $7.9 million at par, the rest at discounts from eighty-eight to eighty per hundred. In addition, the Treasury lost further because many of the bank notes received for the stock were depreciated, particularly after August 1814 when the British captured Washington and specie payments were suspended through much of the nation, New England being the exception. Treasury notes were equally problematic. Of the $35.5 million authorized between mid-1812 and the end of 1814 only $17.2 million were issued. Because of provisions that these notes could be used to pay duties, taxes and debts due the government, they quickly flowed back to the Treasury. Secretary George W. Campbell found it impossible to keep circulation over $6 million, and the department was kept busy redeeming and issuing. Finally in November 1814 the Treasury could not pay interest on notes held in Massachusetts and failed to redeem on time $1.9 million of notes in Boston, New York and Philadelphia. This led to a new Treasury secretary and several attempts to charter a national bank, all unsuccessful.[33]

But, not all economic aspects of the war were bad. Business incorporations, which had averaged 54 per year in 1807–11 and peaked at 83 in 1811, grew to 100 per year during the war with a peak of 157 incorporations in 1814.[34] Cotton factories, which were established at a rate of 6.4 per year between 1807 and 1811, appeared at the rate of thirty-one per year in the war years 1812–1814, and cotton and wool manufactures in New Hampshire, Vermont, Massachusetts, Connecticut, New York and New Jersey incorporated at a rate of sixty-three per year, up from an average of fourteen per year 1807–11.[35] Thus, manufacturing that started as a result of trade restrictions stemming from embargo received an even stronger push from the war.

The years between the Embargo and the Treaty of Ghent began a crucial transformation of the new republic's economy. An emerging manufacturing sector, interruptions of traditional trade flows, and issues regarding the role of government, particularly with respect to a national bank and tariff protection, became the focus of debate and policy as the economy moved beyond 1815.

The American Economy, 1815–18

News of the Treaty of Ghent brought great celebration to a war-weary and economically strapped citizenry. In New York City, festivities went on for more than a week as artisans 'snake-danced tipsy through the streets, their paths lit by shimmering transparencies, of eagles and dollars spilling from a cornucopia'.[36] And for much of the economy the next few years would in fact bring dollars flowing as one measure of real output increased almost 18 per cent from 1815 to 1818.[37] Those parts of the early national economy tied to domestic activity, and particularly to the opening of the old southwest and to western movement generally, did very well. Export trade, domestic trade and transportation, real estate and public land speculation, shipbuilding and western river steamboat construction, and finance including banking, insurance, and the stock market all prospered as the national economy grew and national markets coalesced. According to Walter B. Smith and Arthur H. Cole, 'price indexes for domestic goods in the four big Atlantic seacoast markets came into coincidence in the second quarter of 1817 ... the Atlantic seacoast was once more a unified market for staple products'.[38]

However, not all sectors of the economy shared in the flow of dollars generated by a peacetime economy. The emerging national market and general good times did not benefit manufacturing, the re-export trade, and international shipping. The infant manufacturing sector was mostly overwhelmed by intense British competition, re-exports suffered as the British West Indies were closed to American ships, and intense competition in international freight carrying drove freight rates through the floor, crippling American shipping interests.[39]

To better understand the complex economic developments in this period and how they provided a foundation for the crisis of 1819, several areas of the economy require a closer look. The first is international trade. Stagnant trade of the previous seven years exploded following the Treaty of Ghent. The reintroduction of trade started almost immediately upon news of peace arriving in New York in February 1815. One source indicates that from March through September of that year more than $46 million of domestic products left American ports, giving employment to more than 850 thousand tons of American shipping.[40] Table 1.1 provides trade data for the period.

This was also a time of very favourable terms of trade for the United States, reflecting the increase in American export prices pushed by British and Continental demand and the decline of import prices as British goods flooded the American market. Export prices rose because poor crop yields in Great Britain and Europe increased demand for American agricultural staples, while weather problems in the United States limited supply for the export market.[41] As a result, the value of exports increased much more than did the physical quantities. In addition, exceptionally high demand for cotton further pushed American export prices up in spite of significant increases in cotton production.[42] After adjusting for specie flows, freight earnings, ship sales, insurance and interest, North estimates that the negative trade balances in 1815–18 led to the following annual capital inflows (in millions of dollars): $15.2, $58.1, $10.5 and $25.2[43] with British merchant bankers and factors providing the financing for these increases in overseas debts.[44]

Factors creating this situation include changes in British business conditions; crop yields in America, Britain and on the Continent; the dumping of British manufactured goods; and changes in the American system of distributing goods. In addition, the Tariff of 1816 was mildly protective, particularly with the proviso that coarse cotton cloth, defined as all cotton goods priced less than twenty-five cents per yard, was to be valued for duty purposes at twenty-five cents per yard. The object was to keep cheap East Indian cloth out of the country and thus prevent it from competing with American output.[45]

The British economy experienced substantial prosperity during the war with the United States, and with the defeat of Napoleon a further boom began, interrupted by the Hundred Days, but picking up again following the final victory at Waterloo. A sharp slowdown in late 1816 and early 1817 marred the nation's prosperity leading to the Spa Fields riots, but by mid-1817 a vigorous recovery based largely on foreign trade had begun and continued strongly through 1818. Table 1.2 provides data on the British economy for the years 1815–18.[46]

Britain experienced a 'handsome harvest in 1815', but the next year saw a failure of the wheat crop and below-average yields in barley and oats. Poor crops in 1817 intensified Britain's agricultural problems.[47] As a result of poor yields and subsequent price rises, the Corn Law of 1815 allowed foreign grain into Britain from late 1816 through most of 1817. Ports were closed briefly towards the end of 1817 as prices fell on an erroneous assumption of a solid harvest. However, by early 1818 grain importation was allowed again, and 'the greatest importation of grain in any single year of British history up to that time took place'.[48] The impact on the value of corn imports, on the quantity of wheat and flour imports, and on US grain imports is clear in Table 1.2. The years 1816–1817 also produced 'poor harvests on the continent'. The 1816 harvest in France was so bad that it was regarded as 'actual famine' by one observer.[49] France was in such a critical state 'that a considerable quantity of corn was shipped from England'.[50] In addition, the 'crisis tended toward a deeper level of stress' in the German lands, while in the Hapsburg Monarchy 'famine conditions became widespread and no province escaped lightly', and Switzerland experienced a 'true famine with deaths from starvation'.[51] Table 1.3 provides data regarding French imports of provisions and gives some sense of the slowness of economic recovery on the Continent.

Like their British counterparts, American farmers enjoyed an excellent harvest in 1815. The next three years, however, were all below average, with the wheat crop failing in 1816.[52] In part, the problems of this period were the result of unusual weather conditions. Writing to Albert Gallatin, Thomas Jefferson commented, 'The summer of 1816 was unseasonably cool – as cold indeed as a moderate winter. Killing frost continued into late May. A severe drought that lasted throughout the summer, followed by another frost in August and torrential rains in September, had a devastating effect on the crops.'[53] The result was that the problems with British and European agricultural output combined in the years 1816–18 with relatively slow growth in US farm output to drive up the demand for US staples which meant, in turn, higher prices for American produce. The final factor affecting American agriculture was the re-imposition of the British colonial system following the end of hostilities in 1815. Although some sectors of the economy expected to benefit from trade with the British West Indies once the war was ended, the closing of those ports to American ships and the American response of a new navigation act in 1818 closing US ports to British ships dashed those hopes and devastated important sectors of the economy.[54]

A second economic sector of particular importance in the years before the Panic was American manufacturing, which had its real beginnings in the period between the Embargo and the end of the War of 1812. However, once trade was re-established, British merchants began dumping goods in the American market with the effect of both destroying much of the nation's fledgling manufacturers and initiating a process of revolutionizing the way business was carried out in the United States. Data regarding manufacturing incorporations in the states of New York, New Jersey and Maryland in Table 1.4 indicate the spurt of manufacturing growth during the war and its collapse following the Treaty of Ghent. Anticipating the signing of a peace treaty, British merchants had dispatched ships loaded with goods for the American market to stock warehouses at Halifax and Bermuda. The ultimate goal was the New York market. According to Robert G. Albion, the choice of New York by British merchants and manufacturers was a deliberate attempt to destroy local competition.[55] However, more important were changes in the British factory system, with strong competition encouraging manufacturers to lower costs by taking full advantage of scale economies. This led to excess goods in the domestic market, and foreign dumping grounds, particularly the United States, became attractive options.[56]

With British goods inundating the American market, traditional market mechanisms and relationships dominated by established mercantile firms become overburdened. Thus, the auction system was utilized to dispose of excess goods quickly, and in the process it speeded the remittance of funds and enabled manufacturers to increase output on speculation. Soon auction rooms at Baltimore,

Boston, Philadelphia and particularly New York became sites of intense activity. Although the primary reason for adopting an auction system was to dump excess production as British manufacturers exploited the factory system's scale econo- mies, auctions also provided a mechanism through which false invoices could be used to circumvent tariffs. For example, a manufacturer might sell goods to an agent below costs; the agent would then clear the goods with an American consul at a port of shipment, thus establishing tariff changes. Once clear of customs in the United States, goods were sold to a second agent with a correct price invoice and then taken to the auction room for sale.[57] For the manufacturers and their agents, 'nothing could have been more convenient; the goods paid a low duty, and the agent was spared all the expenses of warehouse rent, clerk hire, and merchant license tax'.[58] Reliance on the auction system also emphasized the importance of credit to the auction houses, rural retailers and wholesale jobbers – those who put together packages of goods for marketing to country retailers. With auctions driving prices down to cost, 'the credit offered to finance the sales provided the jobber or auction house its margin of profit'.[59]

The auction market grew through 1818, when activity peaked at $13.5 mil- lion, and became so dominant that by 1820 one observer suggested that 'business is now so completely systemized that a great proportion of the goods which are consumed in the country are specially manufactured on the other side of the water for Auction'.[60] Throughout this period, a steady flow of memorials and tracts primarily from American importers pointed out the evils of the system. However, in addition to lowering prices, the auction system 'served to introduce new goods, it assisted in forming new tastes on the part of the consumer, and it forced the importing merchants ... to the greatest degree of efficiency, while it probably introduced ... elements of competition and of economy which had never been known before'.[61]

Additional factors affecting the economy in the years 1815–18 included changes in the banking system, federal fiscal policy and the government's land policies, with the latter contributing importantly to the speculative fever of the times. The intense demand for land, pentup during the war and now released as settlers swarmed west, in turn created additional demands for credit from the state-chartered banks. The tremendous volume of land sales also created a flow of bank notes from West to East that generated problems for the federal govern- ment and the banking system. First, the banking system. State-chartered banks continued to expand in the years after the war, and by 1818 their number had grown to 237, a 31 per cent increase over 1815. With public land sales jumping dramatically in 1814–16, see Table 1.5, the Department of the Treasury became concerned because revenue from those sales was mostly in the form of depreciated bank notes from the West and Southwest, while much federal spending occurred in the East where bank notes were more sound.[62] This situation, combined with a growing federal surplus from both land sales and customs revenue, the prospect of a number of federal bond issues maturing in the next few years, and the false belief that the absence of a national bank had made it difficult to raise funds for the war, led Congress to create the Second Bank of the United States in 1816.[63] The first order of business for the new Second Bank was to restore all the nation's currency to par by requiring state banks to resume specie payments. Facing some reluctance by state banks, the Second Bank negotiated an agreement whereby it would expand discounts by $6 million in exchange for the resumption of convertability. Although the process was not completely successful, the discipline of convertability led state banks to restrict their notes and deposits from a total of $67.6 million at the end of 1816 to $60.4 million a year later. However, this was more than made up for by the $20.6 million expansion of the Second Bank's notes and deposits leading to a total expansion of the banking system's money supply of almost 20 per cent for the year 1817.[64] The initial actions as well as subsequent moves of the Second Bank have direct relevance to the Panic of 1819 and will be dealt with in Chapters 2 and 3. Further exacerbating the monetary picture in the years after 1815 were attempts by European countries to return to a specie standard. These efforts meant 'every country was trying to build up gold and silver reserves' thus placing intense pressure on the world's specie supply.[65]

Following a surge in activity beginning in 1814, public land sales continued to expand, jumping again in 1816 before taking off and reaching a peak of some 3.4 million acres in 1818. Table 1.5 provides data regarding acres sold and receipts for the years 1810–25. With the end of the War of 1812 and the closing of the threat posed by the British and by Native American tribes, westward movement began in earnest, propelled by the prospect of enormous gains as cotton and other staple prices rose rapidly. The credit system for purchasing public land was established in 1796 and was operational until 1820, with various changes along the way. Liberal credit policies incorporated in the Act of 1800 enabled purchasers to put down one-quarter of the purchase price within forty days, with another quarter due in two years and the balance in four years.[66] Such terms combined with the land auction system helped to raise the fever among speculators.[67] Moreover, with Congress passing debtor relief acts on a regular basis [twelve acts were passed between 1806 and 1820], speculation in western lands became a regular part of life in some quarters. The amount owed to the federal government rose from about $3 million in 1815 to $17 million in 1819.[68]

Revenues from land sales were driven by the rapid westward movement of population and the intense speculation of Americans hoping to benefit from the tremendous growth in the West. Combined with increased custom revenues resulting from the boom in imports, these land sales enabled the federal government to resume retiring the public debt. In 1816, 1817 and 1818, respectively, the government reduced the federal debt by $3.8 million, $20.0 million and $7.9 million.[69] Because a significant component of this debt was owed to foreigners, the federal government's actions sent funds overseas and likely helped to mitigate inflationary effects of the second Bank's expansion of loans and deposits.[70]

The impact of economic change in the years leading up to the Panic of 1819 was varied. Prices for American exports tended to rise, while prices of imported goods fell; the net effect was mildly rising prices. While much of the economy boomed, manufacturing, the re-export trade and international shipping suffered. The resulting increase in unemployment hit hard, particularly in cities and in the Northeast. In New York, for example, the number of persons in debtors prison jumped from ninety-five in 1816 to 300 in 1817, and during 1817 'more than fifteen thousand persons, about one-seventh of the city's population required some sort of public or private charity relief'.[71] Other regions would experience these increased demands for relief in the years to come.

Virginia, 1800–15

In his 1799 account of travels in the United States, the Duc de La Rochefoucauld-Liancourt described the Richmond economy in the following words: 'The trade of this town consists in the purchase of the country products, and in selling at second hand the articles of domestic consumption, which are generally produced in England'. Elaborating further, he indicated, 'The commission trade may be considered as the real business of the place' and provided details of relations with Norfolk and the hinterland as well as the financing of trade. Importantly, he noted that 'Richmond merchants supply all the stores through an extensive tract of back country'.[72]

In addition to capturing the commercial heart of the capital city's economy, La Rochefoucauld-Liancourt's journal made clear the critical role that staple crop production played in the state's economy. He also noted the beginnings of manufacturing in Richmond, a sector that would become increasingly important as the nineteenth century developed. Commenting about one of Richmond's two flour mills, he observed, 'It is a fine mill, and unites the advantages of all the new inventions'. Finally, La Rochefoucauld-Liancourt described the canal bypassing the falls of the James River, a critical component of the transportation infrastructure so important to moving staples to market and for subsequent export.[73]

While agriculture dominated the Commonwealth's economy and commerce, in Richmond at the beginning of the nineteenth century the roots were already present for three industries, tobacco manufacturing, flour milling, and coal and iron, that would come to define the state's manufacturing future. Tobacco had been the central focus of the colonial Virginia economy and it continued to be a critical component of the state's economy in the nineteenth century. For example, in 1817 and 1818 Virginia was the nation's leading tobacco producer and the source of almost 30 per cent of all US tobacco exports. In 1820, according to the census, twenty-five tobacco manufacturing firms with an average of thirty-five workers each, eighteen slave and seventeen free, were operating in Richmond while Petersburg had forty-seven tobacco screws working and Chesterfield County had seven stemming factories employing 227 men to produce 1.3 million pounds of tobacco.[74]

Flour milling was the second industry to become increasingly important for Virginia's and the nation's economic prosperity. The late-eighteenth-century mills described by La Rochefoucauld-Liancourt grew to 'three sizable Richmond flour producers between 1809 and 1818' and the 1820 census of manufacturing shows hundreds of mills scattered across the state. Some insight to the industry of this period is provided by an 1831 report to the House of Delegates. The document reported that Richmond's five mills' 'leading objective, when employed, is to supply the South American markets'. Meanwhile, Richmond's 'canal flour', the product 'of country mills, whether brought to market by land or water transportation', was shipped from Richmond 'mostly to northern and eastern towns in the United States, and occasionally to Europe'. Flour from 'country mills accounted for about two-thirds of the 242,916 barrels inspected in Richmond during the year 1831'.[75]

The third industry upon which Richmond built its antebellum manufacturing strength was linked to coal and iron. 'The city of Richmond, in Virginia', according to Tench Coxe in his 1794 *A View of the United States of America*, is one of the two 'scenes in the Atlantic counties ... in which coal, iron and waterfalls are yet found in abundance'. As a result, Coxe believed the city 'may be considered in a permanent view as having an incontestable advantage over any more northern sea-port' in the area of iron manufacturing.[76] Coal had been discovered early in the eighteenth century in the Richmond area, and the output of Virginia's mines came to be the primary supply for northern cities and emerging American industry in the first quarter of the nineteenth century. As industrial demands for low-sulphur coal increased, Pennsylvania's anthracite coal overtook the Richmond area's bituminous coal in 1828, although the Virginia product remained a strong competitor until the Civil War. Table 1.6 provides data regarding Richmond coal field production from 1800 to 1825. With abundant coal resources and the James River linking the area to pig iron furnaces to the west, Richmond became the site of a cannon and arms foundry completed in 1809. Although ultimately unsuccessful, the initial attempt to manufacture iron set the stage for the Bellona Foundry, established in 1816 and located twelve miles west of the city.[77]

Although by 1815 Richmond was Virginia's most important commercial and manufacturing centre, other areas of the state saw important economic sectors develop in the early decades of the nineteenth century. For example, naval stores and shipbuilding strengthened Norfolk's economy and port activities through this period. As early as 1795, Norfolk was seen as a booming port. According to La Rochefoucauld-Liancourt, the backcountry products shipped to Petersburg and Richmond by land were subsequently transported to Norfolk by barge for export. 'Thus, this port practically monopolizes the commerce of all Virginia from the Rappahannock, and that of North Carolina well beyond the Roanoke.'[78] Unfortunately, much of this trade was with the West Indies and the combination of European wars, the Embargo, the War of 1812 and the closing of the British West Indies following the Treaty of Ghent meant that Norfolk would not fulfill its potential as a major port city for decades.[79] In the western part of the state, known as the Trans-Allegheny, salt works and tanning became important enterprises while small furnaces and iron works dotted the countryside through the Shenandoah Valley. Finally, flour mills of all sizes could be found across much of the state. Table 1.7 provides a list of the state's counties by region.

Despite these developments in manufacturing and commerce, agriculture continued to overwhelmingly dominate the Commonwealth's economic picture. The 1820 census enumerated the number of Virginians engaged in agriculture, commerce or manufacturing. According to this count, in the Eastern District, east of the Allegheny Mountains, 88.1 per cent of those working in the three sectors were engaged in agriculture while in the Western District of the state the figure was 94.0 per cent.[80] Thus, for all the commercial and manufacturing growth during the first two decades of the century, the Commonwealth primarily remained an agricultural producer with a large enslaved labor force.

Table 1.8 shows Virginia's total, white, enslaved and free black populations from 1800 to 1830 and indicates decennial per centage changes in each component. By 1820, many Virginians had become concerned about the declining proportion of whites, the steady increase in the proportion of enslaved blacks despite the more than 50,000 enslaved individuals transported 'from the Chesapeake to the new states of Mississippi and Alabama during the decade between 1810 and 1820', and the rapid growth in the free black population. Further, the distribution of enslaved people meant 'Virginia was actually two slave states'. East of the Blue Ridge was 'a slave society with proportions of African Americans similar to the states of the Cotton South', while west of the mountains 'slaves formed a small minority' of the labor force. This distinction bred an important intrastate sectionalism that would come to dominate Virginia politics and in the East created 'a distinctly conservative attachment to the social order and, in many planters, a stubborn resistance to change'. In the aftermath of the Panic these differences would play an important role, particularly with respect to poor relief.[81]

Virginia, 1815–18

In the aftermath of the War of 1812, Virginians were not immune to the surge in optimism that swept the nation. In 1815 and again in 1816, the Virginia General Assembly directed its federal representatives to request that Congress 'manifest an interest in internal improvements'.[82] In 1816 the state's legislature created the Fund for Internal Improvements and a Board of Public Works to manage the Fund. Designed to 'provide the proper incentive for private action', the Fund was capitalized at $1,251,761, including 'the state's small existing investment in improvement companies' and 'a substantial amount of bank stock owned by the state, together with any future "bonuses" for the extension, modification or creation of bank charters'.[83] Governor James A. Preston expressed the optimism of the era in his address to the 1817 General Assembly. On the national level, Preston suggested that the republic 'no longer groans under the horrors of a relentless, vindicative, and cruel war. Her councils are undisturbed by the turmoils of passion and violence; and that Hydra, party spirit, is no longer seen to rear its baneful head among us'. Government, according to Preston, was 'prosperous, and between every department there prevails a perfect cordiality'. Furthermore, 'the reign of reason and justice, and of intellectual power, is again acknowledged and restored'. In the economic sphere, Preston believed that 'the agriculturist is in the full enjoyment of the abundant fruits of his toil; the mechanic is rapidly increasing in wealth by his labour and industry; the merchant reaps the advantage of a widely extended and almost unlimited commerce, and receives the just reward of his enterprise'.[84] All was well with the Commonwealth.

However, Virginia's initial optimism, boosted by record tobacco prices in 1816 and a strong export market for wheat and flour in 1817, faded as prices began to fall and foreign markets dried up. The blow to the Commonwealth's optimism was exacerbated when the return to specie convertability pressed by the Second Bank of the United States tightened credit across the state. Details regarding the state's agricultural economy and banking will be provided in Chapters 3 and 4. Virginia's spirit of nationalism also began to wane in light of new federal programs. They consisted of 'a strong navy to protect the nation and prevent the destruction of its coasting trade, a protective tariff to encourage the development of essential industries, a system of roads and canals to facilitate the exchange of goods between the parts of the nation, and a national bank to stabilize and supply currency for business transactions'.[85] In particular, the new tariff schedule was seen as damaging to the Commonwealth's interest, and the re-establishment of a national paper-money-issuing bank was difficult for many hard-money Virginians to accept. By the time of the 1817 congressional elections, many of Virginia's older political leaders were being replaced by younger men 'set against the Clay-Calhoun policies of nationalism and ambitious to restore the fallen prestige of Virginia'.[86]

With the stage set for a resurgence of states' rights and strict construction, the Panic of 1819 helped seal the fate of the Commonwealth. The economic hardship created by the depression exacerbated the troubles created by British trade policy and the American response in the form of navigation acts. Thus, the Panic of 1819 provided additional rationale for disengagement from an interventionist role for the state and cemented Virginia's opposition to nationalist policies.

Summary and Conclusions

Data from the US, Britain and Europe show that the return to peace and subsequent expansion of the Atlantic economy after 1815 spurred rapid growth in the American economy and that of the Commonwealth of Virginia. Although not all sectors of the national economy benefited equally from newly opened trade, and although British navigation laws continued to restrict trade important to the nation's economy, the national and Virginia economies experienced significant growth. Led by agricultural commodities, the booming economy encouraged westward movement that resulted in significant speculation in land and further added to the inflationary pressures already present from the War of 1812. The establishment of the Second Bank of the United States with its restructuring of the banking system and return to specie convertibility further complicated the picture. Efforts by European nations to re-establish a specie standard added further contractionary pressure on the specie supply. As the American economy edged towards the end of the decade, each of these factors played a critical role in creating the economic crisis known as the Panic of 1819 and, more importantly, in initiating the subsequent economic depression.

Tables

Table 1.1: United States Imports, Exports, Re-Exports and Customs Reciepts, 1800–25.

Year	Imports	Exports	Re-Exports	Customs Receipts	Federal Debt
			(millions of current dollars)		
1800	108	107	39	9.1	83.0
1801	132	134	47	10.6	80.7
1802	91	98	36	12.4	77.1
1803	80	88	14	10.5	86.0
1804	102	114	36	11.1	82.3
1805	144	134	53	12.9	75.7
1806	155	148	60	14.7	69.2
1807	167	162	60	15.8	65.2
1808	71	55	13	16.4	57.0
1809	76	88	21	7.3	53.2
1810	110	117	24	8.6	48.0
1811	78	114	16	13.3	45.2
1812	96	75	8	9.0	55.9
1813	30	45	3	13.2	81.5
1814	20	11	0	6.0	99.8
1815	96	81	7	7.3	127.3
1816	163	105	17	36.3	123.5

Year	Imports	Exports	Re-Exports	Customs Receipts	Federal Debt
			(millions of current dollars)		
1817	113	103	19	26.3	103.5
1818	141	116	19	17.2	95.5
1819	105	91	19	20.3	91.0
1820	84	84	18	15.0	90.0
1821	72	76	11	13.0	93.5
1822	92	83	11	17.6	90.8
1823	87	89	21	19.2	90.3
1824	90	90	18	17.9	83.8
1825	106	112	24	20.1	81.1

Source: *Historical Statistics of the United States: Colonial Times to 1970* (Washington, DC: Bureau of the Census, 1975), Series U-1, U-8, U-192, Y-353 and Y-338.

Table 1.2: British Economic Activity, 1815–23.

Year	Business Activity, 1821–5=100	Industrial Production Hoffman Index 1913 = 100	Total	Corn	Wheat /Flour	Grain US	Prices
					Imports		
1815	72.9	9.0	33.0	396	na	na	144.3
1816	66.5	9.2	27.4	406	210.9	na	128.3
1817	74.4	9.5	30.8	2196	1034.4	316.4	130.7
1818	91.1	9.8	36.9	3914	1589.1	187.6	133.9
1819	79.8	10.0	30.8	1613	471.8	47.7	120.3
1820	80.8	10.0	32.4	1388	593.1	91.9	108.7
1821	81.7	11.0	30.8	273	137.7	38.5	101.8
1822	89.4	11.0	30.5	116	47.6	6.2	100.2
1823	97.8	12.0	35.8	41	24.0	4.2	99.3

Imports: Total: official value, millions of Pounds Sterling
Corn: thousands of Pounds Sterling
Wheat and Flour: 1,000 quarters
Grain US: 1,000 quarters
Prices: monthly average of 1821–5 = 100
na = not available

Sources: A. D. Gayer, W. W. Rostow and A. J. Schwartz, *The Growth and Fluctuation of the British Economy, 1790–1850* (Oxford: Clarendon, 1953), pp. 145n, 151, 354; B. R. Mitchell, *European Historical Statistics, 1750–1970* (London: Macmillan, 1975), p. 355; B. R. Mitchell, *Abstract of British Historical Statistics* (Cambridge: Cambridge University Press, 1971), pp. 282, 470 and J. R. McCulloch, *A Dictionary of Commerce and Commerical Navigation*, ed. H. Vathake, 2 vols (Philadelphia, PA: Thomas Wardle, 1841), vol. 1, p. 507.

Table 1.3: European Economic Activity, 1815–23.

Year	Industrial Production 1913 = 100	France Imports Total	Provisions	Iron	Austria Wool	Cotton
		millions of francs		value added in millions of 1913 kronea		
1800				9.3	na	7.4
1802				9.7	na	8.1
1803				8.6	na	9.1
1815	19.2	199	85	na	49.5	na
1816	19.5	243	108	na	na	na
1817	19.9	332	164	na	na	na
1818	21.3	336	145	na	na	na

Year	Industrial Production 1913 = 100	France Imports Total	Provisions	Iron	Austria Wool	Cotton
		millions of francs		value added in millions of 1913 kronea		
1819	19.5	295	141	9.0	52.4	6.2
1820	20.7	335	153	10.6	56.2	8.1
1821	21.9	394	na	9.7	59.2	8.1
1822	21.4	426	na	10.2	na	8.8
1823	20.2	362	na	10.7	54.6	7.2

na = not available

Sources: Mitchell, *European Historical Statistics*, pp. 355, 487; J. D. Post, *The Last Substance Crisis in the Western World* (Baltimore, MD: Johns Hopkins University Press, 1977), p. 156; J. Komlos, *The Hapsburg Monarchy as a Customs Union: Economic Development in Austria-Hungary in the Nineteenth Century* (Princeton, NJ: Princeton University Press, 1983), p. 110.

Table 1.4: Manufacturing Incorporations:
New York, New Jersey and Maryland, 1808–20.

Year	Number of Incorporations New York	New Jersey	Maryland
1808	1	0	1
1809	8	1	0
1810	15	9	1
1811	24	1	0
1812	15	0	1
1813	33	1	0
1814	46	4	2
1815	20	4	5
1816	11	1	5
1817	5	0	1
1818	5	0	0
1819	1	0	1
1820	1	0	0

Source: G. H. Evans, *Business Incorporations in the United States, 1800–1943* (New York: National Bureau of Economic Research, 1948), p. 17.

Table 1.5: Public Land Sales and Receipts, 1810–25.

Year	Acres (thousands)	Receipts (thousands of dollars)
1810	285.8	607.9
1811	575.1	1,216.4
1812	386.1	829.4
1813	505.6	1,066.4
1814	1,176.1	2,462.9
1815	1,306.4	2,713.4
1816	1,742.5	3,692.7
1817	1,886.2	4,478.8
1818	3,491.0	13,122.8
1819	2,968.4	8,238.3
1820	804.1	1,783.2
1821	782.5	1,123.4
1822	710.0	908.0
1823	652.1	847.6
1824	737.0	947.1
1825	999.0	1,392.3

Source: B. H. Hibbard, *A History of the Public Land Policies* (New York: Macmillan, 1924), pp. 100 and 103.

Table 1.6: Richmond Coal Field Production and Distribution, 1800–25.

Year	Total Production (thousands of tons)	Shipped by Canal (thousands of tons)	Received at Philadelphia (thousands of tons)
1800	18.0	na	na
1801	22.0	na	0.3
1802	26.0	na	na
1803	29.5	14.2	na
1804	40.5	13.7	na
1805	42.0	14.8	na
1806	43.0	12.5	na
1807	44.0	14.0	na
1808	45.0	11.5	na
1809	46.0	4.7	na
1810	47.0	0.8	na
1811	48.0	na	na
1812	50.0	na	9.4
1813	52.0	na	0.1
1814	54.0	na	na
1815	56.0	na	7.4
1816	57.0	na	6.0
1817	58.0	na	2.4
1818	59.0	na	3.9
1819	60.0	na	2.9
1820	62.0	na	0.5
1821	64.0	10.0	0.5
1822	54.0	na	0.4
1823	44.0	na	na
1824	67.0	na	4.1
1825	66.7	15.2	4.1

na = not available

Source: W. Hibbard (comp), *Statistical History of Virginia Coalmining: 241 Years of Data from 1748 to 1988* (Blacksburg, VA: VPI & SU, 1989), p. 66.

Table 1.7: Virginia Counties by Region, 1830.

Tidewater	Piedmont	Valley	Trans-Allegheny
Accomack	Albemarle	Alleghany	Brooke
Caroline	Amelia	Augusta	Cabell
Charles City	Amherst	Bath	Giles
Chesterfield	Bedford	Berkeley	Grayson
Elizabeth City	Brunswick	Botetourt	Greenbrier
Essex	Buckingham	Frederick	Harrison
Fairfax	Campbell	Hampshire	Kanawha
Gloucester	Charlotte	Hardy	Lee
Greenville	Culpeper	Jefferson	Lewis
Hanover	Cumberland	Morgan	Logan
Henrico	Dinwiddie	Pendleton	Mason
Isle of Wight	Fauquier	Rockbridge	Monongalia
James City	Fluvanna	Rockingham	Monroe
King and Queen	Franklin	Shenandoah	Montgomery
King George	Goochland		Nicholas
King William	Halifax		Ohio
Lancaster	Henry		Pocahontas
Mathews	Loudoun		Preston
Middlesex	Louisa		Randolph
Nansemond	Lunenburg		Russell

Tidewater	Piedmont	Valley	Trans-Allegheny
New Kent	Madison		Scott
Norfolk (City)	Mecklenburg		Tazewell
Norfolk	Nelson		Tyler
Northampton	Nottoway		Washington
Northumberland	Orange		Wood
Petersburg (City)	Patrick		Wythe
Prince George	Pittsylvania		
Prince William	Powhatan		
Princess Anne	Prince Edward		
Richmond (City)			
Richmond			
Southampton			
Spotsylvania			
Stafford			
Surry			
Sussex			
Warwick			
Westmoreland			
York			

Source: A. G. Freehling, *Drift Toward Dissolution* (Baton Rouge: Louisiana State University Press, 1982), pp. 265–9.

Table 1.8: Population of Virginia, 1800–30.

Year	White	Enslaved	Free Black	Total
(number, per cent of total, and per centage change from previous census)				
1800	514,280	345,796	20,124	880,200
%total	58.4%	39.3%	2.3%	–
%change	–	–	–	–
1810	551,534	392,518	30,570	974,622
%total	56.6%	40.3%	3.1%	–
%change	7.2%	13.5%	51.9%	10.7%
1820	603,074	425,153	37,139	1,065,371
%total	56.6%	39.9%	3.5%	–
%change	9.3%	8.3%	21.5%	9.3%
1830	64,300	469,757	47,348	1,211,405
%total	57.3%	38.8%	3.9%	–
%change	15.1%	10.5%	27.5%	13.7%

Source: G. Tucker, *Progress of the United States in Population and Wealth in Fifty Years* (Boston, MA: Little and Brown, 1843), p. 57; J. D. B. DeBow, *Statistical View of the United States [...] Being a Compendium of the Seventh Census* (Washington: A. D. P. Nicholson, 1854), pp. 45, 63 and 82.

2 AN OVERVIEW OF THE PANIC OF 1819

Contemporary observers indicate that the Panic of 1819 was a traumatic experience for the new republic.[87] For example, John C. Calhoun, discussing the situation with John Quincy Adams in 1820, said, 'There has been within these two years an immense revolution of fortunes in every part of the Union: enormous numbers of persons utterly ruined; multitudes in deep distress; and a general mass disaffection to the government'.[88] In the Boston newspapers, Andrew R. L. Cayton found that 'complaints of Hard Times appear universal' and that what was once a thriving town 'presents a dull and uncheery spectacle – silence reigns in the streets'.[89] Hezekiah Niles in his *Register* reported that a Philadelphia committee found that employment in thirty industries studied declined 'from 9672 in 1816 to 2137 in 1819; weekly wages were down from $58,000 to $12,000', and Niles himself estimated that in New York, Philadelphia and Baltimore some 50,000 were 'either unemployed or irregularly employed'.[90] Niles also reported that in Philadelphia 'houses which rented for 1,200 dollars, now rent for 450 dollars, fuel which costs 12 dollars, now costs 4 1/2; beef 25 cents now 8 cents; other things in proportion'.[91] From Pittsburgh a citizens' committee 'stated that certain manufacturing and mechanical trades in their city and its vicinity, which employed 1960 persons in 1815, employed only 672 in 1819'.[92] And, in Virginia, as in virtually every corner of the Union, property had depreciated dramatically. For example, in Richmond where 'the spirit of land speculation' had been rife, a new town had been 'laid off on paper above the city, called the town of Sidney'. At the outset, 'land sold readily for one thousand dollars per acre'. Once hard times began, such land would not 'bring one hundred'.[93]

Macroeconomic Overview

The young nation's 'traumatic awakening to the capitalist reality of boom-and-bust' reported by these various sources was a complex combination of financial market volatility, swings in international market demand, and federal government financial activity.[94] The actions of the Second Bank of the United States along with those of a number of state-chartered banks have received much scholarly attention. And, the monetary tightening of 1818–19 sounded the alarm for an economy rife with speculation and brought the economic optimism that had fuelled such speculation to an end. The next chapter will analyze in more detail the role of banks in the nation and in Virginia during the Panic of 1819.

Although changes in money and credit were an important component in generating panic across the nation, ultimately it was the collapse of the strong foreign markets for commodities that had fuelled the American economy in the years following the War of 1812 and the rapid repayment of federal debt, much of it to foreign bondholders, that together were the proximate causes of the country's first modern business cycle.[95] One Virginian was well aware of the role of foreign markets in the economic downturn. In a letter to Richard Rush in 1821, James Madison indicated that 'a surplus ... for which foreign demand has failed is a primary cause of the present embarrassment of this Country'.[96]

Chart 2.1 shows the changes in the level of prices and real GNP in the nation from 1815 through 1825.[97] The dramatic deflation experienced during the period is clear as the price index fell from 147 in 1818 to a level of 102 in 1821, a 30.6 per cent decline. The stagnation of real GNP between 1818 and 1821 appears as a plateau in the middle of the diagram. The short-run Aggregate Supply-Aggregate Demand equilibria for the United States for the years 1815–25 are given in Chart 2.2. Each point represents the combination of output (real GNP) and price level for a given year determined by the interaction of short-run aggregate demand and short-run aggregate supply. The resulting figure demonstrates further the sharp deflation following the Panic of 1819 and the slight decline and slow recovery of real GNP between 1818 and 1821.[98]

Measures of aggregate output for this time period are not readily available, and the Berry GNP statistics were for many years the only annual series to be found. Recently, this changed with the publication of Joseph H. Davis's annual index of American industrial production for the period 1790–1915.[99] Each will be discussed in turn.

The Berry data, unfortunately, must be used with great caution. The GNP series is calculated based on the trend of GNP for the years 1910–56 with that trend projected back to 1789 using 'a second-degree logarithmic trend, arbitrarily selected so as to thread its way among R. E. Gallman's estimates for 1839–59 and various contemporary estimates'.[100] Variations from the trend are calculated using a multiple regression based on 'consensus economic patterns' derived from fifty-four data series. For the period of the Panic, only between fourteen and twenty-one of the data series are available and used.[101] As a result of the method employed and the relatively small number of series available for the years between 1815 and 1825, the Berry data is suspect. It does not represent a direct measurement of the economic patterns of the day and therefore must be considered only generally reflective of annual changes in economic activity. However, the Berry data are used here to give a sense of what the economy may have experienced with the Panic and subsequent depression.[102]

The Davis data on industrial production shows a somewhat different pattern for the economy in the years surrounding the Panic of 1819. His index measuring 'the level of physical production in the nation's manufacturing and mining industries' is presented in Table 2.1 and shows an increase of 9.6 per cent between 1819 and 1821.[103] This is much higher than the 2.8 per cent increase in real GNP indicated by Berry for the same period but with the significant fall in prices during those years still means a large fall in nominal output. Chart 2.3 shows the short-run equilibria of the period using Davis's index of industrial production and the Warren-Pearson price index.

Davis's index, while much superior to Berry's, is not without problems for the period of this study. Most importantly, it is an index of industrial production for a time when the farm share of the nation's workforce was over 70 per cent and when some 90 per cent of Virginia's population was engaged in agriculture. Although, as Davis suggests, 'the new index should be broadly indicative of the nation's broader economic conditions because the industrial sector has historically derived demand directly from nonindustrial occupations', in an economy where imports of industrial goods were important, it could mean a substitution of domestic for imported industrial output and mask important declines in the user occupations.[104] Further, of Davis's forty-three production series used to construct the index, sixteen, or 37.2 per cent, were not available until after the period of the Panic, and at least another nine of the series used have nothing to do with Virginia production. Thus, micro data for Virginia in this study may help us better understand the real impact of the depression following the Panic of 1819.

Finally, the macro measures of economic activity by both Davis and Berry show output increasing during the period following the Panic. This suggests that the economic decline of the period was more severe in nominal terms than in real terms. However, the decline in real exports during the depression following the Panic of 1819 suggests that for an economy dominated by agriculture, and for which agricultural exports were critical, the depression was real and possibly was much worse than other nineteenth-century downturns, only two of which saw real exports fall, in each case by much less than real exports fell during the period 1818–21. See Table 2A.2 for changes in real exports. The evaluation of the Panic of 1819 relative to other downturns will be elaborated later in this chapter.

In the events leading up to the Panic of 1819, the banking system played a critical role. Having secured a somewhat shaky return to specie convertibility early in its operations, the Second Bank of the United States proceeded to more than live up to its part of the agreement with state banks by continuing to expand credit until discounts stood at over $41 million by mid-1818.[105] This expansion combined with the dramatic increase in land sales in the west meant that notes of western and southern branches of the Second Bank, which it had decided to redeem at any office as a means of developing a uniform national currency, began to flood eastward, particularly to New York and Boston.[106] Despite large imports of specie, the Bank could not continue to meet the demand for note redemption. Thus, in July 1818, the directors ordered discounts reduced at Philadelphia ($2 million), Baltimore ($2 million), Richmond ($700,000) and Norfolk ($300,000).[107]

Further complicating the financial picture at the time was the retirement of 1803's Louisiana bonds, scheduled to begin in 1818 and to continue through 1821. Such fiscal action on top of the over $20 million in federal debt retired during 1817 meant that substantial government revenues did not reenter the economy directly, thus creating a smaller multiplier impact than if those revenues had been spent directly by the government. Most importantly given the Second Bank's contraction in the last half of 1818, approximately $3.5 million of the roughly $4.5 million in Louisiana bonds retired in October 1818 went as payments to foreigners, and of the total $11 million retired of the entire issue, some $6 million went to foreigners. This flow of funds out of the domestic economy meant that potential domestic spending was lost at a critical time, and it placed additional strains on the Second Bank. Treasury deposits at the bank dropped approximately $6 million between October 1818 and January 1819 to an ending balance of slightly less than $3 million – a two-thirds decline in just three months.[108]

The contraction story's final and most critical element was also international. As Great Britain and Europe prepared for the resumption of specie convertibility in 1819, additional strain was placed on an already very tight world specie supply. The resulting economic slowdowns across Europe combined with the return of good harvests on the Continent and in Britain meant that markets for American staples began to fall sharply. As Tables 1.2 and 1.3 indicate, between 1818 and 1819, Britain's index of business activity fell 12.4 per cent, and both the value of total imports and imports of corn (grain) declined by 16.5 per cent and 58.8 per cent respectively. The quantity of wheat and flour imported fell 70.3 per cent, and importation of American grain declined 74.6 per cent. In the same period the value of French imports dropped 12.2 per cent; the importation of provisions declined 2.5 per cent in 1819 after falling 11.6 per cent between 1817 and 1818. French industrial production also decreased 8.5 per cent while British industrial production increased slightly by 2.0 per cent. Although data for Austria is not complete, in 1819 values added of iron production and cotton output were below the average levels of 1800–1803, and value added of wool production was up slightly from its 1815 level but still below 1814. Table 2.2 shows the importance of British and European markets for the United States during these years.

With a monetary contraction underway, the continued retirement of federal debt, much of it to foreigners, and declines in the overseas markets for American staples, the United States economy was headed for disaster. The extent of that disaster in Virginia and its impact on the Commonwealth are the subject of the remaining chapters. Before beginning that analysis, additional perspective on the Panic of 1819 will be helpful. First, the Panic of 1819 will be considered in terms of Irving Fisher's debt-deflation theory of great depressions. Second, it will be compared with other contractions in the nineteenth and early twentieth centuries.

The Debit-Deflation Theory

In 1933, as the Great Depression was reaching its trough, the economist Irving Fisher published in the journal *Econometrica* an update of his debt-deflation theory of great depressions, first presented the previous year in his book *Booms and Depressions*. Fisher's debt-deflation theory envisions a multi-step series of economic events that create a decline in economic activity and argues that most importantly it is the 'attempts to liquidate debt in the context of over-indebtedness and falling prices' that leads to depressions.[109]

Although Fisher recognized that a number of factors were involved in the great booms and depressions of history, he believed that all 'played a subordinate role as compared with two dominant factors, namely *over-indebtedness* to start with and *deflation* following soon after'. Thus, according to Fisher, 'In short, the big bad actors are debt disturbances and price-level disturbances'. Over-indebtedness has as its starter '*new opportunities to invest at a big prospective profit*, as compared with ordinary profits and interest', combined with 'the great cause of over-borrowing', easy money. Such over-indebtedness, according to Fisher, 'will tend to lead to liquidation, through the alarm either of debtors or creditors or both' and results in a chain of consequences that produce a drop in the price level which, in turn, results in bankruptcies, falling output and trade, and unemployment. Although he does not assign the monetary system a primary role in initiating a deflationary spiral, Fisher does suggest that one of the most important interactions in the deflationary process 'is the direct effect of lessened money, deposits, and their velocity, in curtailing trade'.[110]

The Fisher theory has been extended and formalized by Ben S. Bernanke, who argues that banking panics cause an increase in the cost of credit intermediation. This means that banks must ration credit thereby making it harder for firms to borrow. Based on asymmetric information, Bernanke agues that in panics banks protect themselves by both curtailing lending and switching to more liquid loans. As deflation erodes 'borrowers' collateral relative to debt burdens', the cost of credit intermediation increases and bank further restrict credit. Those most affected by this process are 'households, farmers, unincorporated businesses, and small corporations'.[111]

The Panic of 1819 and resulting depression seem to fit the general outline of the debt-deflation theory quite well. The postwar boom was led by rapidly expanding markets for the nation's commodities and aided by the expansion of bank credit, particularly from the new Second Bank of the United States. The resulting widespread speculation in land, particularly in the west and cotton south, provided the starter for the over-indebtedness that is a critical part of Fisher's theory. And, the alarm sparked first by contractions in the banking sector and completed by the redemption of a significant portion of federal debt to foreigners and, most importantly, by the collapse of foreign markets for America's agricultural goods provided the deflation that brought the economy crashing down. Further, the monetarist focus on monetary contraction and its impact on aggregate demand, while applicable to the initial period of the Panic in late 1819 and early 1819, does not hold for the depression following the Panic of 1819. Monetary data from Table 2.3 suggests that the money supply actually increased over the period 1818–24, a change that would have increased aggregate demand.

The Panic in Comparative Perspective

As suggested in the Introduction, the Panic of 1819 has received relatively little attention from economists and historians. Burns and Mitchell in their National Bureau of Economic Research study of American business cycles chose not to define the Panic of 1819 as a modern cycle and instead began their reference dates with the 1834–8 period.[112] In addition, some scholars of Jacksonian finance have ignored the Panic because they see the downturn itself as relatively short-lived, and because with the help of the Bank of the United States, the banking system as a whole rebounded relatively quickly from the initial contraction.[113] Further, as North suggests, the depression following 1839 'was even more severe' than the 'precipitous depression of 1818'.[114] And finally, with the exception of Davis, recent scholarship on economic instability in the antebellum period has tended to focus on fluctuations after events surrounding the Panic of 1819 largely because of the lack of adequate data for the earlier period.[115] Davis's comparisons of the severity of ante and postbellum business cycles see only the period 1822–3 in the years following the Panic of 1819 as a downturn. And, his measure indicates the 1822–3 depression is the second mildest of the entire antebellum period. Davis's index of industrial production declined by 1.22 in 1822–3 compared to a mean loss of 7.32 points for all antebellum recessions.[116] However, including the issues raised earlier regarding Davis's index, there exist sufficient data to make a tentative judgment regarding the Panic of 1819, and thus to reconsider these decisions.

Tables 2.3 and 2.4 compare the Panic of 1819 with the depression following the Crisis of 1839, the Panic of 1857, the five most important post-Civil War nineteenth-century downturns, the 1920–1 contraction, and the Great Depression of the 1930s.[117] The results suggest a strong parallel with 1839–43, the other early-nineteenth-century depression preceded by extensive speculation in land and a financial crisis, and with 1920–1, a sharp postwar contraction. There is less of a similarity with the other nineteenth-century depressions, and the tables' figures bear out the devastation of the crisis of the 1930s which makes the Great Depression worthy of its title.

Table 2.3 focuses on financial and international trade measures of the economy. Deflation during the Panic of 1819 was not as severe as that experienced during 1839–43 or 1929–33, but it was roughly similar to the decline in prices experienced in the depressions of 1873–9 and 1920–1.[118] In spite of deflation during all of the periods considered, none of the nineteenth-century downturns, particularly 1818–21 and 1839–43, approached the severity of the Great Depression, and none except 1857–8 were as harsh as the 1920–1 depression. This suggests flexible prices were present during the earlier crises which in turn allowed falling demand primarily to affect prices and wages and to have less impact on production, although failures and unemployment were certainly present in the earlier downturns. Chapter 5 will discuss this issue in some depth as it relates to the wholesale and retail business community in Virginia. Finally, the economic dislocations that occurred in 1818–21 and 1839–43 were found largely in particular sectors of the economy, primarily those dependent on foreign markets and those still struggling to survive in the face of competition from more efficiently produced imports – for all practical purposes a large proportion of the Commonwealth's economy.[119]

While the numbers of banks increased 7.2 per cent during 1818–21, in the years 1819–22 the number decreased 6.9 per cent. This is about half the percentage decline during 1839–43 but both fall far short of the drop in banking institutions that occurred during the Great Depression. In the other periods the number of banks actually increased. Although each of the periods of economic crisis involved deflation, and for the most part substantial deflation, in all except 1873–9, 1893–4, and 1895–7 the money supply declined. In particular, the periods 1839–43 and 1929–33 involved substantial drops in money supply. But in 1818–21, despite imperfect monetary data, all indications are that the money supply increased (see Table 2.3.). To have a period of deflation while the money supply is increasing requires a decline in velocity, or the turnover rate of money.[120] The data suggest that velocity may have in fact dropped substantially during the period of the Panic of 1819. Support for a decline in the velocity of specie comes from a remark by Philadelphian Condy Raguet in response to a question from the British economist David Ricardo. According to Raguet, 'persons who had a right to demand coin from the Banks in payment of their notes, so long forbode to exercise it' because 'the whole of our population are either stockholders of banks, or in debt to them. It was not in the interest of the first to press the banks and the rest were afraid'.[121] In such a situation, the velocity of specie should decline as banks hold their stocks, not using them to redeem notes, and individuals, seeing precious metals becoming dear, begin to hoard specie. But, what of the velocity of bank notes? To the extent the stability of banking institutions was an issue, holding bank notes became more costly. For example, Virginia bank notes moved from trading at Philadelphia in a range from par to a 6 per cent premium in 1816 to being valued at a 1.5 to 8 per cent discount by 1819, and they continued to trade at a discount through 1823.[122] As a result, bank note velocity could be expected to decline since individuals would be increasingly hesitant to accept notes whose value was questionable and which might change suddenly. However, the higher cost of holding bank notes should lead individuals to increase the turnover rate as they try to get rid of bank notes as quickly as possible. Yet, Raguet suggested individuals in fact held bank notes in spite of the increased cost because they were unwilling or afraid to press banks for redemption. Thus, it is not clear a priori what might be the direction of change in bank note velocity. However, the magnitude of the general fall in prices as the money supply likely increased suggests a decline in bank note velocity to accompany the suspected drop in specie velocity.

In addition to financial factors, Table 2.3 includes comparisons of changes in the current value of imports and exports.[123] Imports are an indicator of the impact a downturn has on spending in the economy. The dramatic drop in imports during the depression of 1818–21, down 55 per cent, is comparable to that experienced during the post-World War I contraction of 1920–1 but falls short of the decline experienced during the depressions of 1839–43 and 1929–33. The sharp decline in exports between 1818 and 1821, a drop of 41 per cent, suggests the importance of international conditions in the first downturn relative to that of 1839–43, and a similarity in the importance of international factors to the nation's economy during the Panic of 1819 and 1920–1, another severe postwar depression. Again the Great Depression stands alone for the magnitude of the fall in exports.

Table 2.4 provides comparative GNP data from various sources for the contractions being considered. For the most part, the measures of GNP and its components used in the table are derived from Thomas Berry's work and are subject to the concerns expressed earlier. The data suggest the similarity of the 1818–21 and 1839–43 contractions, indicate that each was more dramatic than any of the other nineteenth-century depressions except for the Panic of 1857, and confirm the more severe nature of the 1920–1 and 1929–33 depressions relative to all the nineteenth-century contractions. The latter point supports the argument that flexible prices may have played a role in mitigating the impacts on production of the earlier downturns.

Summary and Conclusions

As the first modern business cycle experienced by the United States, the Panic of 1819 appears to fit Fisher's debt-deflation theory of great depressions well. A wide variety of data show that the Panic of 1819 represents the nation's rude awakening to the globalized market economy of the nineteenth century with its proximate cause being the collapse of foreign markets for American commodities. The depression following the Panic ranks with the depression of 1839–43 as the worst of the contractions experienced by the United States in that century. In some categories, such as the drop in exports and fall in real investment, the Panic of 1819 was the most dramatic of the century.

However, this overview has been based upon limited measures of economic conditions and the problem of adequate data upon which to base an analysis of the Panic of 1819 has still to be addressed. Although at the national level significant holes in the data continue to exist, one of the purposes of this study is to develop sufficient data for the Commonwealth of Virginia to undertake a level of detailed analysis that has been lacking. The following chapters utilize existing data sources as well as develop new data in order to analyze the events surrounding the Panic of 1819 in Virginia.

Tables

Table 2.1: Index of US Industrial Production, 1815–25.

Year	Index
1815	13.584
1816	12.595
1817	13.119
1818	13.838
1819	14.412
1820	14.384
1821	15.792
1822	17.291
1823	17.081
1824	18.559
1825	19.886

Source: J. H. Davis, 'An Annual Index of U. S. Industrial Production, 1790–1915', *Quarterly Journal of Economics*, 119:4 (2004), Table III, pp. 1177–215; p. 1189.

Table 2.2: Percentage of Value of US Exports by Destination, 1815–23.

Year	Europe	United Kingdom	France
1815	71.6	33.9	13.2
1816	71.9	36.6	12.1
1817	65.9	37.5	10.2
1818	73.1	40.9	12.9
1819	67.1	34.3	12.8
1820	68.6	34.3	12.8
1821	65.5	34.5	10.9

Year	Europe	United Kingdom	France
1822	65.6	39.3	9.8
1823	64.7	32.4	13.2

Source: *Historical Statistics of the United States: Colonial Times to 1970* (Washington: Bureau of the Census, 1975), Series U 317-334.

Table 2.3: Comparison of 1818–21 with Other Nineteenth-Century Depressions, 1920–1 and 1929–33: Financial and International Trade Measures.

Contraction Dates		Percent Change			
	Money Supply	Prices	Number of Banks	Imports	Exports
	(a)	(b)	(c)	(d)	(e)
1818–21	na#	-31	+7.2*	-55	-41
1839–43	-34	-42	-12.5*	-73	-26
1857–8	-11	-16	+07.2*	-24	-7
1865–7	-211	-12	+16	+66	+78
1873–9	+4	-32	+1	-31	+36
1882–5	-5	-21	+22	-20	-1
1893–4	+0.5	-10	+0.2	-24	+5
1895–7	+5	-5	+23	+5	+30
1920–1	-6	-37	+0.5	-53	-46
1929–33	-27	-31	-42	-67	-68

na = not available

Notes and deposits of state banks adjusted for the number of reporting banks rose from $63 million in 1818 to $79.8 in 1821. Notes and deposits of the Bank of the United States also rose in the same period from $12.4 million to $13.7 million. Data for the stock of specie is not available. Friedman and Schwartz (*A Monetary History of the United States, 1867–1960* (Princeton, NJ: Princeton University Press, 1963) estimate the stock of specie at $25 million in 1819 and $39 million in 1821. Their estimate of specie held by the public is $4.9–5.2 million in 1819 and $15 million in 1821. Thus it is likely that the money supply actually rose during the period.

Sources: *Historical Statistics of the United States: Colonial Times to 1970* (Washington: Bureau of the Census, 1975), Series (a): X-423/X-415, (b): E-40, E-52, (c): X-580, (d): U-190 and (e): U-193; * W. E. Weber, 'Early State Banks in the United States: How Many Were There and When Did They Exist?', *Journal of Economic History*, 66:2 (2006), pp. 433–55; J. Van Fenstermaker, *The Development of American Commercial Banking, 1782–1837* (Kent, OH: Kent State University, 1965) and J. Van Fenstemaker, J. E. Fuller and R. S. Herren, 'Money Statistics of New England, 1785–1837', *Journal of Economic History*, 44:2 (June 1984), pp. 441–53. Also M. Friedman and A. J. Schwartz, *Monetary Statistics of the United States: Estimates, Sources, Methods* (New York: National Bureau of Economic Research, 1970) and A. F. Burns and W. C. Mitchell, *Measuring Business Cycles* (New York: National Bureau of Economic Research, 1946).

Table 2.4: Comparison of 1818–21 with Other Nineteenth-Century Depressions, 1920–1 and 1929–33: GNP Measures.

Contraction Dates		Percent Change			
	Real GNP	Real Invest	Real CON	Per Real GNP	Capital Real CON
1818–21	+1	-25	+3	-6	-6
1839–43	+16*	-23*	+21*	-5	-5
(Berry)	+7	-21	+7		
1857–8	-9	-18	-9	-12	-11
1865–7	+7	+74	+8	+1	+3
1873–9	+19	-2	+22	+6	+7
1882–5	+5	-8	+6	-3	-2
1893–4	-3**	na	na	-5**	na
1895–7	+7**	na	na	-3**	na

1920–1	-9**	na	na	-11**	na
1929–33	-30*	-91*	-19*	-33**	-22**

na = not available

Sources: Unless indicated otherwise, calculations are based on T. S. Berry, *Production and Population Since 1789: Revised GNP Series in Constant Dollars* (Richmond, VA: Bostwick Press, 1988), Tables 3, 4, and 6. * P. Temin, *The Jacksonian Economy* (New York, Norton, 1969), p.157; ** *Historical Statistics of the United States: Colonial Times to 1970* (Washington: Bureau of the Census, 1975), Series F-3, F-4 and F-27; and A. F. Burns and W. C. Mitchell, *Measuring Business Cycles* (New York: National Bureau of Economic Research, 1946).

Charts

Chart 2.1: Real GNP and Price Level, 1815–25.

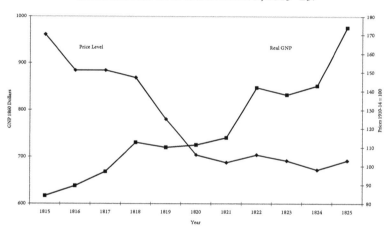

Chart 2.2: Short-Run AS–AD Equilibria.

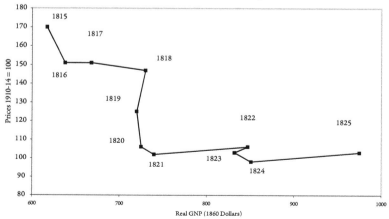

Chart 2.3: Short Run Equilbria with Industrial Production.

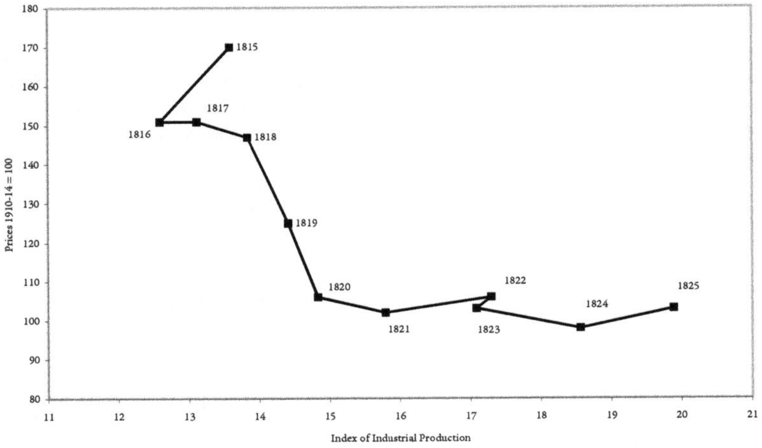

Appendix

Table 2A.1: Comparison of Price Changes in Depressions.

Contraction Dates	Warren-Pearson/BLS	David-Solar	Romer
	percent change		
1818–21	-31	-11	na
1839–43	-42	-21	na
1857–8	-16	-5	na
1865–7	-12	-9	na
1873–9	-32	-17	-21
1882–5	-21	-6	-12
1893–4	-10	-5	-6
1895–7	-5	-0.5	-2
1920–1	-37	-11	na
1929–33	-31	-24	na

na = not available

Sources: *Historical Statistics of the United States: Colonial Times to 1970* (Washington: Bureau of the Census, 1975), E-40, E-52; P. A. David and P. Solar, 'A Bicentenary Contribution to the History of the Cost of Living in America', *Research in Economic History*, 2 (1977), pp. 1–80; p. 16; C. D. Romer, 'The Prewar Business Cycle Reconsidered: New Estimates of GNP 1869–1908', *Journal of Political Economy*, 97:1 (1989), pp. 1–37.

Table 2A.2: Comparison of Real Imports and Real Exports in Depressions.

Contraction Dates	Imports		Exports	
	Warren-Pearson/BLS	David-Solar	Warren-Pearson/BLS	David-Solar
		percent change		
1818–21	-35	-49	-15	-33
1839–43	-60	-66	+11	-7

Contraction Dates	Imports			Exports
	Warren-Pearson/BLS	David-Solar	Warren-Pearson/BLS	David-Solar
		percent change		
1857–8	-10	-20	+10	-0.2
1865–7	+89	+82	+103	+96
1873–9	+3	-17	+101	+63
1882–5	+1	-16	+26	+5
1893–4	-16	-21	+17	+10
1895–7	+9	+6	+36	+31
1920–1	-25	-47	-14	-39
1929-33	-52	-56	-54	-58

Sources: *Historical Statistics of the United States: Colonial Times to 1970* (Washington: Bureau of the Census, 1975), Series E-40 and E-52, and David and Solar, 'A Bicentenary Contribution', p. 16.

Chart 2A.1: Real GNP and Price Level, 1815–25.

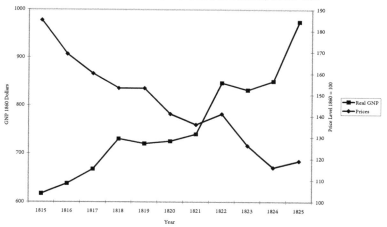

Chart 2A.2: Short-Run AS–AD Equilibria.

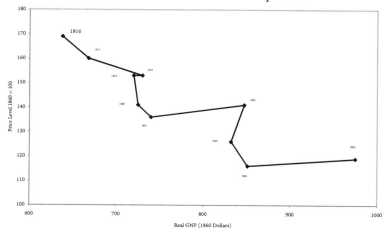

3 BANKING AND GOVERNMENT FINANCE

As the Panic of 1819 gripped the nation, the Commonwealth's leading newspaper, the *Richmond Enquirer*, announced on 21 May 1819, 'we shall for several months keep open a head in this paper, styled "Political Economy"'. The object was 'to excite investigation' because, according to the *Enquirer*, 'The times particularly demand information on the subject of political economy. The country is lamentably deficient in important knowledge.' As the *Enquirer* editorial suggested, 'Never did a thicker gloom hang over the monied transactions of this land. The state of the markets, of trade, of the interest of manufactures, the great problem of the banking system, of the precious metals; there is scarce an individual in this country, who does not feel some interest in these questions.' The announcement concluded, 'Things are winding up; but perhaps *too fast* and in *too much panic*.'[124]

Four days later, the first article under the new banner appeared. 'A deeper gloom was never spread over the commercial world than is seen at this moment', wrote the author of the piece, Economicus. First describing conditions in Europe, he then turned to America. 'Here we find in almost every quarter, an unparalleled embarrassment in the money market'. According to Economicus, the nation's condition could be blamed on the banks. 'It is a melancholy (nay *worse*, it is a disgraceful) fact, that this country, blessed beyond any that the world ever shone upon, has been brought to this condition, principally by monied institutions: by their *multiplication* and *mismanagement*'. Most important was the mismanagement which had 'given birth to the wildest spirit of speculation. Speculation has generated banks; and banks have generated a tenfold spirit of speculation'. This spirit had, in turn, affected the 'moral habits of this nation', including corrupting 'our manners' and undermining our 'republican principles'.[125]

The Introduction indicated that modern economic theory, particularly monetarist and asymmetric information theory, has focused on the role of financial institutions and their credit mechanisms as the source of major contractions in the real economy. The debt-deflation view of great depressions sees 'easy money as the great cause of over-borrowing'; i.e., easy money and liberal loans start the process leading to economic downturns. Further, the debt-deflation view assigns an important part to the contraction of currency and the slowing of velocity as

39

depressions develop. Many of those living through the Panic of 1819 saw the sudden lack of credit playing a critical role in the economic events of the times. As Economicus indicates in the *Enquirer*, many believed the blame for this state of affairs could be placed squarely on the banks. But was this really the case? Were banks across the nation and particularly in Virginia were the state's banks the reason for the existing economic distress?

On the contrary, the primary factor in the crisis of 1819–21 was the loss of foreign markets for American agricultural commodities. However, to the extent banks participated in the speculative boom preceding the downturn, and to the extent they shocked the economy and weakened credit relationships by contracting credit and reducing note circulation in 1816 and 1817 in anticipation of and in response to the resumption of specie convertibility, they exacerbated the driving forces in the depression of 1819–21. Analyzing the part played by Virginia banks in the Panic of 1819 and how the Commonwealth's experience differed from that of other states is the object of this chapter. To understand the role of the state's banks in the years leading up to the Panic, we begin with background on banking in Virginia and the Second Bank of the United States. This is followed by an analysis of the operations of both the Virginia branches of the Bank of the United States and the Commonwealth's own state-chartered banks in the years prior to the Panic and during the subsequent depression. Finally, the chapter concludes with a review of government finances both in the Commonwealth and in the nation during the Panic of 1819.

Banking in Virginia

In the colonial period, a shortage of currency had been a perpetual problem for Virginia, and the lack of a circulating medium resulted in a variety of schemes to use treasury and other notes to expand trade. At times, even tobacco warehouse receipts were used to supplement existing coinage, mostly Spanish coins. While some attempts were more successful than others, the Loan Bank scheme of 1765 and extensive counterfeiting of treasury notes in the early 1760s left many Virginians wary of paper currency and, by extension, of banks of deposit and issue. Likewise, the need for circulating currency during the Revolution led to the printing of paper money by the state. However, overissue created significant inflation, again turning many citizens of the Commonwealth against all paper money schemes. As a result of these experiences, it was not until 1792 that the first bank was chartered by the Virginia legislature: the Bank of Alexandria with capital of $150,000.[126] Meanwhile, citizens of both Richmond and Norfolk petitioned to have offices of the newly established Bank of the United States located in their cities. However, in spite of a 1795 act of the General Assembly authorizing that an office of the First Bank be established in the Commonwealth, it was not until

1799, when a branch was established at Norfolk with a capital of $600,000, that another section of Virginia had a significant banking presence. Moreover, when the District of Columbia was created in 1800, the Bank of Alexandria, which until that time had continued primarily to serve its local area with a capital expanded to $500,000, moved from the control of Virginia to the jurisdiction of Congress.[127]

Despite the fear of banks on the part of many Virginians, the expanding needs of commerce combined with the decline of the Commonwealth's economy relative to those of neighboring states led the General Assembly to charter the Bank of Virginia early in 1804. Following an exceptionally successful stock issue, including 20 per cent subscribed by the state, the Bank of Virginia began operations in October 1804 with its headquarters in Richmond and branches in Norfolk, Fredericksburg and Petersburg. While the early success of the Bank of Virginia brought forth calls for chartering a second state bank, the economic doldrums created by the embargo and the war in Europe put a halt to any serious efforts in that direction. However, with the resumption of trade in 1810 and the failure to renew the charter of the Bank of the United States in 1811, a move strongly supported by the Bank of Virginia, efforts to create a second bank in the Commonwealth reappeared. In 1812, the Farmers' Bank of Virginia was chartered with capital of $2 million and began operation with a main office in Richmond and branches in Norfolk, Lynchburg, Winchester, Petersburg and Fredericksburg.[128]

Following the War of 1812, citizens in the western parts of the state began to press for additional banking services. By that time, Virginia's two banks had a total of eleven branches. However, none was located west of the mountains and only three were to be found in the Valley, two at Lynchburg and one at Winchester.[129] Because these sections of the state were underserved, unchartered private banks carried on extensive operations in western Virginia despite laws restricting their operation.[130] Finally, in February 1816 the General Assembly made unchartered bank operations a misdemeanor subject to fines of $100 to $5,000, effectively ending private bank operations in the Commonwealth. However, because a number of these firms had such large circulations outstanding, the date for recall of notes for thirteen of them was extended until the end of August 1818.[131] The legislature's action also brought twenty-two applications for bank charters to the General Assembly, mostly from the Valley and Trans-Allegheny regions. Included were petitions from Romney to incorporate the Bank of the South Bank of the Potomac, from citizens of Jefferson County to charter a Farmers' Mechanics' and Merchants' Bank, and from others of the now-outlawed private banks.[132] Given the number of applications, the General Assembly appointed a Select Committee to investigate establishing new banks; it in turn recommended chartering banks at fifteen locations, all but two in the Shenandoah Valley and Trans-Allegheny.[133] After defeating a bill based on the commission's recommendations, the General

Assembly, in January 1817, incorporated two new banks and authorized them to have multiple branches, the Northwestern Bank of Virginia at Wheeling and the Bank of the Valley of Virginia at Winchester.[134]

Some insight regarding the operation of Virginia's banks of this period is provided by a report to the General Assembly in 1815 from the committee assigned to consider petitions for new banks. The committee suggested that 'if the accounts of any American bank be examined, it will be seen that more than one half of its outstanding debts are found on what is called its "*standing accommodations*"; that is, on the discounted notes which the Banks may, but it is understood, will not call in at the end of sixty days.' Further, according to the report, 'much of that debt will be found to have arisen from assurance, on the part of the bank, that the actual payment of it, will not be required for many months, and some part of it, for several years'. For the banks' protection, 'the capital adventured, is usually insured against the accidents of the voyage in which it is invested; the payment of the note or bond, on which it is obtained, is endorsed by approved security, and new endorsers may be required, every sixty days, should a change of fortunes be discovered or suspected by the bank in the circumstances of the drawer or endorser'. For Virginia planters, merchants, and manufacturers, this meant that loans and discounts were often based on the personal security of individuals which in turn depended on the real property held, including slaves. As deflation hit the Commonwealth, such security would undergo 'a change of fortune', leading to changes in the terms of any such accommodations and thus giving full play to the debt-deflation mechanism of Irving Fisher.[135]

The Second Bank of the United States

At the same time Virginia was restructuring its banking system, the Second Bank of the United States was created in April 1816 by Congress, and in early 1817 banking operations began.[136] The chartering of a second national bank resulted, in part, because of the failure, by a very close vote, to renew the charter of the Bank of the United States in 1811. The void created by the disappearance of the national bank was quickly filled by state-chartered banks. The number of state banks increased from 117 in 1811 to 143 in 1812 or 22 per cent in the first year after the First Bank of the United States wound up its affairs. By 1816 the number of state-chartered banks grew to 232, or almost double the 1811 total.[137]

With the outbreak of war in 1812 and the drying up of tariff revenues, the absence of a national bank forced the Treasury to rely upon bond sales and the issue of Treasury notes to finance the war effort. Neither proved easy, and following the capture of Washington D.C. by the British in 1814 a general suspension of specie payment swept the country. This further devastated the federal government's finances since it 'was forced to receive its revenues in state-bank paper and treasury notes of all degrees of depreciation'.[138] By the end of the war, Treasury operations were in disarray and the nation's currency was composed largely of 'incontrovertible bank notes of varying degrees of depreciation'.[139] As a result of the disruptions during the war, supporters of a national bank seized the initiative. They were able to overcome the objections of the hard money interest and create a federal institution capable of operating multiple branches across the nation and powerful enough to establish a uniform currency to serve the Treasury's needs and to ensure control of circulation. The Bank was capitalized at $35 million.

The new bank quickly moved to begin operations, to restore confidence in the currency, and to bring order to Treasury deposits and payments. Although stock in the new bank had been fully subscribed, in part thanks to Philadelphia banker Stephen Girard, few of the proceeds were in the form of specie. Important components of the subscription consisted of United States obligations of various types, including the 'entire subscription of the government'. In addition, at the Philadelphia and Baltimore branches payments for the stock were made using balances from the Bank itself. Those balances, in turn, had been created on the security of the Bank's stock being purchased. This led a later report to 'ironically characterize' the transactions as 'an operation of more potency in creating specie, than was ever ascribed to the fabled finger of Midas'.[140]

As a result of the Bank's weak specie position, towards the end of 1816 Congressman John Sergeant was dispatched to London to purchase specie and to secure an agent for dealing with foreign stockholders.[141] This action yielded some two million dollars in specie in 1817 and almost eight million in 1818, but the specie in flow did not prove sufficient to meet the nation's demand for currency. The inadequacy of specie across the country became clear on 20 February 1817, the date Congress required that all payments to the Treasury should be made in specie, 'or in treasury notes, or in notes of the Bank of the United States, or in notes of banks payable and paid on demand in specie'.[142] State banks were reluctant to resume specie payments as early as February, wishing instead to wait until 1 July, but they were persuaded to do so by the Bank, which agreed in return to expand discounts for its customers by $2 million in both New York and Philadelphia, by one and $1.5 million in Baltimore, and by $500,000 in Virginia.[143] Across the nation, the resulting convertibility 'was neither universal nor genuine' as the demand for specie to pay for large net imports, the drop in carrying trades income as the sector faced increased foreign competition, and the demand for silver for the China trade continued to create specie shortages.[144]

However, the Bank did live up to its promises to expand loans. This action, combined with growing commerce across the nation and widespread land speculation in the South and West, meant the Second Bank of the United States moved its portfolio into a position that would ultimately produce a panic in financial markets. Difficulties arose because of the Bank's attempt to redeem at par the notes of all its branches wherever presented, the speed and extent of the loan expansion, and the reality that much of the increase took place in the rapidly developing areas of the Old Northwest and in the cotton-producing South. As a result of the rapid extension of credit by the Second Bank, state banks in the developing areas felt little pressure 'to contract credit and retire their note issues'. In addition, Treasury receipts from taxes on an expanding import trade and the proceeds from speculative land sales were building credits in southern and western branches of the Bank which the Treasury ultimately had to transfer from these debtor areas in order to satisfy their creditors in the East.[145]

The result was a massive flow of bank notes from west to east. Traditional analysis of this period has focused on the 'course of exchange' to explain the flow. The underlying factors include 'a continuing balance of trade' against the western and southern sections of the country and western land sales that meant 'large balances were accumulated in favour of the Treasury in the frontier areas, and the bank had to transfer these funds to the East, where the Treasury made use of them'. Further, the price increases of 1817–18 inhibited the 'interregional acceptance of bank notes' and hastened the eastward flow because 'only those notes [eastern] were truly redeemable in specie'.[146] Peter Temin has expanded upon this explanation by considering various means the financial system might use to settle interregional trade balances. He concluded that the note flow was not the result of previously existing deficits in western and southern accounts but was instead the normal two-way financing of interregional trade. Arthur Frass has suggested that the flow of notes from West to East was the result of the Second Bank's effort to introduce a uniform currency. The Bank's endeavor meant that 'currency flows automatically eliminated the initial discrepancy' in regional prices and 'initiated the process that produced the adjustments in the underlying price structure necessary for a longer term equilibrium'.[147]

Regardless of the underlying reasons generating the note flow, the situation reached crisis proportions in mid-1818 when eastern branches of the Bank of the United States refused to redeem in specie any notes but their own issues, including notes of other branches of the Second Bank. Meanwhile, the directors of the Second Bank instituted a policy of reducing discounts by $2 million at both the Philadelphia and the Baltimore offices, by $700,000 at the Richmond office, and by $300,000 at the Norfolk office. With this move, the Panic of 1819 soon began.[148]

The actions of the Virginia branches of the Second Bank of the United States and how they interacted with the operations of Virginia's state banks in the period leading up to the Panic and through the resulting depression are analyzed next. Did Virginia state banks overexpand along with the Second Bank, as was the case with a number of state-chartered banks in other states, or did Virginia's banks play a different role in the Panic and subsequent depression?

Virginia Banks and the Panic of 1819

The opening of the Second Bank of the United States at the beginning of 1817 and the effort to re-establish specie convertibility later that same year marked the beginning of events that would lead Virginia into the depression known as the Panic of 1819. Virginia's banks had little trouble resuming specie payments, in part because of their actions during 1816. As one historian suggested, the Commonwealth's banks 'were able to open their vaults with little inconvenience to the public'.[149] This is confirmed by the discount for Virginia bank notes in New York of only three-fourths of one per cent in April 1817, and their trading at par by August of that year.[150] Branches of the Second Bank of the United States were not established in Virginia until after the February 1817 resumption of specie payment, with offices created at Norfolk and at Richmond in October of that year. Loans and discounts at these branches quickly expanded so that by June 1818 they totaled almost $4.5 million (see Table 3.1). Part of this expansion was mandated by the agreement between state banks and the Second Bank that stipulated in exchange for the resumption of specie convertibility by the state banks, the Second Bank would expand discounts for individuals by $500,000 in Virginia.[151]

Because only some data for Virginia state-chartered banks for the years 1816 and 1817 are available (total loans and discounts cannot be located for year end 1816 and year end 1817, although partial data is available for 1816), the analysis will begin by looking at the period from year end 1815 until year end 1818. This lack of data will prevent a more detailed analysis of the events of 1817 and early 1818 surrounding the resumption of specie payments and the establishment of a Bank of the United States presence in the Commonwealth, but the analysis will still provide important insights into the state of banking in Virginia in the years leading up to the Panic. When considered as a whole, Virginia state banks contracted their loans and discounts 10.6 per cent or $919,499 between the end of 1815 and the end of 1818 (see Table 3.3). Two points are important to consider. First, it is likely that loans and discounts had dropped even more sharply in 1816 in anticipation of the resumption of specie convertibility before rebounding a bit once banks adjusted to the realities of convertibility. This is supported by partial data from *Niles' Register* that shows the bank's discounts and state debt declining 28.0 per cent between 1 January and 11 November 1816.[152]

The dramatic decline in notes and deposits, down 48.4 per cent during the year 1816 before recovering 5.1 per cent in calendar year 1817 and then declining 4.7 per cent in 1818 for a 43.1 per cent fall between year end 1815 and year end 1818, and the sharp increase in the specie reserve ratio, from 0.05 at the end of 1815 to 0.30 at the end of 1816 before levelling out at about 0.20 for the remaining years prior to the panic, provide further evidence of the volatility of the financial sector in the Commonwealth during the period preceding the panic (see Table

3.3). This may be part of the explanation for the drop in prices experienced in 1817 before they recovered at the beginning of the next year. Another part of the explanation for the price declines in 1817 is the adjustment following their sharp rise resulting from the loss of much of the 1816 crop because of exceptionally bad weather, which in turn led to a 31.6 per cent fall in Virginia exports although exports increased 7.0 per cent for the nation as a whole. Chart 3.1 shows changes in the Richmond commodity price index for 1817 and 1818.[153]

A second point to consider is the decline in loans and discounts by the state-chartered banks between year end 1815 and 1818. This decrease was offset by the expansion of loans and discounts in late 1817 and early 1818 by the Virginia offices of the Second Bank of the United States. As a result, total loans and discounts in the state still increased significantly from approximately $8.6 million provided by the state-chartered banks alone at year end 1815 to the $11.2 million outstanding at year end 1818 from the state banks and the offices of the Second Bank of the United States combined, an increase of 22.8 per cent (see Tables 3.3 and 3.4). This likely explains in part the resurgence in prices in early 1818 and their slight upward trend through the end of the year (see Chart 3.1).

The striking decline in notes and deposits by Virginia state-chartered banks between year end 1815 and year end 1818 requires more explanation. During a period in which the Virginia branches of the Second Bank were introducing their notes to the Commonwealth and were, following the initial distribution, increasing their notes and deposits modestly, Virginia's state-chartered banks contracted notes and deposits by almost $3.5 million or 40.3 per cent, and increased their specie reserves dramatically during 1816 from 5 per cent to 30 per cent before easing back to a 0.19 reserve ratio at year end 1817 (see Tables 3.2 and 3.3). As indicated earlier, this action by Virginia's banks was in response to the resumption of specie payments in February 1817 as mandated by Congress and negotiated by the Second Bank with the state banking interest. This meant that notes and deposits from the combination of state-chartered banks and Bank of the United States branches in Virginia dropped from about $8.5 million at year end 1815 to about $5.1 million by late 1817 and early 1818, approximately a 40 per cent decline. Such action would have put pressure on the Commonwealth's merchants during 1818, the year preceding the Panic. The loss of circulating currency would have meant that merchants had to turn increasingly to using credit when dealing with customers rather than relying on cash. Finally, although the return to specie convertibility affected circulation dramatically, the resumption appears to have been more successful in Virginia than in some states since the notes of the Commonwealth's banks circulated in New York and Baltimore at less than one per cent discount soon after the resumption and were circulating at par by mid-summer of that year.[154]

The tightening, mild expansion and retightening of credit that took place in Virginia through 1816, 1817 and early 1818, combined with the shrinking of the circulating medium by Virginia banks during the period, set the stage in the Commonwealth for the actions of the directors of the Second Bank. In response to the overextension of credit and the flow of notes eastward, orders came from the Bank in July 1818 that the Virginia branches were to reduce their discounts. The Richmond office was directed to reduce discounts by $700,000, or 23.0 per cent of its June loans and discounts, and the Norfolk branch of the Bank to reduce discounts by $300,000, or 20.9 per cent of its June loans and discounts. A further demand was made in October of the same year that the Richmond branch reduce discounts an additional $400,000. Such action created additional problems for Virginia's already stressed credit system. Although the Virginia state-chartered banks had managed to reverse the trend of their notes and deposits and reserve ratio between 1817 and 1818, the damage done by the earlier contraction largely remained, and by the end of 1818, the actions of the Second Bank sent a clear signal of further financial contraction to the Commonwealth's citizens. This combined with the collapse of markets for Virginia's commodities during the same period to cause prices to begin their precipitous drop. The Richmond commodity price index fell from a level of 85.19 in mid-October 1818 to a trough of 44.19 in February 1821, a 48.1 per cent fall. The sharp contraction of loans and discounts by the Second Bank's Virginia branches continued through 1819 (see Table 3.1). But, with the Commonwealth's state banks keeping loans and discounts almost level through the year, down 2.0 per cent, the total contraction of loans and discounts in the state for 1819 was a more modest 9.4 per cent (see Tables 3.3 and 3.4). However, for an already weakened credit system, the impact further exacerbated changes coming from commodity markets and generated a dramatic decline as seen from the perspective of the state's merchant community.

From this point in time onward, the banking system in Virginia played an even more neutral role as the economic crisis developed. As data in Table 3.4 indicate, the combined operations of Virginia's state banks and the Virginia branches of the Bank of the United States kept loans and discounts almost constant from 1819 through 1821, while notes and deposits actually increased. Thus, while the Commonwealth's banking system played a role in setting the stage for the economic hardships faced by Virginians, once the downturn had begun, except for the abnormally high reserve ratio in 1819 that was largely in response to demands placed on the state bank's specie by actions of the Second Bank's branches in the Commonwealth, the state banks did little to exacerbate the situation.[155] Likewise, except for a mild expansion by the state's banks during 1821, the system did nothing to speed recovery. Thus, the search for reasons behind the sharp deflation must be found elsewhere.

The Second Bank of the United States Again

At the national level, the Second Bank did not play a neutral role in the depression following the Panic of 1819. A reassessment of the role of Langdon Cheves, who in 1819 became President of the Second Bank of the United States, by the economic historian Edwin Perkins suggests that while Cheves 'can be spared blame for precipitating the panic, the monetary policies he pursued after the crisis had materialized were inappropriate for a quasi-central bank or for any large bank holding up to one third of the total reserves of the banking system'. In particular, Perkins finds that the Second Bank accumulated over $7 million in specie by the end of 1820 and that 'at least $4 million of that total represented excess reserves, which could have been used to increase the nation's supply of notes and deposits by up to 17 percent'. Thus, Perkins believes that Cheves and the Second Bank 'could have alleviated much hardship, prevented hundreds of failures and bankruptcies, and perhaps led the country out of the recession before it became a depression'.[156]

But, banking is not the only component of a modern financial system, and deflationary pressures could also come from the financial operations of governments, federal and state. Thus, before concluding the analysis of the role of Virginia's banking system in the Panic of 1819, the impact of federal government and Virginia state finances requires attention.

Federal and State Government Finance

Reducing the debt created during the War of 1812 was the national government's primary focus in the years following the Treaty of Ghent. Large budget surpluses in 1816 and 1817 resulting from the booming export economy coincided with the expiration of Louisiana Purchase bonds to enable the federal government to make significant progress towards its goal. As Table 3.5 indicates, the federal deficit, which stood at $127.3 million in 1816, was reduced by some $35 million between 1816 and 1819, with many of these funds going to foreign bondholders.[157] For example, of the some $11 million in 1803 Louisiana 'stock' retired between 1818 and 1821, about $6 million was paid to foreigners.[158] The economic impact of these fiscal actions was to further exacerbate the beginnings of the downturn. To the extent federal surpluses were directed abroad to repay foreign creditors, they reduced overall domestic spending. Federal expenditures fell in real terms by 29.1 per cent between 1816 and 1817 and a further 6.8 per cent by 1818. Further, because domestic creditors did not receive these funds, they could not spend or invest their returns in the domestic economy. Having removed spending from the domestic economy in the three years prior to the downturn, the federal government increased expenditures by 27.3 per cent in real terms in 1819, thus providing some stimulus, although far too little to reverse the economic crises already underway. After keeping real expenditures almost constant in 1820, the federal government decreased real spending 10.0 per cent and 8.7 per cent in 1821 and 1822 respectively while keeping the budget virtually balanced over the period 1820–3. Thus, as the depression deepened, the federal government played no important role in either stimulating or contracting the national economy (see Table 3.5).

The Commonwealth's budget during these years was revenue driven, with the combination of licence fees from peddlers, ordinary keepers and merchants plus property taxes on lands and lots, slaves, and horses and carriages providing the bulk of receipts. Expenditures primarily supported government administration and court operations, although the Literary Fund and the Board of Public Works were important beneficiaries of state revenues and thus critical contributors to the state's spending. State budget data for 1816–23 is given in Table 3.6. Although the Commonwealth maintained a large budget surplus in 1818 and the budget year 1820 showed some impact of the downturn, state spending stayed remarkably strong during this time. Real revenues actually increased 13.8 per cent between fiscal years 1818 and 1821, and real spending fluctuated widely with peaks in 1819 and 1821 before levelling off in the aftermath of the crisis. While the drop in spending in the years leading up to the Panic (1816–18) and the sharp decline in 1820 may have contributed to slowing the state's economy, the relatively high real spending in the crisis years of 1819 and 1821 likely helped modify the downturn slightly. Interestingly, subscriptions and loans by the Board of Public Works increased during the period of the Panic, up 57.2 per cent in 1819 and 173.0 per cent in 1820 before dropping back 27.3 per cent in 1821 and remaining at about that level for 1822. However impressive these increases, the total spent by the Board each year was only about 10 per cent of the expenditures from the state, ranging from a low of 3.7 per cent in 1819 to a high of 16.7 per cent in 1820. Action by the Board of Public Works was particularly significant for Norfolk, since the Dismal Swamp Canal was the major recipient of Board funds, receiving 43.6 per cent of the funds actually paid out between 1817 and 1823.[159]

Norfolk and Hampton Roads, which were hit hard by American navigation acts as well as the Panic, benefited during the Panic from federal expenditures.[160] At the close of the War of 1812, Congress took action to reduce the vulnerability of the Chesapeake area by authorizing new fortifications to be built to protect the harbor and ordering a naval expansion as a means of further protecting the nation's shores. Actual construction began in March 1819 on Forts Monroe and Calhoun. At roughly the same time, the Navy Yard at Gosport began building a ship of the line, the *Delaware*, and a forty-four-gun frigate as part of the 1816 act to gradually increase the size of the navy. This federal spending boosted the local economy at a critical time.[161] Table 3.7 shows federal expenditures on various projects in Hampton Roads in 1818–23. Norfolk's strong opposition to 'Mr.

Madison's War' may have played some role in the decision to allocate spending to the area, and the continuing deflation helped these dollars have an even greater impact.[162] Although the concept of countercyclical government spending was not viewed as part of the government's role in this era, for Norfolk and Hampton Roads the impact of both state and federal spending directed at specific local projects helped to modify some of the decline resulting from the combined effect of the navigation acts and the Panic of 1819.

Summary and Conclusions

In the early decades of the nineteenth century, a number of Virginians feared all paper money in general and in particular the banks that issued fiat currency, which might become inconvertible. For many, the Panic of 1819 confirmed their worst fears. But, the question remains: were Virginia's banking institutions in part responsible for the economic crisis that struck the nation and the Commonwealth? The answer is mostly no. Despite much focus by historians on the role of the banking system, the primary factor in the economic crisis of 1819–21 was the loss of foreign markets for American agricultural commodities. However, the banking system was not totally blameless. To the extent that banks across the country participated in the speculative boom preceding the downturn, to the extent they shocked the economy and weakened credit relationships by contracting credit and reducing note circulation in 1816 and 1817 in anticipation of and response to the resumption of specie convertibility, and to the extent the contraction of credit by the Second Bank of the United States in 1818 created a sudden but temporary shock, banks exacerbated the driving force in the depression of 1819–21. However, the ultimate foundation for the crisis lay in foreign markets for American commodities. It was their collapse that created the depression of 1818–21. As the depression developed, the large specie reserve held by the Second Bank during the depression likely exacerbated the downturn, but the cause of the depression cannot be attributed to the Bank or its vilified president, William Jones.

In Virginia, data indicate that a contraction by the state-chartered banks during the resumption of specie payments in 1817 likely weakened the credit system upon which many Virginians depended. However, by the time of the Panic the Commonwealth's chartered banks had stabilized their loans and discounts and notes and deposits. Although Virginia banks maintained a high specie reserve ratio during 1819, the state-chartered banks actually mitigated the decline in loans and discounts from the Bank of the United States offices in the state that year. In addition, an expansion of notes and deposits by the Bank of the United States offices was sufficient to ensure the state's total rose 9.9 per cent despite a mild contraction by Virginia's state-chartered banks. Thus, the banks bear little blame for the events of 1819 in Virginia and the depression that followed.

Likewise, federal and Commonwealth government finances played a relatively small role in the economic events of the time. The levels of spending were small, and as the crisis developed the impacts of their financial operations were neutral to slightly positive.

Although Virginia's banks deserve little of the blame for the economic crisis of 1819–21, they faced substantial criticism from citizens of the Commonwealth. The strengthening of hard money positions that resulted meant that no new bank would be chartered in Virginia until after the General Assembly revised the state's banking law in March 1837 following the demise of the Second Bank of the United States.[163] Attacks on banking began appearing in the middle of 1819, with a series of editorials and letters in the *Richmond Enquirer*, the state's most influential newspaper.[164] Governor Thomas M. Randolph, son-in-law of Thomas Jefferson, attacked paper money and the banks that issued currency in his 4 December 1820 inaugural address to the legislature. Indicating that 'paper can never be a measure of value', Randolph attacked 'the mode in which capital is dispensed by banks'. He added, 'They, beyond all doubt, have a strong tendency to prevent permanent advances by capitalists for the promotion of useful industry, and to facilitate and encourage those employments of money least beneficial to the general interest of society'. Randolph continued, 'But a still greater evil seems to be inseparably connected with the system of banking. Great Fluctuations in the quantity of circulating medium proceed from their vacillating nature, and such changes are productive of the most distressing consequences in society'.[165] In a further attack on banks, Thomas Ritchie, editor of the *Enquirer*, suggested that bank notes should be allowed, if at all, only in large denominations and with complete specie convertibility.[166] Finally, Thomas Jefferson, long a vigorous opponent of banks and their credit, unsuccessfully proposed to the General Assembly through his friend William C. Rives a 'Plan for Reducing the Circulating Medium' for the purpose of 'the eternal suppression of bank paper'.[167]

Attacks on the Commonwealth's banking institutions were not limited to speeches and print. In 1824 when the charter of the Farmers' Bank of Virginia came to the legislature for renewal, there was considerable debate before it was extended. To obtain renewal, the Bank was required to contribute to the Internal Improvement Fund a sum of $50,000 annually.[168] As a further indication of the attitude toward banks, in February 1820, efforts were undertaken by some shareholders to reduce the salaries of the president and branch presidents of the Bank of Virginia. This was defeated, as was a move to reduce the salary of the Farmers' Bank president. However, stockholders did vote by a one-vote margin to reduce the annual salaries of Farmers' Bank branch presidents from $1,000 to $700.[169]

To complete the analysis of causes of the deflation and depression that rocked Virginia and the nation in the period 1819–21, the next chapter turns to the state's agricultural sector and commodity exports.

Tables

Table 3.1: Loans and Discounts, 1818–23: Bank of the United States, Norfolk and Richmond Branches.

Date	Loans and Discounts (current dollars)		
	Norfolk	Richmond	Total
Oct 1817		Branches Established	
Feb 1818	1,144,913	2,870,844	4,015,757
June 1818	1,437,930	3,040,955	4,478,885
July 1818	Bank of the United States resolves to reduce discounts by $700,000 at Richmond and $300,000 at Norfolk at the rate of at least 12 1/2 % of the amount of income on each discount day.		
Oct 1818	Further reduction of $400,000 at Richmond ordered.		
Dec 1818	1,217,541 (-15.3%)	2,258,826 (-25.7%)	3,476,367 (-22.8%)
June 1819	891,094 (-26.8%)	1,846,387 (-18.3%)	2,737,481 (-21.3%)
Dec 1819	805,229 (-9.6%)	1,766,968 (-4.3%)	2,572,197 (-6.0%)
June 1820	779,145 (-3.2%)	1,547,921 (-12.4%)	2,327,006 (-9.5%)
Dec 1820	825,932	1,422,332	2,248,264 (-3.4%)
June 1821	848,270	1,323,001	2,171,271 (-3.4%)
Dec 1821	838,604	1,326,725	2,165,329 (-0.2%)
June 1822	829,951	1,309,233	2,139,184 (-1.2%)
Dec 1822	802,145	1,358,555	2,160,700 (+1.0%)
June 1823	857,139	1,404,753	2,261,892 (+4.7%)
Dec 1823	850,237	1,336,428	2,186,665 (-3.3%)

Sources: United States Congress, House, 'Bank of the United States', House Executive Document 147, 22nd Congress, 1st session, 1835, pp. 22–5 and *American State Papers, Finance*, vol. 3, pp. 387–9.

Table 3. 2: Notes, Deposits and Specie, 1818–23: Bank of the United States, Norfolk and Richmond Branches.

Date	Norfolk			Richmond		
	Notes & Deposits	Specie	RR	Notes & Deposits	Specie	RR
			(current dollars)			
Oct 1817			Branches Established			
Feb 1818	159,289	84,281	52.9	217,953	95,832	44.0
June 1818	172,647	57,802	33.5	289,557	79,606	27.5

Date	Norfolk			Richmond		
	Notes & Deposits	Specie	RR	Notes & Deposits	Specie	RR
			(current dollars)			
Dec 1818	201,897	84,512	41.9	244,093	91,260	37.4
June 1819	107,940	31,736	29.4	146,322	144,072	98.5
Dec 1819	446,758	84,682	18.9	1,179,545	73,378	6.2
June 1820	481,481	86,958	18.1	1,212,640	141,497	11.7
Dec 1820	616,759	115,648	18.8	1,161,714	144,518	12.4
June 1821	656,812	84,540	12.9	1,123,497	163,792	14.6
Dec 1821	691,968	146,907	21.2	1,126,139	165,184	14.7
June 1822	588,280	67,533	11.5	1,223,403	140,103	11.5
Dec 1822	533,258	61,367	11.5	1,155,011	151,411	13.1
June 1823	589,821	98,588	16.7	1,030,556	158,583	15.4
Dec 1823	529,996	97,234	18.3	1,027,329	164,332	16.0

RR=Specie Reserve Ratio

Sources: US Congress, House, 'Bank of the United States', House Executive Document 147, 22nd Congress, 1st session, 1835, pp. 22–5.

Table 3.3: Virginia Banks, 1815–23.

Year End (# Banks)	Loans and Discounts	Notes and Deposits	Specie	Reserve Ratios		
		(current dollars)		VA	ALL	BofUS
1815 (2)	8,647,150	8,546,270	456,329	.05	.17	--
1816 (2)	na	4,408,479	1,344,272	.30	.19	--
1817 (2)	na	5,100,279	952,165	.19	.21	.12
1818 (3)*	7,727,646	4,858,625	1,025,647	.21	.20	.21
1819 (4)	7,576,730	4,206,347	1,939,914	.46	.19	.33
1820 (4)	7,749,798	4,456,530	1,234,427	.28	.21	.61
1821 (4)	8,368,091	5,427,900	1,356,968	.25	.25	.34
1822 (4)	7,287,838	4,300,942	857,845	.20	.15	.37
1823 (4)	7,654,635	4,607,749	969,760	.21	.19	.32

VA=Virginia State Banks
ALL=All State Banks (from Perkins)
BofUS=Bank of the United States (from Perkins)
* Loans and discounts for two banks (Bank of Virginia and Farmers' Bank), other data for three banks (including Bank of the Valley of Virginia).
Note: Farmers' Bank data reported for end of year. Bank of Virginia and Bank of the Valley (beginning 1820) reported for 1 January. Northwestern Bank data reported 1 October beginning 1818. These all combined to provide end-of-year statistics. Data for 1819–23 come from Fenstermaker, *Development*. 1818 data come from *Journal of the House of Delegates 1818–1819* (Bank of Virginia and Farmers' Bank) and *Condition of State Banks* (Bank of the Valley, p. 418). Data for 1816 and 1817 and specie data for 1815 come from *Condition of State Banks*, p. 431 and p. 444. Other data for 1815 come from *Journal of the House of Delegates 1815–1816*, p. 151.

Sources: J. van Fenstermaker, *The Development of American Commercial Banking, 1782–1837* (Kent, OH: Kent State University Press, 1965), pp. 234–5; J. van Fenstermaker, *A Statistical Summary of the Commercial Banks Incorporated in the United States Prior to 1819* (Kent, OH: Kent State University Press, 1965), p. 25; E. J. Perkins, 'Langdon Cheves and the Panic of 1819: A Reassessment', *Journal of Economic History*, 44:2 (1984), p. 457; *Journal of the House of Delegates 1815–16*, p. 151; *Journal of the House of Delegates 1818–19*, p. 165 and United States Congress, House, *Condition of State Banks*, House Document 79, January 8, 1838, 25th Congress, 2nd Session, pp. 411, 418, 431 and 444.

Table 3.4: Loans and Discounts and Notes and Deposits in Virginia, 1818–23.

Year End	Loans and Discounts			Notes and Deposits in Virginia		
	Bus	VA Banks	Total	Bus	VA Banks	Total
			(thousands of current dollars)			
1818	3,476	7,728	11,204	446	4,859	5,305
1819	2,572	7,576	10,149	1,626	4,206	5,833
1820	2,248	7,750	9,998	1,778	4,457	6,235
1821	2,165	8,368	10,533	1,815	5,428	7,243
1822	2,161	7,288	9,449	1,688	4,301	5,989
1823	2,186	7,655	9,841	1,557	4,608	6,165

BUS=Bank of the United States, Virginia Branches
VA BANKS=Virginia State-Chartered Banks

Sources: Tables 3.1, 3.2, and 3.3.

Table 3.5: Federal Budget, 1816–23.

Year	Receipts	Expenditures	Surplus or Deficit	Net Change in Debt
		(thousands of current dollars)		
1816	47,678	30,578	17,091	-3,843
1817	33,099	21,844	11,255	-20,025
1818	21,585	19,825	1,760	-7,937
1819	24,603	21,464	3,140	-4,514
1820	17,881	18,261	-380	-1,028
1821	14,573	15,811	-1,237	+3,559
1822	20,232	15,000	5,232	-2,671
1823	20,541	14,707	5,834	+608

Source: *Historical Statistics of the United States: Colonial Times to 1970* (Washington: Bureau of the Census, 1975), Series Y-335-Y338 and E-52.

Table 3.6: Virginia State Expenditures and Board of Public Works Subscriptions and Loans, 1816–23.

Year (ending Sept. 30)	Virginia Budget				Board of Public Works	
	Revenue		Expenditure		Subscriptions and Loans	
	current	real	current	real	current	real
1816	2,084,753	1,380,631	2,039,300	1,350,530	na	na
1817	1,343,332	889,624	1,342,238	888,899	15,000	10,265
1818	1,187,103	807,553	796,401	541,769	31,500	21,249
1819	1,207,749	966,199	1,137,783	910,226	41,750	33,400
1820	650,981	614,133	577,695	544,995	96,650	91,179
1821	937,568	919,184	870,125	853,064	67,650	66,324
1822	739,700	697,830	779,956	735,808	72,070	67,991
1823	687,253	667,236	763,719	741,475	96,900	94,078

na = not available

Sources: *Journal of the House of Delegates 1816–1817*, p. 145; *1817–1818*, p. 107; *1818–1819*, pp. 105–6; *1819–1820*, p. 119; *1820–1821*, p. 144; *1821–1822, Treasurer's Report*; *1822–1823, Treasurer's Report*; *1823–1824, Treasurer's Annual Report*; *1824–1825, Second Auditor's Report on Canal and Turnpike Companies, January 7*, 1825 and *Historical Statistics of the United States: Colonial Times to 1970* (Washington: Bureau of the Census, 1975), Series E-52.

Table 3.7: Federal Government Expenditures in Hampton Roads, 1818–23.

Year	Expenditures (current dollars)			
	Fort Monroe	Fort Calhoun	Norfolk Customs House	Gosport Navy Yard
1818	–	–	18,000	na
1819	208,210	141,933	13,500	na
1820	–	–	3,052	136,630
1821	396,889	171,293	–	84,909
1822–3	133,235*	152,491*	–	65,400**

* through September 30, 1823
** to November 1, 1822
na = not available

Sources: *American State Papers*, part 6, vol. 1, p. 851 and United States Congress, Senate, *Statement of the Appropriations and Expenditures for Public Buildings, Rivers and Harbors, Forts, Arsenals, Armories and Other Public Works from 1789–1882*, Senate Document 196, 47th Congress, 1st Session, 1883, pp. 88 and 584–5.

Charts

Chart 3.1: Richmond Commodity Price Index, 1817–18.

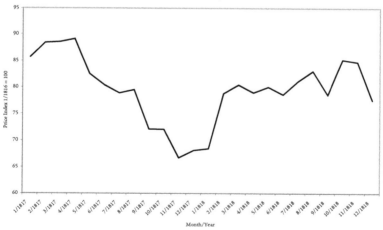

Appendix: Virginia Bank Data

Initial data for Virginia's state-chartered banks was obtained from two studies by J. Van Fenstermaker. The first, *The Development of American Commercial Banking, 1782–1837* provides data for Virginia banks from 1819 through 1837 on pages 234 and 235. Pre-1819 data were found in Fenstermaker's *A Statistical Summary of the Commercial Banks Incorporated in the United States Prior to 1819* on page 25. However, the pre-1819 data do not appear to be complete and do not match with the data provided for 1819–37. Thus a review of the data was undertaken. The 1819–37 data match, with a few minor exceptions, the data found in the sources provided and therefore were used for this study. The earlier data did not match with various sources consulted. Thus a new data set was created for the period from the end of the year 1815 to the end of the year 1818.

The end of the year was used for reporting data to make it clearer when considering changes in various categories during a calendar year. However, not all data were actually reported as end of the year. The Farmers' Bank of Virginia and branches reported data for the end of the year. The Bank of Virginia and branches and the Bank of the Valley of Virginia (beginning 1820) reported for 1 January. The Northwestern Bank of Virginia data were reported for 1 October, beginning in 1818. For each year, these reports were combined to provide an end of the year statistic. Data for 1819–23 come from Fenstermaker, *Development*, and are reported as end of the year. Data for 1818 come from *Journal of the House of Delegates 1818–1819*, page 165, for the Bank of Virginia and Farmers' Bank, and from *Condition of State Banks*, House Document 79, 8 January 1838, 25th Congress, 2nd Session, page 418, for the Bank of the Valley. Data for 1816 and 1817 and specie data for 1815 come from *Condition of State Banks*, pages 431 and 444. Other data for 1815 come from *Journal of the House of Delegates 1815–1816*, page 151.

4 AGRICULTURE, EXPORTS AND LAND

As the year 1821 drew to a close, a meeting of the citizens of Norfolk over-whelmingly passed a series of resolutions regarding the 'pernicious' effects of Congressional actions in 1818 and 1820 that closed American ports to British ships.[170] 'Destroying our commerce, and injuring all classes of our citizens', these navigation acts, according to the resolutions, were 'operating most unequally and partially upon different sections and portions of the Union, burdening the products of agriculture in a fruitless attempt to promote the shipping interest, diminishing the revenue, and threatening, in the issue, to produce many great and lasting evils to the whole nation'.[171] The economic crisis that led Norfolk's citizens to take action resulted from the combined effects of the American Navigation Acts to which the resolutions were directed and the more general impacts of the new nation's first modern business cycle, the Panic of 1819.

A few years before, in early February 1815, a banner in the *Norfolk Gazette and Public Ledger* carried the 'glorious news' of peace ending the War of 1812, brought in fifty hours from New York by the schooner *James Lawrence*. That night, the mayor 'recommended' an illumination that was, according to the fol-lowing Saturday's press, 'more general than ever we saw'.[172] To celebrate the peace in Richmond, Mayor Thomas Wilson ordered an illumination for 1 March. 'The Capital and all the houses of the town were illuminated ... and there was a mile long procession of soldiers and citizens carrying transparencies'.[173] Although the word of a peace treaty brought joy to Virginians and enabled the frigate *Constellation*, blockaded in Norfolk since early in 1813, to sail for New York, it did not erase the concern of some for the future of Virginia's export-based agricultural economy. As a Norfolk editorial regarding the treaty indicated, 'In a commercial view we have gained nothing; for commerce is not even noticed, nor indeed was it to be expected, that commercial objects would be embedded in a treaty of peace and amity'.[174] With the peace, a more rigorous enforcement of British navigation acts restricted the entry of American goods and vessels to British colonial ports, par-ticularly in the West Indies.[175] This led the Norfolk newspaper to 'presume it will be an immediate object of our government to enter into a treaty of commerce and navigation with Great Britain; we hope the attempt will be attended with success, but fear it will not'. The editorialist went on to suggest that 'we may certainly exclude British vessels from our ports, if they exclude ours from theirs, we mean her colonial possessions, but this we must not do at the expense of our agriculture'.[176] However, in retaliation against British action and the failure of negotiations to resolve the issue of American access to British colonial ports, the United States soon passed a series of navigation acts that excluded British ships from American ports at some expense to the Commonwealth's agricultural interest.[177] How the concurrent events of depression in the wake of the Panic of 1819 and the closing of West Indies trade affected the heart of the Commonwealth's economy, agriculture, during these troubled times is the focus of this chapter.

Virginia, Agriculture and Agricultural Prices

The American economy of the period was dominated by agriculture, as was that of Virginia. For the United States in 1820, Thomas Weiss estimates that of the total labour force 71.4 per cent was the farm share, down slightly from the 72.3 per cent share in 1810. In Virginia, the 1820 census found 88.1 per cent of the Commonwealth's population east of the Alleghenies and 94.0 per cent of those west of the mountains engaged in agriculture. Of enslaved Virginians, 40.3 per cent of the state's population in 1810 and 39.9 per cent in 1820, the vast majority worked growing and processing agricultural commodities.[178] The Commonwealth's agricultural sector produced a wide variety of staples, with tobacco, grains, particularly wheat, and naval stores being the state's most important crops. Virginia was the nation's leading source of tobacco and a major wheat producer.[179] Moreover, the export market for these goods was critical for the Commonwealth. In the years 1817 and 1818, Virginia exported 58.9 per cent and 67.2 per cent respectively of the American tobacco inspected for export.[180] If this ratio held for the entire period, the demand for Virginia's chief crop would be highly sensitive to changes in foreign markets. And, change is just what happened to international markets.

Led by an economic downturn in Great Britain, reinforced by recession in Europe, and adversely affected by the operations of the British Corn Laws, the demand for American staples and particularly the agricultural commodities produced in Virginia dropped beginning in 1819.[181] Chart 4.1 indicates the movement in US and Virginia exports for the years 1816–23. Between 1818 and 1821 the real value of the state's exports fell 36.8 per cent compared with a fall of 15.7 per cent for the nation as a whole. The fall in the Commonwealth's exports in 1817 is likely the result of changes in the tobacco market and the unusual weather in 1816 which led, among other things, to the failure of the wheat crop. This will be taken up in detail below. Table 4.1 provides data for exports in current dollars of the nation, the Commonwealth and the port of Norfolk in the years 1816–23 and indicates the annual percentage changes in both current and real terms. The downward-tending roller coaster ride experienced by American and Virginia exports after 1818 is evident as is the impact of the American Navigation Acts that effectively closed the port of Norfolk to international trade, primarily with the British West Indies.[182] From contributing 28.7 per cent and 45.9 per cent of the value of Virginia's exports in 1816 and 1817 respectively, Norfolk by 1821 was providing barely a trickle of goods to foreign markets.

One result stemming from this volatility in the markets for Virginia's commodities was a significant deflation. Chart 4.2 shows movements in a monthly Richmond commodity price index beginning in January 1816 and continuing through the end of the year 1823. The equal-weighted index is based on prices current for six commodities in the Richmond market as reported in the *Richmond Enquirer* on the date closest to the fifteenth of each month. The six prices used to construct the index include corn, cornmeal, wheat, flour superfine, tobacco and hemp. Although prices of a number of other commodities are reported during this time period, none are sufficiently consistent to be used in constructing the index, and the reports before 1816 are too sporadic to allow an index to be developed. The Appendix to this chapter provides additional information regarding the price index and its construction.[183]

The most striking feature of price movements during the period is the spectacular drop during 1819 and 1820. From a high of 85.19 in November 1818, the index fell to a low of 44.19 in February 1821, a 48.1 per cent decline. Prices through 1816, 1817 and 1818 reflected the inflationary run-up of prices during the post-War boom of 1812, and the disastrous harvest in 1816. Although there had been a downward movement of prices at the last half of 1817 associated with the state banks' credit contraction as the system resumed specie convertibility, a fall of 23.9 per cent from a high of 89.15 in April 1817 to 68.08 in December of that year, the Commonwealth was not prepared for the intense deflationary pressures in the wake of the Panic of 1819.

To put the Virginia experience in some perspective, Chart 4.3 shows prices in the United States for the period 1810–30. Inflation during the War of 1812 is clearly evident, although it also appears that by the time the Richmond commodity price index begins, in January 1816, much of the wartime run-up in prices has been removed from the economy. With the coming of the depression of 1819–21, prices in the nation began a long slide which would continue, with a break in the mid-eighteen thirties, until the eve of the Civil War. The impact of the 1819–21 depression appears most clearly in the Warren-Pearson wholesale price index which shows prices by the end of the depression in 1821 moving well below their pre-war level. The David-Solar cost-of-living index indicates a less dramatic fall during the crisis following the Panic of 1819 but confirms the long decline in prices from their wartime highs and indicates again that the decline after 1818 brought prices well below their pre-war levels.

The price declines demonstrated by the Richmond commodity price index appear also to have hit the western portions of the state, however with some lag. Table 4.2 provides information on prices and wages in western Virginia for the years 1816–23 from a study by Donald R. Adams, Jr. Although the price index is provided only on an annual basis, it suggests that prices in the western part of Virginia continued to rise into if not through 1819 and that the deflation following the Panic of 1819 continued into 1822. Further, while the western Virginia and Richmond indexes contain different components, both consist only of agricultural commodities, and corn, wheat and flour, which are components in both, have a weight of 0.28 in the western Virginia index. Thus, while not completely comparable, the two indexes suggest that the deflation in western Virginia was not as extreme as that experienced in the Richmond area and that it occurred with some lag behind the fall in prices in the eastern part of the state. The finding of a lag in the decline in prices in western Virginia is consistent with the comparison of eastern, New York and Philadelphia, wholesale prices with western, Cincinnati, wholesale prices during the period. According to Arthur H. Cole in his study of wholesale commodity prices in the United States, 'the real break in Cincinnati prices is delayed until the latter half of 1819'. Further, he finds 'the decline in Cincinnati prices became less violent following the spring of 1821, but the nadir was not reached until the fall of that year'. Thus, the lag observed in western Virginia prices appears to be part of a general lag in price changes experienced by those regions beyond the mountains tied to the isolation created by the Alleghenies.[184]

In addition to explaining the collapse of the state's commodity prices after the Panic of 1819, two related aspects of the Commonwealth's experience during this period require attention. The first and most important is the behaviour of Virginia's exports from 1819 through 1821. The second is the decline in Virginia's exports in 1817, down 31.6 per cent, while exports for the nation as a whole rose by 7.0 per cent. Chart 4.4 shows the relationships between the Richmond commodity price index and the Commonwealth's total exports for the period 1816–23. While much of the story behind the changes evidenced in the chart has already been told in previous chapters, the major elements bear repeating. Far and away the most critical factor explaining the fall in prices and exports after 1818 was the collapse of foreign markets. At this time Europe was the destination of about two-thirds of America's exports and Britain accounted for about one-third of the total; in 1818 the proportions were 73.1 per cent and 40.9 per cent respectively.[185] As Table 1.2 demonstrates, the decline in British business activity after 1818 and the fall in British importation of corn, wheat and flour and American grain were substantial, with business activity down 12.4 per cent, total imports declining 16.5 per cent, and corn, wheat and flour and US grain down 58.8 per cent, 70.3 per cent, and 74.6 per cent respectively between 1818 and 1819. While wheat and flour and American grain recovered slightly in 1820, by 1821 the fall had resumed and continued through 1823.

Douglass North has suggested that 'relative readjustment of the price level in the United States vis-a-vis United Kingdom prices was the most important influence in the sharp decline of 1818–1820'.[186] This point is verified when changes in the value of exports are compared with changes in the level of prices. For the nation as a whole exports fell 41.5 per cent between 1818 and 1821 while export prices fell 47.9 per cent. This suggests that although the physical amount of exports likely increased slightly, the fall in prices of exported commodities dominated the country's international trade during the years following the Panic of 1819. In Virginia, the story was much the same. The Commonwealth's exports fell a total of 56.1 per cent from 1818 to 1821 and prices of commodities in the Richmond market declined 48.1 per cent between November 1818 and February 1821, again indicating that prices rather than quantities dominated. However, while export quantities for the nation may have increased, in Virginia export quantities appear to have fallen. This is confirmed by one report which indicates that in Richmond 'total inspections [of flour] dropped almost forty per cent from 1819 to 1822'.[187]

Comparing the changes in price of the commodities used to construct the Richmond price index and the value of total Virginia exports for the years 1816–23, it is clear that flour and wheat prices declined beginning in 1819 as did corn and cornmeal, although to a lesser extent. Hemp prices, which jumped sharply at the beginning of 1818, declined during 1819 before recovering in the middle of 1820, and tobacco prices also fell sharply in 1819 but much less dramatically than in 1816–17. These comparisons reinforce the importance of price declines to the behaviour of Virginia exports during the depression of 1818–21.

Examining the Commonwealth's prices and exports in 1816 and 1817 helps to explain the decline in Virginia exports in 1817, a time in which exports for the nation as a whole increased slightly. Prices for flour, wheat, corn and cornmeal in the Richmond market all spike significantly towards the end of 1816 before dropping again in early to mid-1817. This behaviour is the result of the terrible weather in 1816 and subsequent crop failures. For Virginia exports, prices rose as demand increased and supply all but disappeared, and the value of exports fell as the declines in quantity dominated price increases. Prices of hemp and tobacco are exceptions to the pattern experienced by the other commodities. Hemp prices fell during 1816 and 1817 before spiking in 1819, and tobacco prices declined sharply in 1816 and, with the exception of an increase during 1818, remained low for the period of this study. Although hemp appears to have been an important crop for the Commonwealth, its role in the export trade was likely not large. One source indicates that 'as late as 1819 hemp was said to be "a great article of export" from Virginia to the Northern States'.[188] Hemp thus seems to have been produced mostly for the domestic market. Tobacco, however, was an important export commodity for Virginia. But the decline in tobacco prices in 1816–17 was accompanied by a 10.0 per cent fall in the quantity of tobacco exported by the nation as a whole between 1816 and 1817. The combination of falling prices and quantity exported meant that the value of tobacco exported by the United States declined 25.7 per cent between 1816 and 1817. Without specific export data for Virginia, it is impossible to know exactly what role tobacco played in the fall of the state's exports in 1817. However, Virginia did export about 30 per cent of the nation's tobacco, and it is fair to assume the Commonwealth experienced a fall in quantity exported to go along with the price fall observed in the Richmond market, thus further exacerbating the state's export picture in 1817.

The intense deflationary pressure experienced by the Commonwealth in the aftermath of the Panic of 1819 was not limited to agricultural commodities. In a state dominated by agriculture every aspect of the economy was affected by the fall in agricultural prices. Among the most important sectors to feel the effects of the commodity price collapse were the market for land and the labour market, particularly the market for enslaved African Americans.

Land and the Enslaved

Deflation and the collapse of the Commonwealth's exports devastated the market for Virginia real estate. According to Avery Craven, in 1818 'the *Richmond Enquirer* and the *Virginia Herald* carried advertisements for over 21,000 acres for sale', and J. M. Garnett in the *Enquirer* 'placed the total amount in all papers of Virginia at from 600,000 to 700,000 acres'.[189] One estimate suggests that from 1817 to 1829 the value of the state's lands declined from $206 million to $90 million, a 31.1 per cent decline in real terms.[190] Thomas Berry, in his study of flour milling in Richmond, found that for two important mill owners in the city, 'realty assessments each slipped from $80,000 in 1818 to $40,000 in 1819, and $20,000 the following year', while for another individual the tax value of his 'interest in the Columbia mills descended from $25,000 to $5,000'. Finally, it was also during this period that 'Madison was unable to get a loan from the United States Bank, because of the poor security he had to offer' and 'Jefferson mortgaged his home to make good the financial failures of friends'. Both examples show how deflation affected credit markets, making it more difficult to obtain credit as asset values fell and forcing bankruptcies for which cosigners were required to cover losses, again with assets whose value had declined.[191]

Anecdotal observations provide some sense of the impact property markets experienced as the economic crisis swept over the Commonwealth. However, a more detailed and accurate view is possible by analyzing county and city land books. Land books contain the annual reports from the assessor, sheriff, or commissioner of revenue of each county and city and provide information on property assessments, rents received and the resulting taxes assigned to property owners each year. Assessments were to be made at local fair market value. Unfortunately for the purposes of this study, in the course of the 1820 General Assembly the legislature mandated a reassessment of Virginia's agricultural land. The resulting change makes assessment comparisons with earlier years impossible. But, information regarding city assessments does not appear to have been affected, and a number of reports contain information on rents, which also do not seem to have been influenced by the changes in assessments of agricultural land.

Table 4.3 shows the value of real property as assessed in the City of Richmond for the years 1817–25. Here the impact of the Panic of 1819 on property values is clearly evident as assessments fell 49.1 per cent between 1818 and 1819 and decreased again by 50.1 per cent between 1819 and 1820 for a total decline of 74.6 per cent in value of assessed property in the years between the peak in 1818 and the trough in 1820. By 1821 assessments had risen slightly, up 1.4 per cent, and in the following year the value of property continued to rise, up an additional 51.2 per cent. Thus, by 1822 assessed property values in Richmond had recovered somewhat from the trough reached in 1820, but assessments, despite their upward movement, still remained 61.1 per cent below their pre-Panic peak of almost $16 million in 1818. From this point until 1825, assessed real property values changed very little. The rapid fall in assessed value of Richmond real property could well reflect the market value of the city's property or could reflect the assessor overreacting to the economic climate of the time, including the 48.1 per cent fall in the Richmond commodity price index discussed earlier. The behaviour of rents may provide some insight.

The total annual amounts of rent paid on lots and property in Richmond for the period are also presented in Table 4.3. Conceptually, rents represent an expected future income stream from property which, when discounted over some relevant time period, provides the foundation for the value of that property. Thus, for example, if rents are expected to continually decline in the future, the value of property would fall and could be expected to fall faster than the decline in rents since the expectation of ever lower rents in the future comes into play. This appears to be what happened in Richmond. Between 1818 and 1819 assessed value fell 49.1 per cent while the total value of rents fell only 11.4 per cent. Assessed value continued its steep decline the next year, falling a further 50.1 per cent before turning up slightly in 1821 and more dramatically in 1822. Rents, however, continued to fall through the period with a drop of 29.6 per cent between 1819 and 1820 and more modest declines for the following years before finally turning around and increasing in 1824. From the perspective of the assessor, the doom and gloom of news reports regarding the Panic of 1819, the sharp fall in prices as reflected in the Richmond commodity price index, and the downturn in rents could have combined with observed real estate prices to generate a pessimistic view of the future course of rents and property values, leading to significant reductions in assessed values for property.

For other cities in the Commonwealth, tabulations of assessments are not recorded in the land books. However, values of rents are available for some years. Table 4.4 provides information on yearly rents in Norfolk Borough, Petersburg, Lynchburg and Winchester for the years 1815–25. The most complete data are for Norfolk. In the borough, the pattern of annual rents was roughly comparable to Richmond's experience. Rents began to drop between 1819 and 1820, a year later than those in Richmond, and continued their decline until turning upwards in 1824, the same year Richmond rents began to increase. Two aspects of this experience are of interest. First, the drop was not as dramatic as the fall in Richmond rents from 1819 to 1820, but the fall in rents between 1820 and 1823 raced well ahead of those in Richmond. Norfolk rents declined 7.2 per cent in 1819–20, then 12.5 per cent, 11.9 per cent and 9.2 per cent in subsequent years for a total fall of 35.0 per cent between 1819 and 1823. This compares to a decline in Richmond rents of 5.3 per cent in 1822, 1.0 per cent in 1823, and a total of 45.7 per cent for the entire period. The more significant declines in Norfolk rents during the latter years is most likely related to the effects of British and American navigation acts on shipping activity in the port city and the resulting impact on property values and rents.

Available data from Petersburg show annual rents falling 12.9 per cent between 1819 and 1822, the last year for which rents were recorded. Lynchburg experienced the largest drop in annual rents among Virginia cities, down 53.4 per cent between the peak in 1818 and the trough in 1822, while Winchester saw total annual rents decline only 5.4 per cent between 1820 and 1822. Interestingly, Lynchburg's downturn, except for turning upward one year earlier, mirrors that experienced in Richmond and is likely the result of the connection between the two cities provided by the James River and the river navigation improvements of the James River Company. Petersburg and Norfolk, on the other hand, turn down one year later and experience significantly less decline in total annual rents. This is a bit surprising but may be the result of these cities being affected less by the initial impacts of market changes than the commercial centre of the state, Richmond. It also may reflect differences in the response of assessors to the Panic of 1819. The role of the assessor may also help explain the Winchester data. Total annual rents in Winchester did not decline until 1820, at which time they fell only 5.4 per cent before turning up in 1822. In part, this may be the result of the delayed impact of the Panic in the western part of the state, as reflected in the western Virginia price data discussed earlier, but it also might be the case of a local assessor who responded little to market changes of the time. Given the general impact of the Panic of 1819, it is doubtful that any community avoided having local property markets affected. Regardless of the impact of assessors, one point is clear in the rent data. The Panic of 1819 and the decline in markets for agricultural commodities that followed in its wake significantly affected the market for land in Virginia. The 61.0 per cent fall in assessed value in Richmond between 1818 and 1822 may overstate the effects of the economic downturn, but the data on annual rents confirm an important and pervasive fall in property values.

Changes in land values and their impact on ownership of property quickly became a political issue, and the 1820 session of the General Assembly debated a proposed minimum appraisal law.[192] Supporters of the legislation argued that the behaviour of the Bank of the United States and the state's banks had created the problem, not the extravagances of debtors. However, those who contended that a minimum appraisal law did not constitute a proper role for the state, that it served a special interest, and that contracts must be honored carried the day as the bill was rejected by a vote of 113 to seventy-four.[193] At the national level, fourteen out of twenty Virginia House of Representatives delegates supported an act for the relief of public land debtors. Here it could be argued that because government was a party to the contract, it could engage in modifying the contract. However, when the issue of debt relief moved to Virginia where only private contracts were involved, support for the plight of debtors dissipated and the community split with passionate arguments being put forward by both sides. In this case, as well as in two more closely contested stay law debates in the next session of the General Assembly, arguments against state intervention dominated.[194]

As agricultural commodity prices and real property values changed, so did the price for labour. Table 4.2 shows nominal wages in western Virginia from 1816 to 1823. Although data for 1818 and 1819 are missing, the 33.3 per cent drop in wages from 1820 through 1821 and 1822 indicates the impact in labour markets of the Panic of 1819. The 1820 date for the fall in wages in the western portion of the state is consistent with the timing of the decline in western Virginia prices discussed earlier.

A measure of change in the eastern Virginia labour market is the price for enslaved African Americans. Chart 4.5 provides information on prices in Virginia between 1815 and 1825 for those enslaved as recorded in Ulrich B. Phillips's study of the antebellum period, *American Negro Slavery*. The data represent annual 'average prices of prime field hands/unskilled young men'.[195] The run-up in price in the post war period as thousands of farmers rushed to develop cotton lands in the Old Southwest, thereby pushing up the demand for field hands, is clearly evident. One source indicates that between 1810 and 1820 'over fifty thousand slaves were taken from the Chesapeake to the new states of Mississippi and Alabama' and Virginia which had 45 per cent of all southern slaves in 1790, by 1820 had only 28 per cent.[196] The plateau in 1818–19 when the Panic of 1819 and the collapse of the cotton market brought speculation in western lands to a halt is also evident. This pattern mirrors the data in Table 1.5 above, which shows sales of western lands in the years following the War of 1812.[197] As agricultural markets in Virginia and the nation fell apart after 1819, so did the prices for prime field hands. Between 1819 and 1822, prices fell 37.5 per cent. They continued to fall through 1825, at which time prices were down 50.0 per cent from the 1819 peak.

The decline in price not only resulted from the particulars of the Panic of 1819 and the drying up of foreign markets for American commodities but also could have been expected to some extent had the Panic not occurred. Conceptually, the extensive development and cultivation of western land should ultimately cause output to expand, leading commodity prices to decline as supply begins to outstrip demand. This in turn would affect prices for enslaved African Americans. Two factors are at work here. First the expansion into more fertile western lands should increase the marginal productivity of enslaved workers, causing their value, or the net present value of their higher lifetime marginal product, to rise. This is set against the impact of expanded output on commodity prices and in turn the prices of agricultural inputs – land and labour. While Peter Passell and Gavin Wright believe they can state with some confidence that 'there was no major positive effect' of westward expansion on prices of enslaved workers, Laurence Kotlikoff and Sebastian Pinera find it probable that 'eastern wealth declined substantially as more and more slaves moved west' and that 'eastern exports, slave prices, and land prices were highly sensitive to changes in New South land area'.[198] Thus, western expansion would have ultimately brought down prices for enslaved African Americans in Virginia markets. The Panic of 1819 and the collapse of foreign markets for the Commonwealth's agricultural commodities speeded up and exacerbated the process.

Summary and Conclusions

Data on exports, commodity prices, including a Richmond commodity price index, and property prices demonstrate the devastating impact of the Panic of 1819 on Virginia's agricultural economy. A combination of events and policies both abroad and at home crippled the state's exports, destroyed the market for land, and led even the conservative Commonwealth to address the issue of debt relief. It would take most of the 1820s before Virginia would begin to recover.

The intense deflation experienced by the Commonwealth in the aftermath of the Panic of 1819, as indicated by the 48.1 per cent fall in the Richmond commodity price index, affected all aspects of the state's economy. Debt accumulated during the war and particularly during the boom following peace now became a burden to many Virginians as debtors faced repayment in significantly deflated dollars.

Farmers and planters were not the only ones who suffered as the combination of debt and deflation worked on the economy. Merchants who depended on sales to a wide range of citizens, many of whom were forced to curtail spending as markets collapsed around them, also begin to suffer. This study now turns to the impact of the Panic of 1819 on Virginia merchants.

Tables

Table 4.1: Virginia and US Exports: 1816–23.

Year (ending 30 September)	US	Virginia	Norfolk
	(current dollars and percent change current and real)		
1816	81,920,452	8,212,860	2,353,551
1817	87,671,569	5,621,442	2,577,779
	(+7.0%)	(-31.6%)	(+9.5%)
	(real +7.0%)	(real -31.6%)	(real +9.5%)
1818	93,281,133	7,016,246	2,699,111
	(+6.4%)	(+24.8%)	(+4.7%)
	(real +9.3%)	(real +28.2%)	(real +7.6%)
1819	70,142,521	4,392,321	1,152,561
	(-24.8%)	(-37.4%)	(-57.3%)
	(real -11.5%)	(real -26.7%)	(real -49.8%)
1820	69,692,000	4,557,957	663,176
	(-0.6%)	(+3.8%)	(-42.5%)
	(real +17.2%)	(real +22.4%)	(real -32.1%)
1821	54,596,000	3,079,210	298,684*
	(-21.7%)	(-32.4%)	(-40.9%)*
	(real -18.6%)	(real -28.2%)	(real -45.6%)*
1822	61,350,000	3,217,389	na
	(+12.4%)	(+4.5%)	
	(real +8.1%)	(real +.05%)	
1823	68,326,000	4,006,788	na
	(+11.4%)	(+24.5%)	
	(real +14.6%)	(real +28.1%)	

* Three quarters. Percent change from first three quarters of 1820.
na = not available
Real changes based on the Warren-Pearson commodity price index.

Sources: *American State Papers, Commerce and Navigation*, vol. 2, p. 525; T. Pitkin, *A Statistical View of the Commerce of the United States of America* (New Haven, CT: Durrie and Peck, 1835), pp. 52–67; North, *Economic Growth*, p. 233, and *Historical Statistics of the United States: Colonial Times to 1970* (Washington: Bureau of the Census, 1975), Series E-52.

Table 4.2: Western Virginia Prices and Wages, 1816–23.

Year	Price Index (1795=100)	Nominal Wages (dollars per day)
1816	137.6	0.625
1817	129.0	0.755
1818	133.8	–
1819	138.6	–
1820	118.5	0.750
1821	105.5	0.500
1822	90.0	0.500
1823	94.5	0.608

Source: D. R. Adams, Jr., 'Prices and Wages in Antebellum America: The West Virginia Experience', *Journal of Economic History*, 52:1 (1992), p. 215.

Table 4.3: Assessed Value of Real Property and Annual Rents, Richmond, 1817–25.

Year	Value Real Property	Annual Rents
1817	15,901,547	451,751
1818	15,997,973	572,116
1819	8,148,827	506,750
1820	4,068,467	356,857
1821	4,126,299	337,805
1822	6,238,121	334,265
1823	6,205,002	310,383
1824	6,266,259	322,876
1825	6,292,906	na

na = not available

Source: Richmond Land Book, 1817–1825.

Table 4.4: Yearly Rent: Norfolk Borough, Petersburg, Lynchburg and Winchester, 1815–25.

(current dollars).

Year	Norfolk	Petersburg	Lynchburg	Winchester
1815	186,129	na	na	26,819
1816	248,716	na	na	36,304
1817	245,189	na	80,342	39,951
1818	253,246	222,749	105,419	38,567
1819	257,426	224,207	90,867	40,373
1820	238,965	201,748	62,275	40,605
1821	209,038	197,525	50,591	39,876
1822	184,190	195,239	49,085	38,400
1823	167,235	na	51,260	38,948
1824	170,342	na	56,303	38,470
1825	170,220	na	61,320	na

na = not available

Sources: Land Book, Norfolk Borough, Petersburg, Lynchburg and Winchester.

Charts

Chart 4.1: US and Virginia Exports, 1816–23.

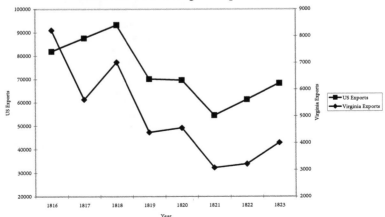

Chart 4.2: Richmond Commodity Price Index, 1816–23.

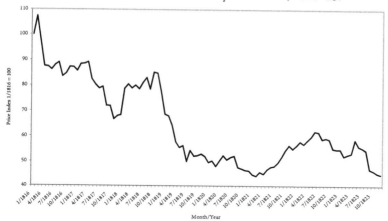

Chart 4.3: United States Prices, 1810–30.

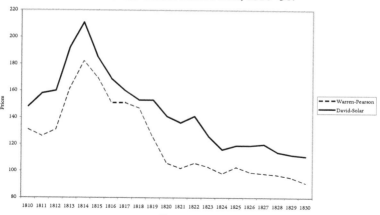

Chart 4.4: Virginia Exports and Richmond Commodity Prices, 1816–23.

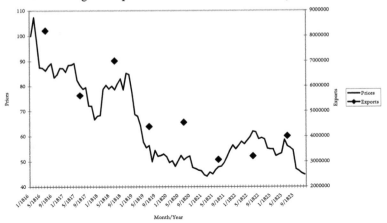

Chart 4.5: Virginia Prices, Enslaved African Americans, 1815–25.

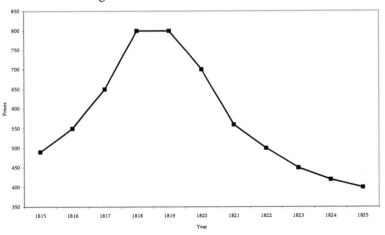

Appendix: Richmond Commodity Price Index

The first step in the construction of a commodity price index for Richmond for the period 1816 to 1823 was the collection of data. As indicated above, prices current in the Richmond market were reported periodically in the *Richmond Enquirer*. Although such reports appeared every few weeks, the prices reported varied considerably over the period, with some items appearing for a time before dropping off the list and others appearing on the list only well after the date at which the index was to begin. In total, nineteen different commodities appear in the listing for at least some part of the period studied. However, only six were reported with sufficient consistency to be used in calculating an index. They include corn, cornmeal, wheat, flour, tobacco and hemp. Of the 576 observations of these six commodities, thirty-seven were missing values. Missing values were interpolated using a simple linear regression. If prices were given as a high and a low for a particular commodity, an average of the two was used for the price that month.

Prices of corn and flour were reported per barrel, cornmeal and wheat per bushel, and tobacco per hundredweight. Prices of hemp were reported per ton. For constructing the price index, hemp prices were converted to price per hundredweight. Beginning in August 1822, corn prices were reported in bushels. These were converted to barrel prices at 3.9 bushels per barrel to keep the price series consistent.

To avoid the problem of possible systematic monthly variations in prices, data were collected for the published date closest to the 15th of each month. Although reporting dates varied considerably, the earliest being 7 November 1820, and the latest 28 March 1817, most fell within three days of either side of the 15th (51 of 96 or 53.1 per cent).

An equal-weighted index was constructed for the period. While a more sophisticated index might be desirable, two factors lead to the decision to use a simple equal-weighted index. The first is the small number of commodities for which data was consistently available for the entire period. The second concerns weights. Although some information on weights for the antebellum period is available, such information is for a large number of commodities in markets such as New York and Philadelphia. None is available for Richmond. Thus, the decision to construct a simple equal-weighted index.

January 1816 was selected as the base month for the index. The resulting Richmond commodity price index is found in Chart 4.2 above.

5 BUSINESS

Writing in May 1819 to George Caskaden, a former Richmond retail merchant who had relocated to Fort St Stevens, Alabama, Benjamin Brand informed him, 'You have been lucky in removing from this place'. Caskaden's good fortune was to avoid the devastating impact of the Panic of 1819 on merchants in the Commonwealth's capital. Describing business conditions, Brand wrote, 'We have gloomy times here – many protests [failures] have taken place since I last saw you, and many more soon expected ... Many have backed out of business.' The financial crisis meant that 'at this time there is very little credit business done. Confidence in each others ability to pay is very slight. (On Saturday it is said there were 12 notes laid over for protest.)' The decline in business activity left 'many store houses ... shut up and written on "For Rent"' and took the bottom out of what had been a speculative boom in property. According to Brand, 'It is thought house rent next year will be about half the present price. Lots out of the business part of the city may be purchased for about ⅓ to ⅒ of what they sold for when you resided here.' For the business community the effect was to create an atmosphere of gloom. As Brand observed, 'Nearly all the trading part of the citizens, both debtors & creditors, have long dejected faces & I suspect many sleepless nights, particularly amongst those who lived in great splendour & extravagance.' Summing up, Brand wrote, 'Times much changed – economy seems all the fashion. – Fine furniture may be purchased at vendue at one half and sometimes one third of the original costs.'[199] John Marshall, putting it more concisely in a letter to Bushrod Washington two months earlier, said, 'We are in great distress here for money. Many of our merchants stop – a thing which was long unknown and was totally unexpected in Richmond'.[200]

Richmond merchants were not alone in their distress. Writing to William and H. Haxall in Petersburg from Norfolk in June 1819, John Cowper indicated 'The failures here, have been as bad as possible'. He goes on to suggest that 'the sudden change in fortune is so large a portion of the community must produce very injurious effects on Society, not only in their own industry lost, but the industry of an infinitely greater number, who depended on them for employment'. One exception, according to Cowper, was Myers and Sons who 'have made arrangements at the Banks to the satisfaction of those institutions, and are going on with their business'. However, for many 'who have been accustomed to active lives, suddenly thrown out of employment, become at first depressed, afterwards desperate'.[201]

Businesses in the Commonwealth suffered as export markets disappeared, commodity prices and land values plummeted, and credit markets tightened. In particular, the importance attached to tight credit by the two observers quoted above suggests the combination of debt and falling prices that form Fisher's debt-deflation mechanism was a critical factor in the events of the time. One measure of the decline in business activity in Virginia is the value of merchant licence revenue collected by the state. Table 5.1 and Chart 5.1 present total Virginia merchant licence revenue annually for the period 1816–24. The figures indicate a dramatic drop in merchant activity in 1819, down 12.5 per cent, and 1820, down 9.9 per cent, with slow recovery in 1821 and 1822, increases of 2.4 per cent and 1.0 per cent respectively.[202] The revenue data for 1823 show another small increase, up 0.9 per cent, but changes in the licensing law make interpretation difficult. This issue will be discussed in detail below. By 1824, merchant licence revenue finally surpassed its 1819 level, but still fell short of the pre-Panic levels from 1816 to 1818.

The sources for statewide merchant licence revenue data are various records and reports of the Virginia Auditor of Public Accounts. Merchant licence fees were established annually by the General Assembly. In the period 1816–22, the legislature set the following fees: 'On every license to sell merchandise of foreign [non-Virginia] growth or manufacture by wholesale and retail, sixty dollars; by retail only, twenty dollars'.[203] Beginning with the 1823 tax year, the legislature created a new class of merchant licences for those selling 'merchandise of domestic [Virginia] growth or manufacture' and set fees at thirty dollars for wholesale and fifteen dollars for retail. The next year the General Assembly returned to a fee system similar to that of earlier years.[204] Unfortunately, for a number of Virginia counties and cities, only information on the total amount of licence revenue collected each year, and not on the number of licences issued annually, is available. Thus, the statewide data for 1823 cannot be adjusted and made comparable to the earlier data. However, this may not present a serious problem.

Given the change in the tax structure in 1823, it is possible that some merchants may have stopped dealing in 'merchandise of foreign growth or manufacture' and limited themselves to domestic goods only, thereby avoiding the higher licence fee, or that some merchants who did not previously purchase licences because they dealt only in domestic goods would purchase the new category of licences. To the extent either of these occurred, the data may understate or overstate the recovery in activity in that year. However, while it is not clear from the record what the legislature's intent was in making the change in 1823, the reality seems to have been virtually no change at all. For example, in the City of Richmond the total number of retail and wholesale licences combined did not change dramatically from the previous year, 257 in 1823 versus 262 in 1822, and only thirty-eight retail merchants and three wholesale merchants chose the new licences, 16.2 per cent and 13.6 per cent respectively.[205] This change reduced the city's retail licence revenues by 4 per cent and wholesale licence revenue by 6.7 per cent over what they would have been if all had purchased the higher-priced licence. In other areas of the state surveyed, none of the new licences were issued. Thus, if the General Assembly had hoped to increase revenues by issuing a new category of licences that would be sold to merchants not previously required to purchase a licence, they failed. The number of licences sold seems not to have changed much, relatively few of the new licences appear to have been sold, and in Richmond total licence revenue declined slightly over what it would have been if all had purchased licences at the old rate. By dropping the new category the next year, the legislature seems to have recognized this failure. For our purposes, therefore, the 1823 data may be considered roughly comparable to data for other years and likely represent a fair indicator of changes in the Commonwealth's business community for that year.

Finally, several concerns arise regarding the data for all years of the study. These focus on the proportion of licences issued between 'wholesale and retail' and 'retail only'. First, if this ratio does not remain roughly the same, the data may be biased. Two factors mitigate this concern. Data for the City of Richmond indicate wholesale licences as a percentage of all licences issued ranged between 9.9 per cent and 12.6 per cent in the years 1817–22, or roughly the same. Further, wholesale licences seem to be concentrated in cities, since none appear in the other surveyed areas of the state. Therefore, they can be expected to be a much smaller percentage of all licences issued in the state. As a result, any variation in licence revenue resulting from changes in the proportion between the two types of licences statewide should be quite small. Secondly, it is possible that some of the decline in 1819 and 1820 may have resulted from merchants stopping their wholesale operations and concentrating on retail only, thereby paying a lower licence fee. To the extent this possibility was a reality in the years 1819 and 1820, the data may overstate the decline in merchant activity during the Panic. Again, data from Richmond for the period 1817–22 indicate that only 11 per cent, seven of sixty, of those who dropped their wholesale licences purchased retail licences the next year.[206] Thus, there is a possibility that variation in the proportion of licences between 'wholesale and retail' and 'retail' may have contributed in some small way to the decline of total licence revenue in the Commonwealth. However, the almost 20 per cent fall in merchant licence revenue between 1818 and 1821 means that the business community of Virginia suffered significantly during the downturn.

To determine more precisely how the Panic of 1819 affected Virginia's business community, merchant licence records for individual cities and counties for the years 1817–23 will be examined. The next section describes the data used for the study. The following section provides a framework for thinking about the decision of licence holders to enter, continue in, or exit the market, and the final section analyzes the experience of Virginia merchants during the period.

Data

For this study, annual reports of merchant licences issued by commissioners of the revenue of Virginia's cities and counties and submitted by them to the Auditor of Public Accounts for the years 1817–23 were reviewed. Because not all returns for all years survived, a search of the records was undertaken and data collected for those counties in which merchant licence records were available for most of the years 1817–23. Retail merchant licence records were collected for Isle of Wight, Kanawha, Middlesex, Pittsylvania and Spotsylvania counties and the City of Richmond, and wholesale merchant licence records for the City of Richmond as no wholesale licences were issued in any of the other areas studied. Although not as extensive a sample as one might wish, the difficulty of finding counties and cities with complete or mostly complete data for the period has limited this study. The sample does, however, include data from each region of the state.

A licence was to be purchased annually for each store or place of business and the fee paid on 1 May of each year. Reports were generally submitted in the following October or November and focused primarily on the fees collected on or around 1 May but also included fees collected up to the time of the report. In addition, revenue collectors would typically provide an addendum to their report indicating partial licence fees that had been received before the 1 May date and after their last report. Thus, it is possible to assign the issue of a partial licence to a particular calendar year. If a licence holder paid a fee any time during the calendar year, they were considered to be in operation during that year. If an individual purchased a partial licence before 1 May of any year and then purchased a full licence on or after 1 May, for the purpose of this study the two were counted as one licence.

Although it would be nice to assume commissioners of the revenue were complete and accurate in the reports submitted to the state's Auditor of Public Accounts, this is unlikely. One potential source of problems is underreporting. As economic hard times hit, revenue collectors might well be under substantial political pressure to look the other way when a merchant did not purchase a licence. Also such pressure might vary considerably across jurisdictions, further complicating the analysis. Unfortunately, there is no way to verify the completeness of the lists. However, to adjust for the possibility of underreporting, the analysis will first provide results based on the data as reported. A second analysis will assume that any licence holder who disappears from the list and reappears at a later date has been underreported. In each such case, the licence holder will be considered as continuing in business throughout the time in question. This will result in two figures for each measure of licence-holder change, one assuming the data as recorded are accurate and reflect that any licence holder dropping from the list in fact stopped business, and a second assuming any licence holder who dropped from the list temporarily was simply underreported, remaining in business but not paying the licence fee. As a result, this technique will provide a high and a low measure for licence-holder continuity, exit and entry in each year.[207]

Analysis will focus on four numbers and three measures of change to describe the experience of the merchant community. The first number is the total merchant licences issued each calendar year. Second is the number of licence holders each calendar year who continued operation from the previous year, meaning they continued to pay the licence fee. Third is the number of licence holders who exited that calendar year, licence holders who had paid the licence fee the previous calendar year but did not pay in the calendar year being considered. And finally, the number of entrants each calendar year, licence holders paying the licence fee for the first time or paying after a break of at least one calendar year from the time of a previous licence purchase (re-entrants).

The three measures are the continuity rate, CR, the entry rate, ER, and the exit rate, XR, where:[208]

$$CR(t\text{-}1) = NC(t\text{-}1) / NT(t\text{-}1)$$
$$ER(t) = NE(t) / NT(t\text{-}1)$$
$$XR(t\text{-}1) = NX(t\text{-}1) / NT(t\text{-}1)$$

when

$CR(t\text{-}1)$ = continuity rate between years t-1 and t
$ER(t)$ = entry rate between years t-1 and t
$XR(t\text{-}1)$ = exit rate between years t-1 and t
$NC(t\text{-}1)$ = number of licence holders who continue between years t-1 and t
$NE(t) = 11$ number of licence holders who enter between years t-1 and t
$NX(t\text{-}1)$ = number of licence holders who exit between years t-1 and t
$NT(t\text{-}1)$ = total number of licence holders in year t-1.

It is important to note the denominator in all three measures is the total number of licence holders in year t-1.

The unit of analysis is the merchant licence. This measure likely correlates highly with the number of retail or wholesale firms. However, several factors are expected to lead the focus on licence holders to overstate the actual behaviour of firms. First, because reports from each commissioner of the revenue are handwritten and list licence holders by name, variations in spelling from year to year create problems. Although every attempt has been made to track licence holders, it is most likely that some will fail to be matched correctly because of differences in the spelling of names from year to year, thus leading to an overstating of the turnover of firms.[209] Secondly, the sale or reorganization of a firm might lead to a new licence holder appearing on the list when in reality the firm had continued. In such cases, it would appear as if a former licence holder exited and a new licence holder entered when in reality the firm continued either under new ownership or in a reorganized state with a new individual purchasing the licence. Finally, from time to time an individual would be found to have purchased two licences, and it appears that some partnerships purchased a licence along with licences purchased individually by the partners. Although the number of such occurrences is very small, their existence means that merchant licences and firms may not correlate perfectly.

Because this is an analysis of licences, not of business firms, each licence is considered individually. This is equivalent to studying business sites, since each location where business was conducted required a licence. Thus, if an individual purchased two licences in one year, each is counted. If in the following year, that individual purchased only one licence, a licence holder is considered to have exited. Likewise, if the holder of a licence in one year purchased two licences the next year, a licence holder is considered to have entered. In the areas studied, this happened only in Richmond among retail merchants, and the number of cases of individuals holding multiple licences is very small, the number each year ranging between two and seven or between 0.8 per cent and 2.6 per cent of licence holders.

Exit as defined here does not necessarily mean a licence holder stopped operation. The individual may have simply stopped selling goods of foreign growth or manufacture and concentrated on selling domestic merchandise, have done this in 1823 but chosen not to purchase one of the new licences, or chosen to close one store while keeping another open. Further, exit does not necessarily mean a firm has gone out of business or gone bankrupt. A change of ownership (sale) or a reorganization with a new individual purchasing the licence appears here as an exit and a new entrance when in reality the firm has continued. As a result of focusing on licences, this study likely overstates the turnover of firms.

To help offset the bias inherent in the method used in this study, where possible every effort has been made to follow licence holders. For example, in Kanawha County the partnership of Hogue and Flanagan from 1817 to 1820 became the licence holder James Hogue in 1821 and in turn became the licence holders James and William Hogue in 1822 and 1823. And, in Richmond the wholesale partnership of Sheppard and Webb that held a licence from 1817 to 1819 dissolved to be replaced by the individual licence holder Lewis Webb in 1820. Lewis Webb continued to purchase a licence through 1823.[210] For the purpose of this inquiry, in such situations one licence holder is considered to have continued throughout the time being studied. Similar cases exist in each area surveyed, but again the cases are few in number. Following licence holders in the manner indicated should help bring the results based on licences closer to the reality experienced by firms in the period studied.

In order to gain additional insights into the data set, the 1819 retail and wholesale merchant licence report for the City of Richmond was compared with the only directory existing for the areas of Virginia studied during this period, *The Richmond Directory, Register and Almanac, for the year 1819* published by John Maddox.[211] While it is expected that a number of merchants may appear in the city directory who did not purchase a licence because such licences are for the sale of 'merchandise of foreign growth or manufacture', we do expect to find most of those purchasing licences in the *Directory*. Comparing the two listings reveals that 145 individuals appear as business persons in the *Directory* who are not found on the 1819 business licence tax list. This includes sixty-four grocers, sixty-three merchants, and eighteen shoe, hat or tailor shops – businesses that might well deal only in good of domestic origin or manufacture. It is also possible, as discussed above, that some of this difference might result from underreporting by the commissioner of the revenue in the panic year of 1819.

When the 187 individuals and partnerships purchasing business licences in 1819 are traced to the *Directory*, fifty-two retail licence holders, or 31.0 per cent, and one wholesale licence holder, or 5.3 per cent, are not found listed in the *Directory*. There are two possible explanations. First, the *Directory* may have been carelessly put together with a number of individuals missed. Secondly, the commissioner of the revenue for the city may have overlooked business operators, inadvertently or on purpose to give some individuals a break because of the distressing times. While it is not possible to rule out some impact from the latter, most likely the former is the source of the differences found. Finally, the *Directory* provides information regarding the types of businesses operated by those purchasing licences. The 116 retail-merchant licence holders who appear in the *Directory* include forty-six grocers, thirty-six merchants, six druggists/apothecaries, three confectioners, two booksellers, and fifteen others.[212] No information besides a street address was provided for eight of the entries. Of the eighteen wholesale-merchant licence holders also listed in the *Directory*, eleven are designated merchants, five auctioneers, one a commission merchant, and one is simply designated a French garden.

Before analyzing the experience of Virginia merchants, it will be helpful to consider what economic theory has to say about the entry and exit of firms.

Modelling Business Turnover

The economic theory of the firm tells us that in equilibrium the typical firm makes a normal profit but zero economic profit. If demand should decrease, firms will make a loss, no longer receiving their normal profit. As a result, firms will leave the market until equilibrium is restored, or until losses are eliminated and economic profits are again zero. Likewise, if demand were to increase, firms would begin to make an economic profit, leading more firms to enter the market until equilibrium is restored and firms earn only their normal profit.[213] For Richmond retail and wholesale merchants in the period of the Panic of 1819, the assumption of competition is likely not far off the mark. In the counties surveyed, the question of competition is more problematic, particularly in the less-populated areas. However, all have multiple merchants operating, and merchants faced competition not only from other merchants in the county but from peddlers and from the possibility that many middling and wealthier farmers might travel to larger towns and cities to shop. Thus, the decline in demand with the onset of the Panic of 1819 and its recovery as the economy bounced back can be expected to have caused firms to exit and then to enter, much as the theory of the firm predicts.

For nineteenth-century merchants the way in which they financed their operations also played an important role, particularly in periods of rapid economic change. A merchant's inventory was typically purchased on credit extended based on notes or real bills, signed by the merchant. For many merchants, particularly in cities, these were short-term notes of sixty, ninety, or even 180 days. Country storekeepers, on the other hand, typically based their operations on longer-term credit, up to one year or more, and the country store often took crops from farmers in exchange for goods. The credit extended to merchants, generally by wholesalers often financed in turn by banks, was often based on personal security, although the bills or notes were also backed by the commodities (real goods) which the merchant obtained. The merchant would then sell the goods with the expectation that the revenues from sales, or in the case of country stores the value of the crops received, would supply sufficient funds, after covering other costs, to repay the bills or notes. If prices declined rapidly, as they did in the period following the Panic of 1819, many merchants would be caught with goods which they could no longer sell at prices high enough to generate sufficient revenue to cover the notes they had signed earlier, and/or the crops they received in exchange would no longer bring an amount sufficient to cover the cost of the goods already advanced to farmers. Such events would generate the protests and distress so clearly described in Brand's letter quoted at the beginning of this chapter.[214]

However, it is possible to dig further into the behaviour of firms to discover more about how they might behave during a downturn such as the Panic of 1819. A recent study by Thomas J. Holmes and James A. Schmitz regarding the turnover of business firms provides a starting point for discussion.[215] A simple model of small business turnover begins with the assumption that the market in question consists of individuals each using their labor endowments to manage a business. In the first period to be analyzed, all individuals are assumed to be new entrants, and each is assumed to have started a new business. At the end of the first period, all individuals must make a decision to stay in the market and continue managing their business or to leave.[216] At the beginning of every additional time period a new generation of individuals enters the market in question, joining those who have decided to continue managing their business. Each new entrant is assumed to start a new business. At the end of each of these additional periods, existing individuals and new entrants must make a decision whether to stay or to leave.

The output or sales of each managed business in any time period is q, which is the sum of a 'match quality component', qM, and a 'business quality component', qB. Match quality 'is specific to a particular individual running a particular business' and is the sum of a permanent component, u, which 'is determined when a business is started', and a temporary component, x. Business quality is 'the same regardless of who runs the business', and is the sum of a permanent component, b, which 'is determined when a business is established', and a temporary component, y. Thus in any period $q = (u + x) + (b + y)$.

Because this analysis of Virginia businesses considers the impact of the Panic of 1819 on individual merchant licence holders, temporary components are the factors of interest. The permanent components, u and b, are assumed independent of temporary changes in economic activity. As economic conditions deteriorate, both temporary components can be expected to change in ways that increase the probability individuals managing businesses in the market will leave while decreasing the probability that they will stay. As economic conditions improve, the reverse will hold. For example, the stress created by bad times might adversely affect match quality component x. If such stress led a particular manager to make poorer decisions than previously was the case or to offend customers by her/his behaviour, output or sales might fall, further exacerbating the situation. Or, business quality component y might be adversely affected by hard times. Say a shop selling luxury goods in a particularly fashionable location finds that their market has disappeared and their location is no longer so fashionable. This would mean a decrease in business quality and would have an impact most similar to the situation described by the standard theory of the firm discussed earlier.

The inclusion of match quality in the model means that in addition to the profit and loss considerations of the simple theory of the firm, factors related to the individuals operating businesses and how such factors might lead those individuals to exit, or to enter, can be considered. For a study that focuses on licence holders, this additional element may be important for understanding changes in the number of licences purchased from one time period to another. In particular, it will be useful for comparing the behaviour of partnerships with the behaviour of individual entrepreneurs.

Analysis

During the years between 1818 and 1822, a period in which the Commonwealth's economy suffered from rapidly declining prices for its products and from a dearth of credit, 71.3 per cent of the merchants operating in 1818 in the capital city, Richmond, disappeared. While a number of those lost were replaced by newcomers, in 1822 there were 13.5 per cent fewer merchant licences issued in the city than had been issued before the onset of the Panic of 1819. And, it would take until the end of the decade for the number of merchants in the capital to exceed the 1818 total. Chart 5.2 provides some perspective on the unusual nature of the Panic years. Richmond retail merchants failing to renew their licences each year between 1815 and 1829 are shown. Clearly the sharp increase in exits during 1819 was different from the general pattern of the period and suggests the seriousness of the hard times brought on by the Panic.

For many merchants, the combination of the deflation of the period with the normal debt under which they operated created real hardships. With the rapid expansion of credit by the Richmond and Norfolk branches of the Bank of the United States during 1818, the situation was exacerbated. As Bernanke has suggested in his study of the role played in the Great Depression by nonmonetary effects of financial crisis, 'The seriousness of the Great Depression was due not only to the extent of the deflation, but also to the large and broad-based expansion of credit in the 1920's.' For Virginia, the impact of the Panic of 1819 was the result of the combination of sharp deflation and the rapid growth of credit in the years leading up to 1819. What follows provides details about the experience of Richmond and Virginia merchants during the Panic of 1819.[217]

1 Retail merchants

Tables 5.2 and 5.4 present information regarding the number of retail licence holders, and the continuation, entry and exit of those licence holders for the City of Richmond and a sample of five Virginia counties for the years 1817–23. The analysis begins with merchants in the City of Richmond.

Data regarding Richmond's retail merchant licences confirm the dramatic impact of the Panic of 1819. The total number of licences issued dropped precipitously in 1819, down 38.5 per cent, and increased slightly the next year, up 5.9 per cent, before recovering more strongly in 1821, up 28.1 per cent, at which point it plateaued for the final three years of the study at about 85 per cent of its pre-Panic total, about 230 vs 250 and 273 in 1817 and 1818 respectively (see Table 5.2). Interestingly, the rate at which licence holders continued, entered and exited from year to year is remarkably steady throughout the period studied, with the exception of all three measures in 1819 and entries in 1821. Continuity rates fall roughly between 0.55 to 0.65 in spite of large changes in absolute numbers. Entries also remain relatively stable at a rate remaining between 0.40 and 0.50 for much of the period. What makes the difference during the years of depression is the rise in exits combined with a fall in licence holders continuing and entering. In the year 1819, 174 licence holders, or 63.4 per cent of 1818 licence holders, failed to renew their licences. This compares to exit rates ranging between 0.37 and 0.46 for other years of the study. In addition, the continuity rate falls to 0.36 and the entry rate to 0.25, their lowest levels between 1818 and 1823. This resulted in licences falling from a total of 273 in 1818 to 168 in 1819, their minimum for the period studied. In 1820, although the exit rate for licence holders is slightly higher than in the other years sampled, excepting 1819, entries jumped to eighty-three from sixty-nine in 1819 and the number and percentage of those reentering, twenty-nine or 35.4 per cent, are the highest of all the years studied. The result is a stemming of the sharp decline in the number of licences issued experienced in the panic year of 1819 and a slight increase in the total number of licences; to 178 from the 1819 low of 168. By 1821, the shakeout of businesses that occurred as the depression hit Richmond had worked itself out and signs of recovery appear. The total number of licences jumped to 228 because more licence holders renewed their licences, 113 up from ninety-six the previous year; entries increased to 115, their highest rate, 0.646, of the period studied; and exits fell to their lowest level and rate of the years studied, sixty-five and 0.365. Thus, the hard times of the Panic appeared to be over. However, recovery was not complete as the number of licences issued still fell short of the level reached prior to the downturn, and it would take Richmond until 1829 to surpass the number of licences issued at the pre-Panic peak of 273 in 1818.

Adjusting for the possible underreporting of licences during the period may be accomplished by assuming that any licence holders that drop out and then return have in reality remained in business each year in between. Thus, a licence holder who failed to purchase a licence in any year but did so in a subsequent year is considered to have continued operating and simply been missed by the commissioner of the revenue. This adjustment changes the magnitudes of various measures significantly, although the basic pattern remains and the earlier analysis still holds. Table 5.3 provides the adjusted data. The number of adjusted licence holders fell 25.3 per cent in 1819 rather than the 38.5 per cent using unadjusted data but fell a further 10.3 per cent in 1820 when the unadjusted data indicate a slight increase. The net effect is that between 1818 and 1820 the number of unadjusted licence holders declined 34.8 per cent while the adjusted number fell 33.0 per cent, a remarkably similar pattern. When the adjusted data is used to consider licence holder behaviour after 1820, the recovery appears much stronger primarily because the number of exits is much lower in 1821 and 1822 than indicated by the unadjusted data. The adjusted exit and entry rates in Table 5.3 confirm the above analysis. The panic year of 1819 does not demonstrate as large a gap between exit and entry rates as does the unadjusted data, indicating, as expected, that, accounting for possible underreporting, the initial impact of the Panic of

1819 was not as severe as suggested by the unadjusted data. Differences between the rates in 1821 and 1822 also suggest that the recovery following the Panic of 1819 was stronger than indicated by the unadjusted data. While it is most likely that the reality of the times lies somewhere between the experiences suggested by the two sets of data, both indicate a dramatic impact on Richmond's retail merchant community as a result of the Panic of 1819 and the system's working out of the effects of sharp deflation combined with the buildup of debt in the years proceeding the Panic.

When data from a sample of five counties is analyzed a more confusing picture emerges (see Table 5.4). In the years for which the most complete data exist, 1817–20, the Panic does not seem to have had the dramatic impact on merchants in these other areas of the state that it had for Richmond merchants. The total number of licence holders in the combined county data remains virtually the same between 1818 and 1819.[218] This, however, masks important differences among the five counties surveyed. Kanawha County saw a 50 per cent drop in licences between 1818 and 1819, from eight to four, because half the 1818 firms exited (exit rate 0.50) and there were no new entrants (entry rate 0). However, recovery was very rapid, with the continuity and entry rates in 1820 hitting their maximums, 1.00 and 1.25 respectively, and with no exits occurring (exit rate 0). For the remaining years of the study, 1820–22, the number of licence holders remains essentially the same.

Middlesex and Pittsylvania counties saw much more modest declines in the number of total licence holders between 1818 and 1819, down 22.2 per cent and 10.7 per cent respectively. In Middlesex, this was the result of a relatively high continuity rate, 0.67, combined with relatively low entry and exit rates, 0.11 and 0.33, while in Pittsylvania the entry rate was at its highest, 0.29, and the continuity and exit rates were at their middle values of the years for which data are available. And, in Isle of Wight and Spotsylvania counties the number of licences issued actually increased between 1818 and 1819. Licences in Isle of Wight jump because the continuity and entry rates are high while the exit rate is at its lowest of the years studied. For Spotsylvania County the Panic of 1819 appears to have had no impact as the number of licences issued and the rates of continuity, entry and exit change very little over the entire period.

To make some sense of the contradictory results from this limited survey of Virginia merchants outside of Richmond, a return to the data in Table 5.1 may be helpful. First, total licence revenue from Richmond as a percentage of total state licence revenue was analyzed. In 1817 and 1818, Richmond contributed 12.0 and 12.3 per cent respectively of total state licence revenue. In 1819 this dropped to 9.7 per cent of the state total or from $6,350 in 1818 to $4,393 in 1819, a 30.8 per cent decline. Revenues then bounced back to 12.2 per cent of the state total in 1820 before rising to 15.9, 14.1 and 12.8 per cent of total state revenue in 1821, 1822 and 1823 respectively. The experience of Richmond's merchant licence revenue stream suggests that its merchants were hit earlier and harder by the Panic than merchants in the rest of the Commonwealth, but that as the downturn spread Richmond merchants recovered more quickly. This is confirmed when changes in Richmond's merchant licence revenue are compared with statewide changes in 1819, 1820, and 1821. For 1819 statewide merchant licence revenue declined $6,473, of which Richmond contributed $2,760, or 42.7 per cent, well above the city's contribution to total revenues from merchant licences. In the next year, statewide revenues decreased $4,485 while revenues from Richmond's merchant licences actually increased $280, and in 1821, with statewide merchant licence revenues up $978, Richmond saw its fees jump $1,660, or 169.7 per cent of the state's total. Thus, while some of the counties surveyed seem to have experienced little impact from the Panic of 1819 (Isle of Wight and Spotsylvania) and others saw moderate declines (Middlesex and Pittsylvania) or came closer to Richmond's experience (Kanawha) throughout the Commonwealth the Panic caused considerable disruption and areas outside of Richmond took longer to recover from the effects of the depression than did the capital city.

Finally, outside of Richmond, information regarding the origins of new licence holders and what happened to licence holders who dropped off the lists is provided in the data from Pittsylvania County (see Table 5.5). When merchant licence holders are checked against holders of ordinary licences, it appears that approximately 40 per cent of retail merchants were also ordinary keepers. However, in the three years for which data exists, no entrants were holders of an ordinary licence in the year or years prior to entry, and only one individual gave up a merchant licence while maintaining an ordinary licence. This suggests that entrants were new to the community while those exiting the retail merchant business dropped out of commercial enterprise within the county, either staying or moving to other localities.

2. Wholesale merchants

Wholesale merchant licence data from the City of Richmond are presented in Table 5.6. The impact of the Panic was indicated by the 36.7 per cent decline in the number of licence holders in 1819, although recovery is much more dramatic than for Richmond's retail merchants with the number of licence holders by 1821 exceeding the number in the year proceeding the Panic. However, unlike retail licence holders, the years 1822 and 1823 saw a return of hard times as the number of licence holders again dropped by a third. This higher level of volatility appears in the rates at which licence holders enter and to a lesser extent exit. For example, entry rates changed from a high of 0.818 between 1820 and 1821 to 0.152 in 1821–2, a level almost as low as that experienced in the panic year of 1819. Of particular note is the role of reentrants who in the panic years of 1819 and 1820 comprised 75 per cent of all entrants, eight of twelve. With a recovery of business confidence in 1821, new entrants dominated as reentrants fell to 28 per cent of all entrants, but in 1822 reentrants were again critical, making up 80 per cent of all entrants that year. This finding suggests wholesale merchants may have moved between purchasing licences and choosing not to purchase much more readily than did retail merchants and could be the result of their having alternative opportunities such that wholesaling was only one part of their business. Remember, among wholesale licence holders listed in the 1819 city directory, five of eighteen were designated auctioneers. The result also could stem from wholesale merchants simply not purchasing licences during the period of the Panic and thus being underreported. This issue will be taken up shortly.

Examples of the volatility experienced by Richmond's wholesale merchants include the 1817 and 1818 partnership of Ludham and Allen that in 1819 become the licence holder Lewis Ludham, who then disappears from the 1820 list. Lewis Ludham, however, returns as a licence holder in 1821 and continues through 1823.[219] The partnership of Ralston and Pleasants appears on the lists for 1817 and 1818 but disappears in 1819, with the partnership Ralston and Sears and several Pleasants as independent merchants found among 1819 retail merchant licence holders. Ralston and Pleasants reappears in 1820 and remains a wholesale licence holder through 1823.[220]

Assuming that wholesale merchants who drop from the list of licence holders only to return at a later date (reentries) actually remained in business and were underreported during the period in which they failed to appear on the list again changes the numbers substantially, although the pattern remains roughly similar. Table 5.7 provides the adjusted data.[221] When the adjusted number of licence holders and exits are considered, the decline in wholesale firms during the Panic of 1819 is still quite clear, although the drop in 1819 is not as sharp, and, as a result the recovery by 1821, not as remarkable. The reason is found in the exit and entry data. The panic year of 1819 saw the smallest number of licence holders because while there were six exits, down from the nine of the previous year, there were no entries, thus causing the total number of Richmond wholesale licences to fall to twenty-four. The next year, 1820, exits were almost as high, five, but entries resumed with four new licence holders entering the market, leading the total number of licences to fall once again. The recovery in 1821 reversed this pattern with only two exits, the lowest of the period studied, but with thirteen new licence holders entering, the highest of the period. Again as with retail licences, the reality of the wholesale merchant experience during the Panic of 1819 most likely lies somewhere between those indicated by the two data sets. And, while the Panic of 1819 did not have as dramatic an effect on the wholesale merchant community as it did on retail merchants, the decline in wholesale merchant licences in 1818 and 1819 certainly suggests hard times for those doing business in the Commonwealth's capital.

3. Partnerships

The experience of partnerships among retail and wholesale merchants and what this tells us about the role partnerships played for early-nineteenth-century merchants are also questions of interest.[222] Little attention has been paid to this form of business organization in the antebellum period with the exception of Naomi Lamoreaux's groundbreaking study of Boston.[223] Focusing primarily on the 1840s, Lamoreaux discusses the potential problems and advantages of partnerships and suggests that 'the popularity of small partnerships that so many Bostonians formed during the early nineteenth century seems not to have resulted from any real economic advantage that such firms had over single proprietorships'. Among the limitations of partnerships Lamoreaux presents are unlimited liability, the short time horizon of partnership agreements, the possibility of the death of a partner and a number of moral hazards, most importantly the unscrupulous partner. Advantages of having a partner include securing a critical input, bringing capital to the firm and obtaining some 'complementary capability'. One possible advantage that Lamorueaux does not discuss, particularly for merchants at a time when lenders 'strongly preferred granting credit on the basis of personal rather than collateral security and typically demanded that a firm's debt be endorsed individually by its partners', is the increased access to credit that a partnership might bring. It will be argued below that this factor, combined with other possible advantages of partnerships, may offset the disadvantages and be important to improving the match quality of firms (licence holders), thereby increasing their ability to survive during the Panic of 1819.[224]

The analysis again begins with the City of Richmond. Table 5.8 provides information on the number and percentage of partnerships among Richmond's retail and wholesale merchants and the continuity rate of partnerships.[225] For wholesale merchants, partnerships are an important factor with the percentage of partnerships ranging from 40.9 per cent of all licence holders in 1823 to 57.9 per cent in 1819. That the ratio is highest in 1819 suggests partnerships may have been in a better position to weather the downturn. This is confirmed when the continuation experience of partnerships is considered (see Table 5.8). Of those wholesale licence holders continuing from one year to the next, the continuity rate among partnerships moves in a pattern much like that of wholesale merchants as a group. Importantly, the partnership continuity rate is higher in every year except 1823 than the rate at which Richmond's individual (non-partnership) wholesale merchants continue, indicating partnerships are typically stronger, meaning they survive at a higher rate, than do individual licence holders.[226] This finding may be linked to the role of match quality in partnerships. If partnerships improve match quality, for example because partners bring a wider range of skills to the business, improve the personal security on which credit is based, or diversify risk among several individuals, as economic conditions make it more difficult for firms to operate, other things being equal, those with the highest match quality will be more likely to survive. It can be argued that this is just what was happening with Richmond's wholesale partnerships during the Panic of 1819.

Among Richmond's retail merchants, partnerships are less prevalent than among the city's wholesale merchants, with partnerships as a percentage of all retail licence holders ranging from a low of 9.4 in 1823 to a high of 18.0 in 1820 (see Table 5.8). However, when the partnership continuity rate is considered, it appears that they were better able to weather the hard times. The percentage of partnerships continuing from year to year exceeds the continuity rate for individual (non-partnership) retail licence holders in every year except 1822, when they are virtually equal. Further, the difference between the two reaches its highest level, 0.377, in the panic year of 1819.[227] Again, this suggests the importance of partnership arrangements for surviving economic hard times and points to the more important role partnerships play in improving match quality for retail merchants than for wholesale merchants in such periods of economic distress.

Comparing the rate at which Richmond merchant partnerships survived, dissolved or disappeared during the Panic of 1819 and the following depression, 1818–22, with Boston partnerships in the period 1845–50, a remarkably similar proportion survived. However, substantial differences in the percentage of firms (licence holders) that dissolved and disappeared are found.[228] In Boston, when all firms are considered 33 per cent survived, 59 per cent dissolved and 9 per cent disappeared. The proportion of partnerships among merchants and shopkeepers that survived, dissolved and disappeared are 32 per cent, 62 per cent and 7 per cent respectively. The survival rate for Richmond's wholesale merchant partnerships from 1818 to 1822 was 33.3 per cent while the city's retail merchant partnerships survived at a rate of 24.4 per cent.[229] The proportions of Richmond's wholesale and retail partnerships that dissolved over the period, 23.5 per cent and 19.5 per cent respectively, were much lower rates than those experienced by Boston firms.[230] The difference stems from the rate at which Richmond merchant partnerships disappeared during the Panic of 1819. Of the city's wholesale partnerships, 41.2 per cent disappeared while none of the members of 56.1 per cent of Richmond's 1818 retail partnerships could be found in the 1822 licence list. Although some of this difference may be the result of differences in the size and stage of development between the two cities in the time periods studied and possibly of the differences in sources, city directories vs merchant licences, a part can surely be assigned to the devastating impact of the Panic of 1819 on the city's business community.[231]

Partnerships among retail merchants performed a much more varied role in the counties surveyed. Middlesex County had no partnerships during the period, while Isle of Wight County had only a handful scattered among the years for which data are available, eight, or 13.1 per cent of all licences issued, a proportion lower than found in Richmond. In Spotsylvania County, partnerships ranged between 12.9 per cent of all licence holders in 1819 to a low of 4.7 per cent in 1821. In all cases, the percentage fell well below the proportion of partnerships found among Richmond's retail merchants.[232] Retail merchant partnerships in Pittsylvania County, on the other hand, exceed the proportion of partnerships found among retail merchants in Richmond for the years in which data exist. The percentages of partnerships among licence holders are 18.8 per cent, 28.6 per cent, 28.0 per cent, and 38.9 per cent for the years 1817 through 1820. And, in Kanawha County retail merchant partnerships varied dramatically from a low of 11.1 per cent of licence holders in 1821 to a high of 50.0 per cent in 1819. However, in each year except 1821 the ratio of partnerships exceeded that found among Richmond's retail merchant community.

What do these different findings mean? Although the sample of counties is quite small, making any general conclusions questionable, the data suggest that partnerships were a smaller fraction of licence holders in the Tidewater counties surveyed than in Richmond, while in the counties sampled from the Piedmont (Pittsylvania) and Trans-Allegheny (Kanawha) regions, partnerships were more prevalent among licence holders than in Richmond. One possible explanation might be that being located in more established areas, such as Tidewater, outside a major city yet with access to well-developed transportation and financial/banking networks and not facing the intense competitive environment of the city may reduce the advantages of partnerships, including using partners to improve the firm's personal security base and/or for the diversification of risk. This suggests that partnerships do not increase match quality in these areas as much as they do in the city or in less accessible, less developed areas. Further, higher risk associated with more distant and less accessible areas may have increased incentives for partnerships, while financing mercantile operations in areas more distant from financial networks and banking offices may have increased the advantages of partnerships. In Virginia at this time banking offices were located mainly in the eastern part of the state, with none to be found in the Trans-Allegheny region and only three west of the Blue Ridge, two in Lynchburg and one in Winchester.[233] Thus, partnerships may have increased match quality in Pittsylvania and Kanawha counties, thereby explaining the higher proportion of partnerships in those areas.

But, outside of the City of Richmond, did partnerships increase the survivability of merchants in the years surrounding the Panic of 1819? The earlier discussion of Richmond's experience suggested partnerships increased match quality, leading to higher survivability rates. Even if factors in the Tidewater meant partnerships were not as beneficial as in other areas, partnerships still should be expected to survive at a higher rate than merchants in general survive, if they increase match quality. This is generally the case. In Spotsylvania County, partnerships outsurvived (continued at a higher rate) individual retail merchants in every year except one, 1821 and in Pittsylvania County in every year except 1819. Also in Pittsylvania in 1820, the year in which the most dramatic fall in the number of licences issued occurred (from twenty-five to eighteen), every partnership operating was a survivor from the previous year. Thus, the evidence, while not as strong as that from the City of Richmond, supports the role of partnerships in increasing match quality and therefore survivability.

For Kanawha County, in what is now the state of West Virginia, the evidence is less clear. In the years surrounding the Panic of 1819, 1818–20, partnerships and independent retail merchants survived at a similar rate. However, in 1821 and 1822 no partnerships survived from one year to the next. Several factors may help explain these results. First the number of cases is very small: in five of the seven years studied there were three or fewer partnerships in the county. Second, partnerships, while an important proportion of licence holders, were highly volatile with a great deal of shuffling occurring, including individual merchants moving in and out of partnerships and members of partnerships often changing partners. For example, in 1819 only four licences were issued, two of those to partnerships. One partnership, Hogue and Flanagan, had continued from the previous year; the other, Bureau, Scales and Company, was new, but Bureau had been a partner in Summers and Bureau the year before. This suggests that in an area more remote from the transportation and banking networks of the eastern part of the state and more closely connected to the economy of the Ohio River, merchants realized the importance of partnerships but in the volatile economy of a frontier region changed their business partners more often.

4. Comparison with Other Time Periods

The final question to be considered is the relationship of Virginia merchants' experience during the years surrounding the Panic of 1819 to the experience of merchants in other places and of other time periods, particularly those of severe economic turmoil. Table 5.9 provides bankruptcy and business failure data for the cities of London and Paris and for France in the period 1815–23. In both London and Paris, the period of the Panic of 1819 was a time of economic distress and saw a sharp increase in business exits.[234] London bankruptcies rose 56.3 per cent in 1819 while Paris business failures rose 33.8 per cent the same year following a 74.7 per cent rise the previous year. These compare to a 69.4 per cent increase in exits of Richmond retail and wholesale merchants combined in 1819 and further confirm the international dimension of the downturn at the end of the second decade of the nineteenth century. Interestingly, the London bankruptcy numbers, while dramatic, are not as high during this downturn as those experienced in the sharp downturn of 1815 and 1816 at the end of the Napoleonic wars.

Although data for French bankruptcies is not available until 1820, the level during the early 1820s was relatively low compared to what would occur later in the decade.[235] One possible explanation for this is that the impacts of the traumatic experience of a subsistence crisis at the end of the Napoleonic wars and the subsequent downturn at the end of the decade already had eliminated many

firms, thereby enabling the stronger surviving firms to experience a lower level
of failure. Later in the decade, following a recovery, firms may have been more
susceptible to an economic downturn and failed at a higher rate. Unfortunately
in all these cases data for the total number of firms are not available, thus making
the determination of a turnover rate impossible.

Bankruptcy data present some comparison problems with the Virginia data.
Licence holders who do not renew their licences have not necessarily stopped
operating. A licence holder might choose to concentrate on domestic goods, thus
not requiring a licence, ownership might change, or a firm might be reorganized
with a new licence holder named in the tax list. And, all firms that stop operating do not do so because they are bankrupt. Thus, the turnover rates found in
Richmond can be expected to be higher than bankruptcy rates. For example, in a
study of English bankruptcy during the downturn of 1810–11, Ian Duffy found
that bankrupts per thousand people ranged from 1.6 in Liverpool to 0.1 elsewhere.
London experienced 1.0 bankrupts per thousand people while Manchester's rate
was 1.5 per thousand.[236] In comparison, Richmond experienced turnover rates
among its merchants ranging from a high of 15.9 exits per thousand people in
1819 to a low of 5.8 per thousand people in 1821. Table 5.10 summarizes the
Richmond turnover rates both in terms of exits per thousand people and the exit
rates of licence holders.

United States business failure rates, defined as business failures, meaning 'concerns involved in court procedures or voluntary actions, probably ending in loss
to creditors', divided by 'total number of industrial and commercial enterprises
listed in the Dun and Bradstreet *Reference Book*', typically ranged between 1 and
2 per cent during periods of economic distress in the years between 1857 and
1970.[237] This business failure rate is comparable to a bankruptcy rate among firms
and is dramatically lower than the exit rate in Richmond between 1818 and 1823.
Several factors explain this difference. The Richmond data includes only retail
and wholesale merchants, not all businesses, and an exit in the Richmond data, as
explained above, does not necessarily mean bankruptcy.

A more appropriate measure for our purpose is the 'death rates' for the United
States business population in the years 1900–41 as given in A. D. H. Kaplan's
Small Business. These rates, calculated from Dun and Bradstreet's *Vital Statistics
of Industry and Commerce*, 'include transfers of ownership or changes in legal
organization' as well as true liquidations of business. In fact, Kaplan finds that
'more than a third of the prewar business discontinuances were changes of ownership rather than liquidations of the enterprise.' Over the period 1900–41, 'death
rates' ranged from a high of 230 per thousand listed firms in 1910 to a low of 115
per thousand in 1919, or between 11.5 per cent and 23.0 per cent, significantly
lower than that of Richmond's retail and wholesale firms in the years surrounding
the Panic of 1819. Again the focus of the Richmond study on retail and wholesale

merchants during a period of significant economic disruption might explain the differences.[238]

Retail stores in 207 Indiana towns in the 1930s, the decade of the Great Depression, come closer to matching the experience of this study's Richmond licence holders during the Panic of 1819. Of the stores entering business in 1930, a study by G. W. Starr and G. A. Steiner found that 26.8 per cent were still in business in 1937, the year the study ended, an exit rate of 0.732. Survival rates ranged from a high of 50.4 per cent for drug stores, exit rate 0.496, to a low of 15.5 per cent for restaurants, exit rate 0.945. General stores and department stores each survived at a 24.2 per cent rate while groceries, the most common business at about 40 per cent of the stores surveyed, survived at a 30.1 per cent rate, exit rates of 0.758 and 0.699 respectively. The first year was the hardest on new firms with 24.9 per cent discontinuing operation. By the end of three years, 53.2 per cent of the stores studied were out of business, a three-year exit rate of 0.532.[239]

Another study of firm turnover, and one that allows us to consider exits through time, looks at businesses in Poughkeepsie, New York, between 1844 and 1926 based on city directories. When the period as a whole is reviewed, 32.5 per cent of retailing firms and 22.4 per cent of wholesaling firms were found to discontinue operation in their first year. By the end of three years, 55.0 per cent of retailing firms and 43.7 per cent of wholesaling businesses had dropped out. Most interestingly, when the data is divided into thirty-year periods, 1844–73, 1874–1903 and 1904–33, there is not a significant variation in the survival rates for different kinds of business. For example, the percentage of confectionary stores that exited in the first three years of operation were eighty, seventy-one and seventy-six respectively for the three periods. And during the same three periods, 65, 43 and 54 per cent of grocery stores exited in the first three years of operation.[240]

Several studies of small businesses in the United States in the 1970s and 1980s provide additional information on turnover, particularly the role of firm age and size in determining turnover rates. Some relevant results are presented in Table 5.11. The first, a study for the Small Business Administration, sampled small businesses existing in 1976 and tracked them through 1986 using the United States Establishment Longitudinal Microdata file. For firms aged four years or younger, approximately 45 per cent had exited by 1980 and at the end of the ten-year study about 65 per cent had been lost. Older firms dropped out at a lower rate with between 50 and 60 per cent being lost by 1986. For the smallest firms, those with one to four employees, almost half had dropped out by 1980 and 70 per cent were gone by 1986.[241] Additional information on business turnover is found in a second study, the Census Bureau's 1982 survey 'Characteristics of Business Owners', as reported by Thomas J. Holmes and James A. Schmitz. The survey of 1982 businesses was conducted in 1986 and 'included a question about the status of each firm in 1986'. Non-minority-male, founder-owned businesses of age two or fewer years had a turnover rate of 49 per cent, meaning firms either discontinued or sold, while similarly defined turnover rates for older founder-owned firms ranged from a high of 30 per cent for firms aged twenty-three years or more to a low of 23 per cent for firms aged seven to twelve years. Non-founder firms experienced higher turnover rates, particularly firms aged zero to two years, 66 per cent, and three to six years, 48 per cent, but were only 4.2 per cent of the firms aged zero to two years and 8.4 per cent of those aged three to six years.[242]

Finally, three studies of merchants in the late eighteenth century provide a further basis of comparison. John Tyler's analysis of persistence and change among Boston merchants in the period 1771–90 finds that between 1771 and 1780, 66 per cent of merchants left, including the departure of Loyalists at the beginning of the Revolution. High rates of exit continued in the 1780s with 43 per cent of merchants leaving between 1780 and 1784 and 47 per cent leaving between 1784 and 1790.[243]

Philadelphia merchants also experienced substantial turnover during the Revolution, as Thomas Doerflinger documents in his study *A Vigorous Spirit of Enterprise*. Considering elite merchants, Doerflinger finds that 61 per cent of the 1791 group had not been in the city in 1774, while only 42 per cent of the 1774 elites had not been in the city in 1756. Further emphasizing the disruption of the Revolution, he finds that of the 1756 elite merchant group, 42 per cent were still merchants, either elite or non-elite, in 1774, meaning 58 per cent were non-merchants in the city or had left the city, while of the 1774 elite group 26 per cent were still merchants by 1791, meaning 74 per cent were non-merchants or had left. Two additional pieces of information confirm the higher turnover of the Revolutionary period. Among 1756 merchants in Philadelphia, 69 per cent were 'still in the city eleven years later', while of the city's 1785 merchants, 'about 30 per cent of them had left the city by 1791' and 'of those staying in the city roughly 33 per cent were no longer merchants.' These numbers convert to a 0.31 exit rate between 1756 and 1767 and approximately a 0.47 exit rate between 1785 and 1791.[244]

In Annapolis between 1783 and 1793 Edward Papenfuse finds that among 1783 residents, 19 per cent had moved and 65 per cent had remained by 1793. The fate of the remainder is unknown. When those listed as merchants or store-keepers are considered, a slightly smaller percentage, 17.1, are found to have moved and 82.9 per cent to have remained in 1793 for an exit rate of 0.171 over the decade (there were no unknowns among these two groups).[245]

What do these various studies of continuity and turnover in the United States tell us? A summary of the findings regarding American business turnover or exit rates for various locations and different time periods is provided in Table 5.12. One of the most striking comparisons is the remarkable consistency of the exit rates for all Richmond merchants between 1818 and 1822, 0.712, and in 1819, 0.610, with those found during other periods of exceptional economic disruption. In Philadelphia between 1774 and 1791 and Boston between 1771 and

1780, during the turmoil of the Revolution including the removal of Loyalist merchants, turnover rates were 0.74 and 0.66 respectively, while in 207 Indiana towns during the depression years between 1930 and 1937 the exit rate was 0.732. For very young, age zero to two years, and small, one to four employees, firms in the United States between 1976 and 1986, a period that included the sharpest recession since the Great Depression, the turnover rate was between 0.65 and 0.70.

Because these studies all involve longer time periods than does the Richmond study, seventeen, nine, seven, and ten years respectively vs four years, and because turnover rates increase with time, the comparison suggests that the disruption for Richmond merchants during the Panic of 1819 was at least as severe as for merchants during the Revolution, for retail stores during the Great Depression, and for small businesses during the late 1970s and early 1980s. And, it is possible that the Richmond disruption was more severe, since a comparable turnover rate occurred in a shorter time period.

Summary and Conclusions

Merchant licence data for Virginia, and particularly for the capital, Richmond, indicate a substantial volatility among licence holders and that this volatility increased significantly with the onset of hard times during the Panic of 1819. Retail merchants in the City of Richmond appear to have been hit hardest, although the remainder of the Commonwealth did not avoid problems either as credit was tightened before the year of the Panic or as the depression following the Panic worked itself through the economy. Throughout the state generally and particularly in Richmond, partnerships had a marginally better chance of survival, especially for retail merchants in the panic year of 1819. Yet, few merchants, in partnerships or not, were able to avoid the 'long faces' Benjamin Brand wrote of in his 1819 letter to a former Richmond retail merchant.

Most important, however, is the comparison of Virginia merchants' experience during the Panic of 1819 with that of small businesses throughout much of our nation's history. The volatility experienced by Virginia merchants in the years surrounding the Panic of 1819 is comparable to that of merchants and small businesses during other periods of economic distress, whether it be the Revolutionary War, the Great Depression, or the sharp downturn of the early 1980s.

This result has important implications for our current economy. At the present time, small businesses employ 'half of all private sector employees', 'pay more than 45 per cent of total US private payroll', 'create more than 50 percent of non-farm private gross domestic product (GDP)', and 'generate 60 to 80 percent of net new jobs annually'.[246] Given the importance of these firms to the nation's employment picture, and given the volatility of small business, particularly in periods of economic crisis such as the Panic of 1819, if the specter of the business cycle reappears, the United States could experience substantial exits, particularly of small business, and the employment growth so critical to a healthy economy could come to a crashing halt.

Tables

Table 5.1: Virginia Merchant Licence Revenue, 1816–24.

Tax Year	Licence Revenue	
	Current Dollars	Percent Change
1816	52,487	
1817	50,560	-3.7
1818	51,826	+2.5
1819	45,353	-12.5
1820	40,868	-9.9
1821	41,846	+2.4
1822	42,244	+1.0
1823	42,610	+0.9
1824	46,783	+9.8

Sources: Auditor of Public Accounts, *Receipts Journal*, 1816–19; *Daybook* 1820; *Auditor's Reports to the General Assembly*, 1821–24.

Table 5.2: Retail Merchant Experience: Richmond 1817–23.

Licences	1817	1818	1819	1820	1821	1822	1823
Number	250	273	168	178	228	233	235
Continue		153	99	92*	113	140	138
Exit		97	174	76	65	88	95
Enter		120	69	83	115	93	97
Re-enter		na	12a	29a	21b	20c	19d
Percent**			17.4	35.4	18.3	21.7	19.6
Rates		1817/18	1818/19	1819/20	1820/21	1821/22	1822/23
CR(t-1)		.612	.363	.548	.635	.614	.592
XR(t-1)		.388	.637	.452	.365	.386	.408
ER(t)		.480	.253	.494	.646	.404	.416

na = not available

* The ninety-two licence holders from 1819 who continue in 1820 purchase a total of ninety-five licences. Lewis Convert, who purchased one licence in 1819, purchases three in 1820, and the partnership of D, G, and S Pleasants purchased one licence in 1819 while Daniel Pleasants and Samuel Pleasants each purchased a licence in 1820 and the partnership did not.

** percent of entries

a: all after one year

b: 11 after one year, 8 after two years, 2 after three years

c: 9 after one year, 5 after two years, 6 after three years

d: 8 after one year, 5 after two years, 4 after three years, 1 after four years

Source: Auditor of Public Accounts, Licence Returns 1817–23, Virginia State Archives.

Table 5.3: Adjusted Retail Merchant Experience: Richmond, 1817–23.

Licences	1817	1818	1819	1820	1821	1822	1823
Number	250	273	204	183	257	250	235
Continue		165	147	129*	163	178	157
Exit		85	126	72	20	79	93
Enter		108	57	54	194	72	78
Rates		1817/18	1818/19	1819/20	1820/21	1821/22	1822/23
CR(t-1)		.660	.538	.647	.891	.693	.628
XR(t-1)		.340	.462	.353	.109	.307	.372
ER(t)		.432	.209	.265	.514	.280	.312

* The 129 licence holders from 1819 who continue in 1820 purchase a total of 132 licences. Lewis Convert, who purchased one licence in 1819, purchases three in 1820, and the partnership of D, G, and S Pleasants purchased one licence in 1819 while Daniel Pleasants and Samuel Pleasants each purchased a licence in 1820 and the partnership did not.

Source: Auditor of Public Accounts, Licence Returns 1817–23, Virginia State Archives.

Table 5.4: Virginia Retail Merchant Experience, 1818–23.

I. Isle of Wight
(Tidewater)

Licences	1817	1818	1819	1820	1821	1822	1823
Number	10	9	15	12	na	14	na
Continue		3	7	8	na	6	na
Exit		7	2	7	na	8	na
Enter		6	8	4	na	8	na
Rates		1817/18	1818/19	1819/20		1820/22	
CR(t-1)		0.300	0.778	0.533		0.500	
XR(t-1)		0.700	0.22	0.467		0.500	
ER(t)		0.600	0.889	0.267		0.667	

II. Middlesex
(Tidewater)

Licences	1817	1818	1819	1820	1821	1822	1823
Number	7	9	7	na	6	na	6
Continue		3	6	na	2	na	3
Exit		4	3	na	5	na	3
Enter		6	1	na	4	na	3
Rates		1817/18	1818/19		1819/21		1821/23
CR(t-1)		0.429	0.667		0.286		0.500
XR(t-1)		0.571	0.333		0.741		0.500
ER(t)		0.857	0.111		0.571		0.500

III. Spotsylvania
(Tidewater)

Licences	1817	1818	1819	1820	1821	1822	1823
Number	81	83	85	83	86	95	80
Continue		54	57	60	60	70	63
Exit		27	26	25	23	16	32
Enter		29	28	23	26	25	17
Rates		1817/18	1818/19	1819/20	1820/21	1821/22	1822/23
CR(t-1)		0.667	0.687	0.706	0.723	0.814	0.663
XR(t-1)		0.333	0.313	0.294	0.277	0.186	0.337
ER(t)		0.358	0.337	0.271	0.313	0.291	0.179

IV. Pittsylvania
(Piedmont)

Licences	1817	1818	1819	1820	1821	1822	1823
Number	32	28	25	18	na	na	na
Continue		24	17	14	na	na	na
Exit		8	11	11	na	na	na
Enter		4	8	4	na	na	na
Rates		1817/18	1818/19	1819/20			
CR(t-1)		0.750	0.607	0.560			
XR(t-1)		0.250	0.393	0.440			
ER(t)		0.125	0.286	0.160			

V. Kanawha
(Trans-Allegheny)

Licences	1817	1818	1819	1820	1821	1822	1823
Number	11	8	4	9	9	8	na
Continue		5	4	4	4	3	na
Exit		6	4	0	5	6	na
Enter		3	0	5	5	5	na
Rates		1817/18	1818/19	1819/20	1820/21	1821/22	
CR(t-1)		0.450	0.500	1.00	0.444	0.333	
XR(t-1)		0.545	0.500	0	0.556	0.667	
ER(t)		0.273	0	1.25	0.556	0.556	

na=not available

Source: Auditor of Public Accounts, Licence Returns 1817–23, Virginia State Archives.

Table 5.5: Retail Merchant Experience: Pittsylvania County, 1818–20.

Retail Merchants	1818	1819	1820
Number	28	25	18
Number Holding Ordinary Licence	12	12	7
percent	43%	48%	39%
Number Continuing (from previous year)	24	17	14
Number of Entries	4	8	4
Entries from Ordinary Licence	0	0	0
Reentries	na	0	2
Number of Exits (from previous year)	8	11	11
Exits to Ordinary Licence	1	0	0

na=not available

Source: Auditor of Public Accounts, Licence Returns 1817–20, Virginia State Archives.

Table 5.6: Wholesale Merchant Experience: Richmond, 1817–23.

Licences	1817	1818	1819	1820	1821	1822	1823
Number	35	30	19	22	33	29	22
Continue		21*	16	13	15	24	16
Exit		14	14	6	7	9	13
To retail licence		1	3	0	1	2	0
Enter		8	3	9	18	5	6
From retail licence		0	0	0	2	0	0
Re-enter		na	3a	5b	5a	4c	2a
Percent**		100%	56%	28%	80%	33%	
Rates		1817/18	1818/19	1819/20	1820/21	1821/22	1822/23
CR(t-1)		.600	.533	.684	.682	.727	.552

Licences	1817	1818	1819	1820	1821	1822	1823
XR(t-1)		.400	.467	.316	.318	.273	.448
ER(t)		.229	.100	.474	.818	.152	.207

na=not available

* The twenty-one licence holders from 1817 who continued in 1818 purchased twenty-two licences. The 1817 partnership Baker and Finney apparently dissolved and licences were purchased by the partnerships of Baker and Folsom and James Brown and W. Finney.

** per cent of entries

a: all after one-year absence

b: two after two-year absence, others after one-year absence

c: one after two-year absence, others after one-year absence

Source: Auditor of Public Accounts, Licence Returns 1817–23, Virginia State Archives.

Table 5.7: Adjusted Wholesale Merchant Experience: Richmond, 1817–23.

Licences	1817	1818	1819	1820	1821	1822	1823
Number	35	30	24	23	34	29	22
Continue		26*	24	19	21	28	18
Exit		9	6	5	2	5	11
Enter		3	0	4	13	1	4
Rates		1817/18	1818/19	1819/20	1820/21	1821/22	1822/23
CR(t-1)		0.743	0.800	0.729	0.913	0.853	0.621
XR(t-1)		0.257	0.200	0.208	0.087	0.147	0.379
ER(t)		0.086	0.000	0.167	0.565	0.029	0.138

* The twenty-six licence holders from 1817 who continued in 1818 purchased twenty-seven licences. The 1817 partnership Baker and Finney apparently dissolved and licences were purchased by the partnerships of Baker and Folsom and James Brown and W. Finney.

Source: Auditor of Public Accounts, Licence Returns 1817–23, Virginia State Archives.

Table 5.8: Richmond Merchant Partnerships, 1817–23.

Year	Retail Merchants			Wholesale Merchants		
	Number	Percent Total	P'ships CR	Number	Per cent Total	P'ships CR
1817	44	17.6	na	15	42.9	na
1818	41	15.0	0.773	17	56.7	0.733
1819	29	17.3	0.683	11	57.9	0.588
1820	32	18.0	0.655	11	50.0	0.727
1821	36	15.8	0.656	15	45.5	0.727
1822	26	11.6	0.611	15	51.7	0.800
1823	22	9.4	0.731	9	40.9	0.533

Per cent Total=partnerships as a percentage of all licence holders in that year.

P;ships CR = partnership continuity rate.

na=not available

Source: Auditor of Public Accounts, Licence Returns, Virginia State Archives.

Table 5.9: Bankruptcy and Business Failures: London, Paris and France, 1815–23.

Year	London Bankruptcy	Paris Business Failures	France Bankruptcy
1815	1759	107	na
1816	2145	122	na

Year	London Bankruptcy	Paris Business Failures	France Bankruptcy
1817	1578	146	na
1818	1012	255	na
1819	1582	341	na
1820	1385	216	950
1821	1268	na	1050
1822	1132	na	1060
1823	988	na	1370

na=not available

Sources: A. D. Gayer, W. W. Rostow and A. J. Schwartz, *The Growth and Fluctuation of the British Economy 1790–1830* (Oxford: Clarendon, 1953), pp. 121, 147 and 205n; T. M. Luckett, 'Credit and Commercial Society in France, 1740–1789' (Phd dissertation, Princeton University, 1992), p. 223, and L. Marco, 'Faillites et Crises Economiques en France au XIXe Siecle', *Annales ESC*, 2:2 (1989), pp. 355–78; p. 364.

Table 5.10: Richmond Merchant Exit Rates, 1818–23.

Year	Exits per thousand people*	Exit Rates Retail	Exit Rates Wholesale
1818	9.6	0.388	0.400
1819	15.1	0.634	0.467
1820	6.9	0.458	0.316
1621	5.8	0.365	0.318
1822	7.5	0.386	0.273
1823	8.1	0.408	0.448

* Retail and wholesale combined. Annual Richmond population interpolated from 1810, 1820, and 1830 censuses (except 1820).

Sources: Tables 5.2 and 5.6.

Table 5.11: US Small Business Turnover, 1976–86.

	1976–86 Percent Surviving				
	1978	1980	1982	1984	1986
Size (employees)					
1–4	66.2	47.5	43.3	35.8	30.9
5–9	81.0	69.2	63.9	57.0	51.2
Age (years)					
0–2	76.9	56.2	49.3	40.4	34.4
3–4	71.9	52.1	47.1	39.9	34.7
5–9	71.6	56.7	52.2	45.3	40.2
10–19	73.9	62.4	58.5	52.0	46.9
20+	74.1	63.9	60.1	53.9	48.8

Age of Firm (years)	1982–6 Per cent discontinued Founder	Non-founder	Per cent sold Founder	Non-founder
0–2	46	59	3	7
3–6	26	36	3	12
7–12	20	23	3	14
13–22	22	18	4	11
23+	26	16	4	13

Small Business=tax returns for proprietorships, parnerships, and sub-chapter S corporations. 80 per cent of these businesses had no employees.

Sources: J. Popkin and Company, 'Business Survival Rates by Age Cohorts of Business' (United States Small Business Administration, RS Number 122, 1989), Tables 1 and 2, and T. J. Holmes and

J. A. Schmitz, Jr., On the Turnover of Business Firms and Business Managers', *Journal of Political Economy* 103:5 (1995), calculated from Table 1, pp. 1005–38; p. 1009.

Table 5.12: Summary of Turnover Rates.

Place and Years		Exit Rate
Philadelphia	1756–67	0.31
	1774–91	0.74
	1785–91	0.47
Boston	1771–80	0.66
	1780–4	0.43
	1784–90	0.47
Annapolis	1783–93	0.171
Poughkeepsie	1844-1926	
	Retail by third year	0.550
	Wholesale by third year	0.437
Indiana	1930–37	0.732
	1930–3	0.532
United States	1976–86 (age 0–2)	0.656
	1976–86 (1–4 employees)	0.691
	1982–6 (founder, age 0–2)	0.49
Richmond	1818–22 (all licences)	0.712
	1819 (all licences)	0.610

Sources: See text.

Charts

Chart 5.1: Virginia Merchant Licence Revenue, 1816–24.

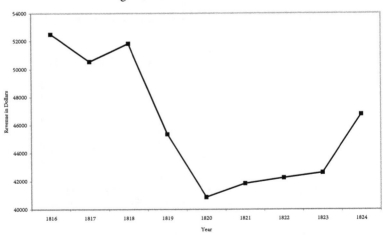

Chart 5.2: Richmond Retail Merchant Exits, 1815–29.

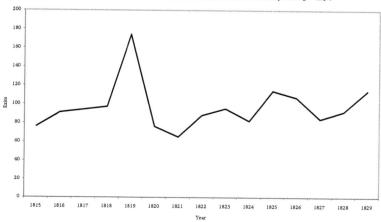

6 POOR RELIEF

With the onset of the Panic of 1819, Virginia found itself in the midst of substantial financial volatility combined with the much more significant loss of foreign markets for the state's agricultural staples. It was the latter that sent prices plummeting and stalled the Commonwealth's economy. Deflation coupled with debt created during the expansion following the end of the War of 1812 created a sharp decrease in business activity, falling property values and a general gloom across the Commonwealth. As a result, some Virginians looking for reasons behind the state's diminished prosperity blamed the people. For example, Governor James Preston in his letter to the General Assembly at the beginning of the 1819–20 session suggested that 'we have rushed upon our own ruin' as a result of our 'love of ease and extravagance, and inordinate desire to grow suddenly rich'. Further, we have 'thoughtlessly and imprudently ... availed ourselves of the facilities heretofore demanded as indispensable for our national advancement'. Yet, according to Preston, 'we can neither be ignorant of the causes, nor of the proper remedies to relieve us from the consequent embarrassments'. For the Governor the remedies were to 'unite in our efforts to return to our habits of industry and oeconomy'.[247]

However, urging renewal of the old ways of industry and suggesting individuals practise 'oeconomy' did little to help those made destitute by the depression. Instead of pointing a finger at people and urging them to improve their lot, others in the Commonwealth seemed willing, at least initially, to extend a helping hand to those less fortunate. According to one scholar who has written about Virginia at the time of the Panic, in Richmond the 'extraordinary high prices' of food and fuel in 1816–17 led to an extra three-month allowance for distribution to outdoor paupers. In addition, as the downturn developed in 1819 and beyond, the city continued to spend 20 to 25 per cent of its budget on the poor.[248] In Petersburg, 'from 1820 to 1823, the bill for poor relief averaged more than five thousand dollars a year, a sum triple or quadruple the normal expense'.[249] Yet, this positive response did not hold as the Commonwealth's economy stagnated in the 1820s.

Once the Panic had passed, poor relief disbursements appear to have levelled off or begun to fall in Petersburg and Richmond along with a dramatic drop in poor rates after the mid-1820s. For example, in Petersburg, 'radical cuts were called for' and 'in 1823, the outdoor relief system was abolished'.[250] This appears to be the beginning of a backlash that would lead to less and less public support for the poor in the 1820s and continuing in the years leading up to the Civil War.[251] Thus, while the initial public response to the poverty created by the Panic was generous in these two cities, ultimately it appears that the 'Panic and its aftermath destroyed the sense of community and consensus that had been so prevalent in the 1780s and 1790s among the elite' in Richmond and Petersburg.[252]

But, was the experience of these two urban centres reflective of the state as a whole? In order to answer questions regarding how Virginia's system of poor relief accommodated the Commonwealth's experience with its first modern boom-bust cycle and to determine what changes occurred in public and private support for the poor in the years following the Panic of 1819 throughout the state, this chapter will analyze poor relief data from a number of the state's counties and cities for the period 1816–28.

Virginia's Poor Laws

After operating informally for some time, Virginia's system of poor relief was formally established in 1631–2.[253] The colony's mechanism for supporting the poor was generally similar to the English Poor Law of the time but with some interesting differences. The Church of England in Virginia was responsible for providing poor relief through its parishes, with churchwardens and vestry making the decisions and establishing the poor tax as part of one general parish levy. This differed from the English system in which separate Overseers of the Poor bore responsibility for aiding the poor and established a separate poor rate. Payment in Virginia was in tobacco, and many of those with the lowest incomes, slaves and the indentured, were not eligible for relief.[254] In 1723, a parish union plan enabled smaller parishes to group together for providing poor relief, and through the mid-1700s a number of petitions were presented to the legislature to create poorhouses or workhouses. Many of those established seem to have been short-lived.[255]

In 1776 the Church of England in Virginia was disestablished in an act that forbade 'collection of parish levies for support of the Church', but 'specifically ordered the vestries to continue collecting for poor relief'. With some vestries no longer operating, the General Assembly in 1778 ordered local tax collectors to provide for the poor, and in 1780 Overseers of the Poor were established in each county for the purpose of providing poor relief. It is this system that was operating at the time of the Panic of 1819.[256]

On 10 February 1819, the General Assembly passed 'an act reducing to one act, the several acts providing for the Poor, and declaring who shall be deemed

Vagrants', to become effective 1 January 1820. Apparently designed primarily as a 'house cleaning' measure, the legislation came at a time when attention to the economy had increased in the wake of the problems encountered in 1817 and 1818 but before the full impacts of the banking panic and collapse of commodity prices changed the demands on the system. A review of this act will yield a better understanding of the mechanisms created to provide poor relief at the time. The heart of the system was the Overseers of the Poor, and as one governor suggested, 'Our poor laws, in their practical operation, are entirely local, confined exclusively within the limits of the counties and towns.'[257] Individuals or families seeking relief were to apply to the overseer of their district and, if refused, could apply to the court which in turn could 'direct the overseers to receive him or her upon the lists of poor'. After establishing how overseers in each county were to be elected, when they should meet, and how they should organize, the General Assembly specified that the overseers determine the funds available to support the poor. According to the General Assembly, they shall 'levy and assess, upon all such taxables in their county, as are subject to county levies' and 'settle, the amount of the poor rate upon each such taxable in specie'. In addition, 'the overseers of each district shall provide for the poor, lame, blind and other inhabitants of the district, not able to maintain themselves ... the expense of which shall be provided for in the succeeding levy'. Corporation (town) courts in the Commonwealth were given the power to appoint 'overseers of the poor within their respective corporations', with the appointed overseers to 'have the same powers, perform the same duties, and be subject to the same penalties, as overseers in the several counties'.[258]

Overseers of the Poor were empowered to appoint a collector of the poor rate and were to settle their accounts with the courts in December of each year, with any balance unappropriated to 'be deducted from the rate to be made for the ensuing year'. In addition, overseers were authorized to 'bind out' as apprentices 'the poor orphans in their district, and such children within the same, whose parents they shall judge incapable of supporting them'. The same held for bastard children. Overseers could refuse to provide for anyone migrating into the state within the last three years and were given the power of removal 'to the county or district where he or she was last legally settled' any person 'strolling' from another county, district, or town. County and city courts were also 'empowered, whenever they shall judge it necessary, to provide or build a poor-house and workhouse for the reception of the poor, and for the reformation of vagrants'. Vagrants were defined as 'any able bodied man, who, not having wherewithal to maintain himself, shall be found loitering, and shall have a wife and children, without means for their subsistence' or 'without a wife or child, not having wherewithal to maintain himself, shall wander abroad, or be found loitering, without betaking himself to some honest employment'.[259]

Finally, in addition to specifying myriad details for the working of the system, the act required that the proceedings of the overseers' annual meeting should 'contain a distinct account of the number, names and situation of the poor, of the expenditures of the proceeding year, the amount to be assessed for the succeeding year, and the rate per tithe of such assessment'. The reports were to be 'carefully filed and preserved by the respective clerks'.[260]

Data

Information from Overseers of the Poor records for Virginia's counties and cities are available in the Archives of the Library of Virginia. Reports of the proceedings of overseers from each county and city were generally sent to the State Auditor of Public Accounts. However, the actual submission of such reports appears to have been somewhat spotty. As a result, in 1829 the General Assembly required overseers to begin submitting annual reports and requested that each county and city also prepare a special report indicating annually back to 1800 the total number of whites and free blacks 'maintained at public charge', 'the number of poor maintained at poor or work houses, with the amount of the annual expense of their maintenance', 'the number of poor boarded out, or otherwise supported, with the amount of the annual expense of their support' and 'the amount of poor rates levied annually for their support'. This latter record is the source for data used in the analysis presented below.[261]

Some or all of these data are available for eighty-nine of the Commonwealth's counties and cities for the period of the Panic and afterwards. All recorded data for the years 1816–29 were collected from the Virginia Auditor of Public Records archives. For a number of units the data are incomplete, with some years having partial data reported and other years having no data recorded. Thus, analysis was conducted first using all information available, and second including only those units for which complete data relevant for the analysis being conducted is recorded for the years 1816–28. The Appendix to this chapter provides details of the data set, including a list of all cities and counties for which data were found and, for each measure used in the analysis, an indication of which localities provided complete and continuous data for the period 1816–28.

The issue of overseers underreporting the number of recipients and the amounts expended is important since, as was discussed earlier regarding business licences, antebellum records are problematic. Unfortunately, no way of estimating the extent of underreporting exists. However, if underreporting were random, it should impact the econometric analysis only by reducing the fit of regressions.

Poor Relief in Virginia

A variety of measures provide insight into the workings of Virginia's system of poor relief in the early decades of the nineteenth century. The pauper rate, or the number of persons receiving relief, either indoor or outdoor, per thousand population, is available for almost seventy counties across the Commonwealth.[262] Table 6.1 provides mean pauper rates for the years 1816–28 for all counties for which data are available and for the forty-eight counties for which pauper rates may be calculated for each year of the period. Means are generally low, between one-quarter and one-half of one per cent of the population, with the range being quite large. For example, during the depression years 1819–21 the maximum pauper rate for a locality was 35.49 or 3.5 per cent of the population and the minimum was 0.18 or 0.002 per cent of the population. The data indicate that pauper rates increased moderately with the onset of the depression following the Panic of 1819; the mean increased 7.2 per cent for all reporting units and 3.9 per cent for the forty-eight counties/cities sample. Interestingly, both data sets show more significant increases in the pauper rate during the 1820s as the Commonwealth's economy stagnated. Mean pauper rates rose from the depression years 1819–21 to the period 1822–8 by 14.6 per cent for all reporting units and 8.5 per cent for the forty-eight units with continuous data.

Regional differences in pauper rates among the forty-eight localities with continuous data are given in Table 6.2. There are important variations not only in the rates themselves but also in the behaviour of pauper rates over time. The Tidewater clearly had the highest pauper rates with Trans-Allegheny having the lowest. This difference between the eastern and western parts of the state may be the result of the western movement of the able-bodied seeking land and opportunity and leaving behind those more likely to require relief. In addition, it also may result from the differential impact of the commodity price collapse on those regions most closely tied to foreign markets and home to the businesses that processed, prepared and shipped the commodities. It also may be the result of the eastern portion of the state having a more well-developed system of poor relief than those counties on the frontier.[263] While pauper rates in Virginia as a whole rose with the onset of depression following the Panic of 1819, in the Piedmont and the Valley pauper rates actually fell. Also, as the 1820s continued, pauper rates rose in general except in the Valley where the pauper rate fell 12.4 per cent. In part, the small size of the sample in the Valley may affect the results. In addition, in the Piedmont and the Valley localities may have been more reluctant to offer public assistance and communities may have taken care of their own through informal means. Also, the Valley's connections to Pennsylvania and Philadelphia markets may have helped to partially insulate the region from the general stagnation experienced by the Commonwealth. Finally, the relatively large increase in pauper rates in the Trans-Allegheny in the years following the depression may be the result of the delayed impact of the Panic in that region, observed earlier in prices and merchant licences.

Those receiving assistance from the overseers seem to have been largely the young, the old, and women. For example, in Fauquier County in 1816 the list of those in the poorhouse included eight children and twenty-one adults. Of the adults, 61.9 per cent were women and seven of the twenty-one adults were age seventy or over. Lancaster County supported an even higher percentage of the young in 1821. According to the overseers' records, 57.8 per cent of the forty-five individuals receiving aid were children – sixteen orphans and ten other children. Of the nineteen adults being supported, 57.9 per cent were women. By 1828, the percentage of children assisted had dropped to 30.6, including six orphans and nine others, the proportion of women among those receiving relief remained roughly the same (51.4 per cent), and two blacks – 'Old Shaderick' and 'Eve, a negro woman' – received support from the Overseers of the Poor. Almost half of those on the poor list in Lancaster County between 1820 and 1860 spent no more than two years receiving aid while 70 per cent spent less than four years on the list.[264]

Another measure of the workings of the poor relief system during this period is the poor rate, the tax rate set by Overseers of the Poor to fund their activities. Once set, poor rates were collected typically by the sheriff based on the number of tithables. Table 6.3 provides information on poor rates for all localities for which data were reported, a maximum of twenty-two, as well as for the eighteen counties and cities for which poor rates are provided each year of the period 1817–28.[265] Means for the periods 1816/17–18, 1819–21 and 1822–8 show that nominal poor rates fell during the Panic in the sample of eighteen cities and counties or remained virtually constant, up 0.2 per cent, for all reporting localities and fell for both samples in the years after the depression. However, real poor rates actually rose during the depression years 1819–21, with means up 10.7 per cent for all reporting localities and up 4.1 per cent for the eighteen for which continuous data are available. Real poor rates also continued to increase in the years following the downturn, with means rising 5.5 per cent and 3.8 per cent for all reporting localities and the subsample of eighteen respectively.

To complete this initial view of the operation of Virginia's system of poor relief, Table 6.4 provides data from all reporting cities and counties on the mean number of individuals receiving outdoor and indoor relief.[266] The data yield important insights into both the Commonwealth's system of poor relief and the impact of the depression following the Panic of 1819 on the operations of that system.

White Virginians were the vast majority of those served by the poor law since slaves were generally the responsibility of their owners and free African Americans were a relatively small portion of the population.[267] The mean number of whites receiving outdoor relief in all reporting localities, which ranged between sixty-two and sixty-eight counties and cities for the years 1817–28, rose moderately, up 5.2 per cent, from the period 1816–18 to the depression years of 1819–21. However, rather than dropping as the economy recovered, the mean number of whites receiving aid continued to increase through the 1820s, with the mean number served increasing 21.9 per cent between the years 1819–21 and 1822–8. This, combined with the pauper rates from Table 6.1, suggests that for those cities and counties providing outdoor relief, the depression of 1819–21, the slow recovery, and the stagnant economy of the 1820s combined to place an increased stress on those at the bottom of the economic spectrum and forced more and more individuals and families to seek assistance from the local Overseers of the Poor. When data from the sub-sample of twenty-seven counties and cities that have data from every year of the period are reviewed, a similar pattern emerges; mean numbers of white outdoor relief recipients went up 3.9 per cent between 1816–18 and 1819–21 and up 15.6 per cent between 1819–21 and 1822–8.

Free blacks, although a relatively small proportion of those receiving poor relief, experienced a significant increase in mean numbers served with the onset of the depression of 1819–21, an increase of 27.2 per cent in all reporting counties and cities, between twenty-four and thirty-four localities for the years 1816–28. This is mirrored by the 22.6 per cent increase reflected in the data for the nine localities that have continuous data for the period. These results suggest that those free persons most discriminated against and therefore most likely to be at the very bottom of the economy were among those most affected by the depression and thus forced to turn to the overseers for relief. As the Commonwealth moved beyond the depression years, the mean number of free blacks receiving support in all reporting counties and cities fell slightly, down 4.4 per cent, but still remained significantly above the pre-depression level. When data from the nine cities and counties that reported every year between 1816 and 1828 are considered, the mean number of free blacks receiving outdoor relief rose slightly in the years following the depression, up 3.1 per cent. Although mixed, these results suggest free blacks continued to require assistance through the 1820s at a level close to that of the depression years.

Finally, the mean number of poorhouse inmates rose dramatically during the depression years and then fell as the 1820s progressed. The mean number of individuals in poorhouses increased 24.9 per cent between 1816–18 and 1819–21 in all reporting localities and only fell 5.5 per cent for the years 1822–8. This pattern is confirmed in data from the four cities and counties for which continuous reports exist. Mean poorhouse inmates rose 38.2 per cent during the depression years 1819–21 and fell 8.2 per cent in the period 1822–8. Although these results give further credence to the findings of Susanne Lebsock and Robert M. Saunders that the years following the Panic of 1819 witnessed a pulling back from previous levels of support for the poor, they are not reflective of the state's actions in general and demonstrate the problem of looking only at areas using poorhouses as their primary poor relief mechanism. In the provision of outdoor relief the picture is quite different with more (white) or roughly the same number (free black) being served in the years following the depression as during the depression years. In order to determine how Virginians reacted to the increased demand for poor relief during the Panic of 1819 and whether the experience of the depression led localities to step back from their commitment to helping the poor, we now turn to measures of the generosity of poor relief.

Two measures of the generosity of poor relief in Virginia provide further insight into the pattern of localities' efforts to assist the poor during the years surrounding the depression of 1819–21. The first, real per capita relief spending, is, according to Joan Hannon, 'the simplest measure of the financial resources devoted to the public relief system'.[268] Tables 6.5, 6.7 and 6.8 provide information regarding mean total, outdoor and poorhouse real expenditures per thousand population for the years 1816–28. Mean total and outdoor real expenditures increased in the depression years of 1819–21 and then continued to rise in the 1820s. This is the case for both all reporting counties as well as those counties that have data for each year of the period. However, when mean real poorhouse expenditures per capita are considered, the picture changes. While there was a significant increase in mean real expenditures per thousand population from the pre-depression years of 1816–18 to the depression period of 1819–21, especially in the eight cities and counties for which there are continuous data, once the depression was over, mean poorhouse expenditures fell. This decline, which was 12.6 per cent for all reporting localities and 16.1 per cent for the eight counties and cities with continuous data, supports the contention that in the aftermath of the Panic of 1819 there was a backlash leading to lower levels of support for the Commonwealth's poor. However, this only applies to per capita poorhouse expenditures. Total and outdoor mean real expenditures, which rose with the onset of the depression, continued to rise as Virginians responded compassionately to the plight of the poor as the decade of the 1820s developed. Again the findings of Lebsock and Saunders that support for the poor was reduced in the years following the depression, while true in the provision of poorhouse relief, is not the case across the Commonwealth, particularly in those localities where outdoor relief was the primary mechanism of caring for the poor.

Mean real total expenditures per thousand population by region for the forty-four cities and counties with continuous data are presented in Table 6.6. Several points require comment. The first is the large difference in total expenditures per capita among the regions, particularly between Tidewater and Trans-Allegheny. This again suggests important differences between eastern and western portions of the state in the nature of the demand for poor relief and in the abilities of the regions to supply relief for the poor. A second point is the general increase in per capita support for the poor during the depression years 1819–21, with Tidewater leading the way with an increase of 14.3 per cent. The exception is

Trans-Allegheny, where per capita expenditures fell 6.7 per cent. In the years following the depression, Tidewater changed per capita expenditures very little, down 0.4 per cent, while the other regions continued to increase per capita spending on poor relief, especially Trans-Allegheny where per capita spending rose 48.3 per cent. The pattern in Trans-Allegheny likely reflects the delayed timing of the impact of the depression in the western part of the Commonwealth. Most importantly, the evidence demonstrates that in no region was there a pulling back from support for the poor.

A second measure of the Commonwealth's generosity towards the poor is real expenditures per recipient.[269] Mean real total, outdoor and poorhouse expenditures per recipient are given in Tables 6.9. 6.11 and 6.12. All three measures indicate the increased generosity of Virginians as economic hard times following the Panic of 1819 swept across the Commonwealth. For both all reporting counties and cities and those with continuous data for the period, mean real expenditures per recipient rose between the years 1816–18 and the depression years of 1819–21. Total expenditures were up 38.1 per cent for all reporting localities and 15.6 per cent for those with continuous data, outdoor expenditures increased 39.3 per cent for all and 13.9 per cent for continuous, and poorhouse expenditures rose 16.1 per cent for all and 18.5 per cent for continuous. Thus, in the depression years of 1819–21 not only were more citizens of the Commonwealth provided relief by the Overseers of the Poor but also both per capita spending for poor relief and spending per recipient rose. The onset of hard times yielded compassion for those affected by the depression. But, what happened in the years following the depression as the state's economy languished?

A comparison of mean expenditures per recipient between the depression years 1819–21 and the period 1822–8 yields a mixed picture. Mean real poorhouse expenditures per recipient fell 15.4 per cent for all reporting localities and 19.4 per cent for those with continuous data, again confirming that Lebsock and Saunders correctly saw the cuts in poorhouse relief in their studies of Petersburg and Richmond. However, mean real total and outdoor expenditures per recipient rose between 1819–21 and 1822–8 in those cities and counties with continuous data. Mean real outdoor expenditures per recipient increased 11.3 per cent while mean real total expenditures per recipient moved up 11.5 per cent. This again suggests the increased generosity of Virginians during the 1820s. A problem appears, however, when similar calculations are made for all reporting units. In this case, real mean expenditures per recipient fell 14.7 per cent for outdoor relief and 8.4 per cent for total expenditures, just the opposite of the findings from continuous data. Although this difference is troubling, the results from all reporting localities should not be given the same weight as the continuous data. Results from the sample of cities and counties with continuous data are more reliable since data for all reporting units have much larger standard deviations resulting from cities and counties moving in and out of the sample as holes in the data appear. Finally, it must be noted that although mean expenditures fell for all reporting units during the 1820s, the mean for 1822–8 was still well above the mean for the pre-depression years 1816–18.

Information regarding regional differences in real expenditures per recipient for the thirty-one localities with continuous data is provided in Table 6.10. Except in the Tidewater region, real spending per recipient rose during the depression years 1819–21, particularly in the Valley and the Piedmont, up 26.5 per cent and 29.6 per cent respectively. In the Tidewater region, per recipient expenditures dropped slightly, down 4.6 per cent. This, combined with the increase in per capita spending, suggests that more poor were being served during the depression in the Tidewater but each recipient was given a bit less. As the 1820s progressed, real per recipient spending rose in all regions except the Trans-Allegheny, where it fell slightly, down 4.3 per cent. The pressure of a 21.8 per cent jump in the pauper rate as the delayed impact of the depression hit likely made it difficult for these frontier counties to sustain their earlier level of generosity. The Valley increased per recipient expenditures 32.4 per cent in the five localities surveyed, making it by far the most generous for each recipient of the state's regions.

What do these various measures of Virginia's poor relief tell us about the impact of and response to the depression of 1819–21? With the collapse of commodity prices and the onset of hard times in the Commonwealth, the pauper rate rose as did the mean number of people receiving aid, both outdoor and in poorhouses. Some of this rise may have resulted from the 1819 revision of the Poor Law. While primarily bringing together existing legislation into one act, the legislation provided more consistency across the state in the way relief was provided and likely increased public awareness of the system. In spite of any impacts from the revision of the law, the 3.9 per cent increase in the pauper rate, 5.2 per cent increase in mean white outdoor relief recipients, 27.2 per cent rise in mean free black outdoor relief recipients and 24.9 per cent increase in mean poorhouse inmates combine to indicate that the depression following the Panic of 1819 had a substantial impact on a number of Virginians, particularly those at the bottom of the economic ladder. In addition, there were important regional variations in the pauper rate with mean rates rising in the Tidewater and Trans-Allegheny but falling in the Piedmont and the Valley. The measures also show that citizens of the Commonwealth responded with great compassion. Real poor rates rose as localities struggled to meet the needs of the poor, up 3.8 per cent in the eighteen county/city survey. Real total expenditures per capita increased 12.1 per cent in the forty-four cities and counties with continuous data, with the most dramatic changes being in real poorhouse expenditures per capita, which were up 26.9 per cent for all reporting units and 51.2 per cent in the eight localities with continuous data. The final measure of generosity, real expenditures per recipient, demonstrates both the intensity of the problem and the humanitarian response found across the Commonwealth. Mean real total expenditures per recipient in units with continuous data increased 15.6 per cent from 1816–18 to 1819–21 – 13.9 per cent for outdoor recipients and 18.5 per cent for poorhouse inmates. This rise in real spending per recipient was true for all regions except the Tidewater, where it declined slightly, down 4.6 per cent, although real spending per capita in the Tidewater did rise during the depression. Thus, not only did the depression create economic hardships for many Virginians, it also led citizens of the Commonwealth to respond with great compassion to the plight of the less fortunate.

In the years following the depression, however, changes began to occur. Rather than returning to its previous level as the depression ended, the pauper rate continued to rise, up 8.5 per cent across the state, as did the mean number of whites receiving outdoor relief, up 21.9 per cent. Only in the Valley did the pauper rate fall, down 12.4 per cent, although both real spending per capita and real spending per recipient in the region rose, up 8.1 per cent and 32.4 per cent respectively. The mean number of free blacks receiving outdoor relief fell slightly, down 4.4 per cent, as did the mean number of poorhouse inmates, down 5.5 per cent. Real poor rates continued to climb, rising 5.5 per cent in all reporting units and 3.8 per cent in the sample of eighteen cities and counties. Both measures of the generosity of poor relief in Virginia, mean real total expenditures per capita and mean real total expenditures per recipient, continued to rise in the state as a whole after the depression. They also rose in each region, with the exceptions of per capita spending in the Tidewater, which remained virtually constant, and per recipient spending in Trans-Allegheny, which fell slightly. The general increase statewide was the result of the generosity of outdoor relief, which continued to increase in the period 1822–8, up 11.1 per cent per capita and 11.3 per cent per recipient. It is in the poorhouses where change occurred. Not only did the mean number of individuals served in poorhouses fall in the years following the depression, decreasing 5.5 per cent, both mean real expenditures per capita and mean real expenditures per recipient fell, 16.1 and 19.4 per cent respectively.

Other questions regarding the operation of the Commonwealth's system of poor relief and questions concerning the statistical significance of the trends observed may be answered using the data collected. To do so requires constructing a model of poor relief and testing that model with the available data.

A Model of Poor Relief

A model of Virginia's antebellum poor relief system begins with supply and demand and is based on work by Joan Hannon and Lynne L. Kiesling and Robert A. Margo.[270] The supply of poor relief is determined at the county or city level where at the time of this study, as we have seen, locally elected Overseers of the Poor set poor rates and made decisions on funding applications for assistance.

The Commonwealth's laws provided the structure, and local officials used that framework to provide actual relief. The decisions of local overseers involved both the amount of support and its duration. Unfortunately, the data set contains only information on expenditures and number of recipients annually, thus eliminating consideration of duration from the analysis. In providing relief for members of their community, overseers 'had to balance a sense of compassion with a sense of economy'.[271] Thus, the outcome in any locality of the overseers deliberations may be considered as maximizing what they considered 'a socially optimal level' of public support for the poor, assuming that 'taxpayers are altruistic towards the poor [public relief is a normal good] and that the level of relief available from private sources, while positive, may not be socially optimal'. The model also assumes that supply depends on the tax base which is limited and poor relief has diminishing marginal utility to the taxpayers.[272]

From the viewpoint of the Overseers of the Poor, the demand for poor relief is the number of applicants seeking relief and the duration for which they seek to be supported. Again, because the data set has no information on duration of relief, it will be ignored. Assuming poor relief is a normal good to recipients, it is expected that increases in expenditures per recipient will bring greater numbers of applicants to the Overseers. Other factors affecting demand include available substitutes, particularly in the form of private relief, which is expected to be preferable to public relief; the demographic structure of the local population, in Virginia most importantly the proportion of children and the aged, since these groups dominated poor relief rolls; and economic factors such as the cost of living, the wage rate, the unemployment rate and the performance of the local economy.[273] Annual county and city data for these variables simply are not available, and census-based measures of the age composition of local populations are highly correlated with the regional dummy variables.

The simultaneous equation system resulting from the supply and demand model unfortunately cannot be identified. Thus, reduced form equations for the pauper rate, total poor relief recipients per thousand population, and for various measures of the generosity of relief expenditures, particularly real total expenditures per capita and per recipient, will be tested. Independent variables include population growth rate, dummy variables for the four regions of the state identified in the 1830 Virginia Constitution, dummy variables for the existence in a locality of outdoor relief, a poorhouse, or both, a dummy variable for cities and towns, and a time trend. Equations will be tested using real values.

Population growth rates are included because they affect both demand and supply structural equations. On the demand side, population growth means an increase in those who might seek poor relief, while on the supply side, it provides a measure of the increase in taxables and therefore potentially the city or county's ability to support the poor. Higher levels of population growth may also represent a more dynamic economy, thus indicating the community's growing wealth and ability to provide poor relief. Thus, the sign of this variable is expected to be positive. For the purpose of this study population growth rates will be determined from the differences in the population recorded in the 1820 and 1830 censuses.

The four regions of Virginia defined in the 1830 Constitution are Tidewater, Piedmont, the Valley and Trans-Allegheny. Each is assigned a dummy variable, and in testing the model Tidewater will be dropped, meaning that the sign, size and significance of the coefficients of the remaining three will provide information on those regions relative to Tidewater. A second set of dummy variables will identify the type of poor relief provided in each locality. A dummy variable will be created for each city and county in which outdoor relief is provided, for each locality that provides relief in a poorhouse, and for each city and county that provides both outdoor and poorhouse relief. When testing the model, the outdoor dummy will be dropped, meaning that the sign, size and significance of the coefficients of the variables tested will indicate performance relative to those localities providing outdoor relief. An exception will be made when testing poorhouse expenditures. In these cases, the poorhouse dummy will be dropped rather than the outdoor dummy, meaning that the size, sign and significance of the remaining dummy variables for type of assistance provided will indicate performance relative to those localities providing poorhouse relief. Finally, two additional dummy variables will be added to the model, one for cities and towns and the second a time trend. The city/town variable will indicate ways in which these entities differ from counties while the time trend may capture changing attitudes of the overseers and the community towards the provision of poor relief as well as changes in the availability of private relief. Because heteroscedasticity is expected, regressions will be run using Huber-White heteroscedasticity consistent variance estimators.

Results

Initial tests of the model will consider the pauper rate (pr). The reduced form equation is:

$$pr=f(popg2030, rpied, rval, rtran, ph, both, town, time)$$

where,

popg2030=population growth rate,
rpied=dummy variable for the Piedmont region,
rval=dummy variable for the Valley region,
rtran=dummy variable for the Trans-Allegheny region,
ph=dummy variable for poorhouse,
both=dummy variable for both poorhouse and outdoor relief,
town=dummy variable for cities and towns, and
time=time trend.

Table 6.13 provides the results for all reporting cities and counties. All variables are significant at the 0.01 level. The population growth rate has the expected sign while regional variables indicate important differences in the pauper rate between the Tidewater, the omitted region, and those tested. The three tested regions all had statistically significantly lower pauper rates than the Tidewater with the Trans-Allegheny having the greatest difference. This confirms the importance of the results from Table 6.2 discussed earlier. Localities with poorhouses had significantly lower pauper rates while those areas offering relief through both poorhouses and outdoor mechanisms had significantly higher pauper rates than areas offering only outdoor relief. The poorhouse finding may be the result of the poor's abhorrence of poorhouses and/or the possibility that those areas with poorhouses were the most parsimonious when it came to serving the poor. Localities with both poorhouses and outdoor relief experienced significantly higher pauper rates than did areas only providing outdoor relief. This suggests that supplying poor relief through more than one mechanism increased both the opportunities for serving the poor and their use of the system. Whether the locality providing relief was a city or town rather than a county made an important difference, with pauper rates in cities and towns being significantly greater than those found in counties. Finally, the time trend is significant, reflecting the upward trend in the pauper rate indicated in Table 6.1. How much this tells us about the attitudes of Overseers of the Poor is difficult to say, except that as the economy stagnated through the 1820s, the equilibrium of supply and demand for poor relief rose, suggesting a compassionate response by overseers. Tests of the generosity of poor relief may tell us more about this issue.

One measure of generosity, real total expenditures per thousand population (rtepp), is the dependent variable in the second specification of the model to be tested. The reduced form equation from the model takes the form:

$$\text{rtepp} = f(\text{popg2030, rpied, rval, rtran, ph, both, town, time})$$

where the independent variables are the same as the previous model. Results of the regression for the data set including all reporting cities and counties are given in Table 6.14. All variables except the population growth rate and the regional dummy for the Valley were significant at the 0.01 level. Regional variables indicate significant differences in real total expenditures per capita between the Tidewater, the omitted region, and the Piedmont and the Trans-Allegheny, both of which had lower real expenditures per thousand population, as was seen in Table 6.6. Interestingly, the Valley demonstrated no statistically significant difference from the Tidewater, suggesting that the generosity of poor relief in the region was comparable to that in the Tidewater and above that of the remaining regions. Table 6.6 shows the regional differences which appear in the size of the coefficients.

As expected, localities with poorhouses spent significantly less per capita on poor relief while those areas offering both poorhouse and outdoor relief had significantly higher levels of real expenditures per capita than areas offering only outdoor relief. The poorhouse finding suggests the savings possible to localities by focusing their provision of relief through poorhouses and confirms that such areas were the most parsimonious when it came to serving the poor. Localities with both poorhouses and outdoor relief spent significantly more per capita than did areas only providing outdoor relief. This suggests that increasing the number of mechanisms for supplying poor relief significantly increased the cost per capita. Whether the locality offering relief was a city or town rather than a county made an important difference, with real expenditures per thousand population in cities and towns significantly greater than those found in counties. Finally, the time trend is significant and positive, reflecting the upward trend in the real total expenditures per capita indicated in Table 6.5. This suggests that as the Commonwealth's economy stagnated through the 1820s, equilibrium real total expenditures per capita for poor relief rose, again indicating a compassionate response from the public to the plight of the poor.

Tables 6.15 and 6.16 report regression results for real outdoor expenditures per capita and real poorhouse expenditures per capita respectively. In the test of poorhouse expenditures, the dummy variable for outdoor relief was substituted for the poorhouse dummy. With a few exceptions, the results confirm what was observed with real total expenditures per capita. One difference involves the regional dummy variables. In the outdoor relief equation, the variable for the Valley remains insignificant, but the sign changes from negative to positive, suggesting per capita outdoor expenditures in that region might be higher than in the omitted region, Tidewater. A second difference is found in the poorhouse results. The time trend remains positive but becomes highly insignificant. This suggests there was no compassionate response from areas providing relief through poorhouses as the 1820s progressed and confirms the findings in Table 6.8 of an initial increase in per capita funding for poorhouses but then a pulling back in the wake of the depression of 1819–21.

A second measure of generosity to be tested is real total expenditures per recipient (rtepc). The reduced form equation is:

$$rtepc = f(popg2030, rpied, rval, rtran, ph, both, town, time)$$

where the independent variables remain the same as in previous models. Regression results are found in Table 6.17. As with earlier tests of generosity, the population growth rate is not significant nor in this case is the time trend. The latter differs from what was found in the previous tests and adds strength to the argument that changes in the overall cost of poor relief in Virginia during the period were related more to increases in the numbers served than to the amount of support given to each recipient. Regional variables reverse their pattern from that found with real total expenditures per capita. The Valley is now significant at the 0.01 level while the Piedmont and Trans-Allegheny are not significant. This confirms the observation from Table 6.10 that the Valley was significantly more generous on a per recipient basis than was the Tidewater region while the other two regions were not significantly different statistically from Tidewater. Localities with poorhouses spent significantly more in total per recipient than did cities and towns providing outdoor relief. When combined with the earlier finding that total spending per capita was significantly lower in localities with poorhouses relative to areas providing outdoor relief, this result brings into question the cost effectiveness of poorhouses as a means of providing poor relief. Localities using poorhouses spent more for each recipient but spent less per capita than areas providing outdoor relief, suggesting the existence of a poorhouse constrained those seeking aid by limiting appeals to the overseers. While this helped to keep per capita cost down, poorhouses remained significantly more costly on a per recipient basis. Finally, the dummy variable for localities having both poorhouse and outdoor relief was not significant and the same is true for the variable for cities and towns. Thus, recipients did not receive significantly more or less on a per recipient basis in areas providing both types of relief than what they received in areas providing only outdoor relief.

Regression results for real outdoor expenditures per recipient and real poorhouse expenditures per recipient are provided in Tables 6.18 and 6.19. As for the earlier test of poorhouse expenditures per capita, the dummy variable for outdoor relief was substituted for the poorhouse dummy variable. Some interesting differences appear from the results for real total expenditures per recipient and help us better understand variations in the provision of poor relief across the Commonwealth. When considering real outdoor expenditures per recipient, the regional variables are all positive and significant at the 0.01 level. These results again confirm the statistical significance of the differences observed in Table 6.10 that the Tidewater was the most parsimonious with relief per recipient while the Valley was the most generous. As might be anticipated, localities with poorhouses gave significantly less outdoor relief per recipient than did cities and towns providing outdoor relief, and areas providing both forms of relief provided significantly more per recipient than localities providing outdoor relief. As with real total expenditures per recipient, neither cities and towns nor the time trend were significant.

Having analyzed Virginia's support for the poor during the depression following the Panic of 1819 and in the decade of the 1820s, we now turn to responses in other parts of the nation to the plight of the poor in this period.

Comparison with Other Cities and States

Important differences are found when poor relief efforts in other parts of the country are compared with the pattern of poor relief in Virginia between 1816 and 1828, a period that includes the Commonwealth's response to the Panic of 1819 and its subsequent support of the impoverished in the years following the depression. For example, in Philadelphia the depression following the Panic of 1819 also brought changes in poor relief. However, where Virginians tended to increase support for the needy, in the Pennsylvania city, 'the most immediate concern of welfare officials during the depression was not how best to aid the poor, but how to reduce the cost of welfare'.[274] This trend continued through the 1820s as real expenditures per recipient decreased 20.8 per cent between 1820 and 1829, something that happened only for poorhouse recipients in Virginia.[275]

In New York City and New York state, relief for the needy increased in the years following the War of 1812. But, with the Panic this changed. An annual census of individuals served by most of New York City's specialized institutions assisting the destitute conducted by John Stanford, chaplain at the city's almshouse, showed the total number receiving indoor assistance grew from 3,021 in May 1818 to 3,710 in January 1821, a 22.8 per cent increase. However, funding for poor relief followed the pattern observed in Philadelphia.[276] Real poor taxes per thousand population declined 26.7 per cent in the city and 20.9 per cent in the rest of the state between 1819 and 1822, and average real expenditures per recipient in the New York City poorhouse declined 23.9 per cent from five years 1815–19 to the period 1820–3.[277] One bright point was various decisions by the New York City Council to increase 'donations to private charitable institutions', which jumped from $3,820 in 1816–17 to $5,280 in 1818–19, a 38.2 per cent increase.[278] As New York moved beyond the depression years, poor relief recipients as a percentage of the population grew in both New York City and in the rest of the state, but real per capita expenditures and real spending per recipient fell both in the city and across the state.[279] Finally, throughout this period in New York the burden of poor relief 'was unevenly distributed, so that the area around the Atlantic coast and the Hudson River, with less than half the state's population, supported far more than half of its poor', and the majority of recipients were women and children as 'widows, single mothers, and orphans received the bulk of public assistance'.[280]

A pattern of declining support similar to that found in New York was experienced at the Newport, Rhode Island, Asylum. Expenditures decreased one-third between 1819 and 1820 and continued to drop at least through 1824.[281] Danvers, Massachusetts, also saw support for the poor fall from an approximate per capita cost of forty-eight cents in 1803 to thirty-six cents in 1820, a real decline of 27.8 per cent. However, the number of poor receiving relief rose from an average of fifty-four in the years 1810–17 to an average of seventy-two in the depression years of 1819–21. Unlike throughout much of Virginia where the number of recipients rose in the years following the depression, the number of poor relief recipients in Danvers fell to an average of fifty-seven in the period 1825–9.[282] The uneven distribution of the burden of poor relief observed in New York was also found in Massachusetts. In a survey conducted for the legislature in 1821, Josiah Quincy found that 'Boston relieved as many as six hundred persons annually, while small communities maintained five to forty charges each.'[283]

In the north, the Panic of 1819 brought calls for economy and a reduction in support of the poor while in Virginia the hard times following 1819 tended to see increased spending for poor relief. This difference might be explained in part by the northern experience following peace in 1815. With a flood of British goods, American manufacturing was devastated. As a result, these cities were forced to deal with increased poverty while Virginia was still benefiting from the high prices of its agricultural staples. By the time the Panic hit, the reaction against poor relief that would come in some parts of Virginia in the mid-1820s and to much of the state in the 1830s may already have been operating in these northern cities.

Moving from the northeast to other sections of the nation, Daniel C. Vogt found differences in the cost of poor relief in Mississippi, where the more urban Natchez City and Adams County had 'significantly higher relief costs than the more rural counties'. In addition, he also found regional differences in that 'the more established counties of the southwest (Adams, Jefferson and Wilkinson) had higher costs than the new counties of the central part of the state (Madison)'. The urban-rural and established-newer locality differences mirror those found in Virginia. Finally, in an event that may have been related to the Panic of 1819, Vogt found that the Natchez Hospital, 'a semi-private institution chartered in 1805 for the care of the poor ... apparently closed in 1819 for lack of funds and reopened in August 1821'.[284]

In an adjacent area of the Old Southwest, Virginia's Governor Preston's ideas found a home with Alabama's Madison County Bible Society. The Society 'offered up to the county's poor the ideas of hard work and discipline and the promise of a heavenly reward'.[285] However, the City of New Orleans, which in 1817 had set aside fifty dollars per month to assist the poor, in 1821 allocated $3,000 and sixty cords of wood for poor relief and in 1824 made a grant of $1,600 'to the Poydras Female Asylum to care for twenty-four children in the city's care'.[286]

Finally, an indicator of the increase in demand for poor relief in Charleston, South Carolina, during the 1820s is found in the 'increasing number of dependent children supported by local communities'. This led the political economist and president of South Carolina College, Thomas Cooper, to argue 'in his lectures on the Elements of Political Economy that the state should sanction no marriage without proof of the couple's ability to provide for and educate their children'.[287]

Although these findings from other states in the south provide some basis for comparison with Virginia regarding the impact of the Panic of 1819 on poor relief, much more research is needed. In both the south and west too little is known about the pattern of support for the poor and of changes in that support as the Panic hit and the economy recovered through the 1820s. Was the Commonwealth's example of generosity in the face of economic crisis the norm, or did Virginia stand in contrast with other states in the region and in the west as it did with the northeast?

Private Sector Responses to the Poor

In order to complete the analysis of poor relief in Virginia, the private sector response to the problem of poverty in the wake of the Panic of 1819 as an addition to or substitute for public relief requires consideration. With the withdrawal of public support for the poor across much of the nation, private charities increased their efforts, and in some localities their combined spending surpassed that of public agencies.[288] Gail S. Murray has suggested that such private organizations can be categorized into several general types. The first is mutual aid societies 'created by workingmen's associations, fraternal orders, religious groups and ethnic societies'. A second group is composed of those that 'targeted specific clientele for aid, such as prostitutes or seamen'. The third category includes all 'charities for the general relief of the poor', and the final group consists of private organizations that 'established and ran institutions that served the poor, such as orphanages, schools, and houses of industry'.[289]

In Virginia, the Panic and its aftermath saw the formation of a number of relief organizations to expand the work undertaken by existing societies such as the Female Orphan Society of Norfolk (established 1804), the Petersburg Female Asylum (established 1812), and Richmond's Female Humane Association (established 1815).[290] Societies for the relief and prevention of poverty were formed in Petersburg (by 1821), Norfolk (by 1822), Alexandria (in 1822), Winchester (in 1824), Richmond (in 1827) and Williamsburg (by 1828) while the Petersburg Benevolent Mechanics Association was formed in 1825, and Bethel Unions to aid seamen were organized in Richmond (in 1821) and Norfolk (in 1823 and 1828).[291] Interestingly, most of these organizations operated in cities and towns, areas in which the costs of public relief were highest and in which the greatest reduction in public poor relief occurred. The decline in Virginia local government support for the poor in the years following the Panic in these areas may indicate a loss of the sense of community. However, at the same time private aid societies increased efforts to ameliorate the conditions of the poor, suggesting a desire to affirm the community's responsibility for its needy. The tension between public and private responses to the problem of poverty in the aftermath of the Panic of 1819 found in some areas of the state, particularly localities that used poorhouses as the primary mechanism for dealing with the poor, may be the result of different perceptions of community and communal responsibility between a male-dominated local government sphere and the realm of private aid dominated by women.

Summary and Conclusions

In the 1820s and 1830s, Americans examined the traditional premises of poor relief and began to reverse their positions. Historically, poverty had not been seen as a social problem nor were paupers considered a danger to society. Further, the community was assumed to be responsible for their own; strangers were, however, a different matter. In the aftermath of the Panic of 1819, poor relief came to the fore as legislatures in Massachusetts (in 1821) and New York (in 1824), the city of Philadelphia (in 1827) and other areas initiated investigations of the poor as 'a social problem, a potential source of unrest and the proper object of a reform movement'.[292] As one author has suggested, it should not be 'surprising that serious discussions of the causes of poverty and the wisdom of alms-giving first appeared in the depressed years which followed the Napoleonic Wars'. It was a time of 'greatly increased expenditures for poor relief and large numbers of unemployed served to stimulate widespread comment on evils which generally hitherto had been of negligible proportions'.[293] The investigations, discussions and subsequent movement away from the humanitarian foundations of public and private relief efforts carried with them a strong moral reform overtone with attention focused particularly on the 'deserving poor'. At the time, Boston, New York, Philadelphia and Baltimore all underwent a similar pattern of change.[294]

Although Virginia, like the rest of the nation, suffered tremendously from the hard times following the Panic of 1819, the response to poverty in the Commonwealth during the depression years was quite different. Virginians reacted with compassion and generosity towards those affected by the economic downturn. Likewise, during the 1820s support for the poor across the state was at odds with the pattern of relief found in the northeast and along the mid-Atlantic coast.

During the depression of 1819–21 the pauper rate rose across Virginia as the number of whites and free blacks receiving outdoor relief jumped and poorhouses became crowded. Yet as other areas of the country responded to the crisis by tightening their belts, counties and cities throughout Virginia increased real spending per capita, and in all regions except the Tidewater increased real expenditures per recipient. The slight decline in real spending per recipient in the Tidewater, down 4.6 per cent, combined with the region's relatively large jump in per capita real spending suggests the Tidewater was dealing with many more poor and giving each relief recipient a bit less.

In the years following the depression, however, changes began to occur. Rather than returning to its previous level as the depression ended, the pauper rate continued to rise, up 8.5 per cent across the state, as did the mean number of whites receiving outdoor relief, up 21.9 per cent. Only in the Valley did the pauper rate fall, down 12.4 per cent, although real spending both per capita and per recipient in the region rose, up 8.1 per cent and 32.4 per cent respectively. The mean number of free blacks receiving outdoor relief fell slightly, down 4.4 per cent, as did the mean number of poorhouse inmates, down 5.5 per cent. Real poor rates continued to climb, rising 5.5 per cent in all reporting localities and 3.8 per cent in the sample of eighteen cities and counties. Both measures of the generosity of poor relief in Virginia, mean real total expenditures per capita and mean real total expenditures per recipient, continued to rise after the depression in the state as a whole and in each region with the exception of per capita spending in the Tidewater, which remained virtually constant, and per recipient spending which fell slightly in the Trans-Allegheny. The general increase statewide was the result of the generosity of outdoor relief, which continued to increase in the period 1822–8, up 11.1 per cent per capita and 11.3 per cent per recipient. Only in the poorhouses did changes occur which matched the pattern of poor relief in the northeast and mid-Atlantic. Not only did the mean number of individuals served in poorhouses fall in the years following the depression, both mean real expenditures per capita and mean real expenditures per recipient fell.

Finally, like in other parts of the nation, important regional and urban/rural differences in the provision of poor relief were found in Virginia. The oldest and most developed region, the Tidewater, had statistically significant higher pauper rates than did the rest of the Commonwealth, while the Piedmont and the Valley were relatively close to one another and Trans-Allegheny had by far the lowest rate. Some of this regional variation may be the result of the differential impacts of the collapse of commodity markets. The Tidewater depended heavily on export markets both for its agricultural products and for its many businesses that processed, prepared and shipped those products. The Piedmont and Valley, with more limited access to export markets, would have been impacted to a lesser extent than the Tidewater while the more transportation isolated and self-sufficient Trans-Allegheny was likely least affected.

In addition, pauper rates jumped most significantly in the western part of the state in the years after the depression, suggesting the delayed impact of the Panic in areas more distant from the coast. Important differences in real spending per capita and per recipient are also found between eastern and western regions of Virginia. The Tidewater spent more per capita than did other regions, although interestingly real per capita expenditure in the Valley was not statistically significantly different. On a per recipient basis, all regions spent statistically significantly more than did the Tidewater with the Valley leading the way. As would be expected, cities and towns spent significantly more on the poor than did counties and had significantly higher pauper rates.

Although the pattern of support for the poor in Virginia during the depression following the Panic of 1819 and into the 1820s is at odds with what we know of policy in the northeast and mid-Atlantic, the Commonwealth was not immune to pressures to reform the system. Rising pauper rates and subsequent increases in the cost of supporting those seeking relief led Virginians to search for ways to economize and to make the system more efficient. The General Assembly's action in 1829 to require annual reports from Overseers of the Poor also included a request for a summary of each county's and town's expenditures and number of paupers supported back to 1800. The Auditor of Public Accounts then used this information to prepare a special report to the legislature summarizing the results and making a series of recommendations. Among the report's findings was that 'in those counties where poor houses have been established, it will be found with few exceptions, that after their creation, the number of paupers has been greatly reduced'. Further, the decrease in the number of paupers 'has not been attended with a proportional reduction in expense'. In reality, 'although the total average expenditures has been less after the establishment of poor houses, the average cost of supporting each pauper has been increased'. These findings are consistent with the results of the current analysis.[295]

In spite of the report's findings, it suggested that 'the poor house system, where the experiment has been fairly made, is generally preferred to that by which the paupers are aided at their several places of abode, or are let out for maintenance to the lowest bidder'. Such a position was supported by a number of arguments. They included (1) that 'without a regular asylum, the poor are scantily and insufficiently maintained'; (2) that boarding out 'operates as a premium to idleness, and has a direct tendency to encourage pauperism'; (3) that collecting paupers together in a poorhouse ensures 'applicants unworthy of relief are excluded'; and (4) that outdoor relief 'is attended by wasteful and injudicious disbursements of the poor fund' as well as fraud. The report concluded with a set of recommendations for 'legislative consideration'. Most significant was that 'each county shall be required to purchase a farm of convenient size, to erect thereon suitable buildings, and to provide the necessary farming and other implements, for the employment and support of the poor'.[296] How the General Assembly dealt with the problem during the 1830s is a topic for a future work. Suffice it to say that following a report in 1830 that found 'fifty-nine counties and two towns maintained poorhouses, while forty-three counties and one town had no such institutions', the legislature on, 5 March 1833, voted to encourage overseers to establish poorhouses. It is not clear what effect this had, if any, on the actual operation of the system since the legislation provided that 'any person to be provided for or assisted by an overseer or overseers, may either be kept at the place of general reception, or may be supported or assisted elsewhere, as he or they deem best'.[297]

This completes the analysis of the Panic of 1819 and its impact on Virginia's economy and the people of the Commonwealth. We now turn to putting the experience of Virginia and the nation during the Panic and following depression in the perspective of the broader events of the time and analysing how the Panic of 1819 affected society, politics and public policy both in Virginia and in the nation in subsequent decades.

Tables

Table 6.1: Virginia Pauper Rates, 1816–28.

Year	All Reporting Counties/Cities		Forty-eight Counties/Cities
	N	Rate	Rate
1816	56	3.43	3.41
1817	60	3.79	3.81
1818	59	4.08	3.67
1819	61	4.04	3.89
1820	63	4.01	3.65
1821	66	4.08	3.76
1822	66	4.40	3.99
1823	67	4.66	4.04
1824	66	4.72	4.06
1825	66	4.46	3.98
1826	68	4.66	4.15
1827	66	4.75	4.09
1828	68	4.75	4.34
Mean			
1816–18		3.77	3.63
1819–21		4.04	3.77
% change		+7.2	+3.9
Mean			
1822–8		4.63	4.09
% change from 1819–21		+14.6	+8.5

Sources: Auditor of Public Records, Overseers of the Poor, Annual Reports, 1829, Virginia State Archives.

Table 6.2: Virginia Pauper Rates by Region, 1816–28.

Year	Region and Number of Counties/Cities			
	Tidewater	Piedmont	Valley	Trans-Allegheny
	(15)	(17)	(5)	(11)
1816	5.80	2.81	3.10	1.24
1817	6.90	2.88	3.24	1.34
1818	6.58	2.69	3.18	1.44
1819	7.23	2.66	3.19	1.31
1820	6.74	2.61	2.85	1.38
1821	7.04	2.45	3.18	1.57
1822	7.81	2.63	2.60	1.55
1823	7.31	3.16	2.33	1.72
1824	7.37	2.96	2.50	1.93

| Year | Region and Number of Counties/Cities | | | |
	Tidewater (15)	Piedmont (17)	Valley (5)	Trans-Allegheny (11)
1825	7.01	2.97	2.74	1.96
1826	7.48	3.13	2.74	1.82
1827	7.46	3.19	2.76	1.51
1828	7.89	3.31	3.13	1.61
Mean				
1816–18	6.43	2.79	3.17	1.34
1819–21	7.00	2.57	3.07	1.42
% change	+8.9	-7.9	-3.2	+6.0
Mean				
1822–8	7.48	3.05	2.69	1.73
% change, 1819–21	+6.9	+18.7	-12.4	+21.8

Sources: Auditor of Public Records, Overseers of the Poor, Annual Reports, 1829, Virginia State Archives.

Table 6.3: Virginia Mean Poor Rates, 1816–28.

| Year | All Reporting Counties/Cities | | | Eighteen Counties/Cities | |
	N	Rate	Real Rate	Rate	Real Rate
1816	15	0.393	0.233	na	na
1817	18	0.512	0.320	0.512	0.320
1818	20	0.442	0.289	0.435	0.284
1819	20	0.490	0.320	0.492	0.322
1820	22	0.450	0.319	0.459	0.326
1821	22	0.401	0.295	0.404	0.297
1822	22	0.379	0.269	0.380	0.270
1823	22	0.395	0.313	0.400	0.317
1824	22	0.429	0.370	0.441	0.380
1825	22	0.387	0.331	0.396	0.338
1826	22	0.397	0.334	0.388	0.326
1827	22	0.388	0.323	0.372	0.310
1828	22	0.409	0.359	0.396	0.347
Mean					
1816–18		0.449	0.281	0.474	0.302
1819–21		0.447	0.311	0.452	0.315
% change		+0.2	+10.7	-4.6	+4.1
Mean					
1822–8		0.389	0.328	0.396	0.327
% change, 1819–21		-10.9	+5.5	-12.4	+3.8

Eighteen Counties: Tidewater: Chesterfield, Fairfax, Northumberland, Richmond County, Spotsylvania, Westmoreland; Piedmont: Amherst, Bedford, Fauquier, Loudoun, Louisa; Valley: Bath, Frederick, Lynchburg Town; Trans-Allegheny: Cabell, Giles, Grayson, Lee.
Other Counties: Tidewater: Elizabeth City; Trans-Allegheny: Kanawha, Monongalia, Wythe.
Rates in dollars. Real values calculated using the David-Solar cost of living index.

Sources: Auditor of Public Records, Overseers of the Poor, Annual Reports, 1829, Virginia State Archives; P. A. David and P. Solar, 'A Bicentenary Contribution to the History of the Cost of Living in America', *Research in Economic History*, 2 (1977), pp. 1–80.

Table 6.4: Mean Number of Whites and Free Blacks Receiving Outdoor Poor Relief and Average Poorhouse Population, All Reporting Units, Virginia, 1816–28.

Year	Mean Number Whites	Mean Number Blacks	Mean Poorhouse Population
1816	30.46	2.47	22.33
1817	32.53	2.54	22.33
1818	33.98	2.50	31.00
1819	34.65	2.80	33.83
1820	33.51	3.39	28.00
1821	33.86	3.35	32.63
1822	36.54	2.93	28.89
1823	41.21	3.17	30.70
1824	41.52	3.06	31.58
1825	42.94	2.61	30.00
1826	41.68	3.24	29.54
1827	43.35	2.85	30.71
1828	42.97	3.40	26.85
Mean			
1816–18	32.32	2.50	25.22
1819–21	34.01	3.18	31.49
% change	+5.2	+27.2	+24.9
Mean			
1822–8	41.46	3.04	29.75
% change, 1819–21	+21.9	-4.4	-5.5

Sources: Auditor of Public Records, Overseers of the Poor, Annual Reports, 1829, Virginia State Archives.

Table 6.5: Virginia Mean Real Total Expenditures per Thousand Population, 1816–28.

Year	All Reporting Counties/Cities		Forty-four Counties/Cities
	N	Mean	Mean
1816	66	76.80	86.95
1817	67	103.87	112.79
1818	71	107.86	111.35
1819	73	107.72	111.97
1820	71	117.86	116.22
1821	73	113.17	120.40
1822	75	106.25	116.23
1823	76	126.47	130.53
1824	73	125.99	132.00
1825	70	118.51	117.76
1826	75	120.02	119.40
1827	71	115.44	111.78
1828	69	121.91	125.86
Mean			
1816–18		96.18	103.70
1819–21		112.92	116.20
% change		+17.4	+12.1

Year	All Reporting Counties/Cities	Forty-four Counties/Cities
Mean		
1822–8	119.23	121.94
% change, 1819–21	+5.6	+4.9

Sources: Auditor of Public Records, Overseers of the Poor, Annual Reports, 1829, Virginia State Archives.

Table 6.6: Virginia Mean Real Total Expenditures per Thousand Population by Region, 1816–28.

Year	Region and Number of Counties/Cities			
	Tidewater	Piedmont	Valley	Trans-Allegheny
	(19)	(16)	(6)	(3)
1816	120.62	58.81	80.04	37.79
1817	158.68	75.15	107.82	32.82
1818	150.03	76.68	113.66	46.74
1819	157.12	72.45	109.57	41.53
1820	161.86	78.09	112.87	37.22
1821	171.79	79.77	110.88	30.71
1822	170.82	67.33	111.18	41.40
1823	186.00	87.47	108.36	53.19
1824	173.46	96.72	126.00	69.59
1825	145.57	92.94	113.27	82.97
1826	150.79	92.88	116.49	67.84
1827	144.19	85.81	118.64	31.39
1828	169.84	83.37	146.65	32.41
Mean				
1816–18	143.11	70.21	100.51	39.12
1819–21	163.59	76.77	111.11	36.49
% change	+14.3	+9.3	+10.5	-6.7
Mean				
1822–8	162.95	86.85	120.08	54.11
% change, 1819–21	-0.4	+12.9	+8.1	+48.3

Sources: Auditor of Public Records, Overseers of the Poor, Annual Reports, 1829, Virginia State Archives.

Table 6.7: Virginia Mean Real Outdoor Expenditures per Thousand Population, 1816–28.

Year	All Reporting Counties/Cities		Thirty-Eight Counties/Cities
	N	Mean	Mean
1816	60	69.21	78.06
1817	61	96.24	102.42
1818	66	97.48	100.24
1819	68	94.89	94.15
1820	65	103.49	99.47
1821	67	97.86	103.05
1822	68	93.95	102.67
1823	69	113.72	118.22
1824	65	114.13	116.81
1825	63	109.22	106.86
1826	68	109.76	108.44
1827	64	104.74	101.78
1828	63	110.84	114.19

Year	All Reporting Counties/Cities		Thirty-Eight Counties/Cities
	N	Mean	Mean
Mean			
1816–18		87.64	93.57
1819–21		98.75	98.89
% change		+12.7	+5.7
Mean			
1822–8		108.05	109.85
% change, 1819–21		+9.4	+11.1

Sources: Auditor of Public Records, Overseers of the Poor, Annual Reports, 1829, Virginia State Archives.

Table 6.8: Virginia Mean Real Poorhouse Expenditures per Thousand Population, 1816–28.

Year	All Reporting Counties/Cities		Eight Counties/Cities
	N	Mean	Mean
1816	12	76.37	72.27
1817	12	90.74	95.91
1818	13	94.21	91.93
1819	13	108.55	117.35
1820	15	109.41	137.18
1821	15	113.67	138.73
1822	16	98.75	121.79
1823	16	110.30	129.79
1824	16	111.17	134.03
1825	16	88.43	89.03
1826	17	90.45	99.71
1827	17	87.83	90.52
1828	16	89.33	105.25
Mean			
1816–18		89.11	86.70
1819–21		110.54	131.09
% change		+26.9	+51.2
Mean			
1822–8		96.61	110.02
% change, 1819–21		-12.6	-16.1

Sources: Auditor of Public Records, Overseers of the Poor, Annual Reports, 1829, Virginia State Archives.

Table 6.9: Virginia Mean Real Total Expenditures per Recipient, 1816–28.

Year	All Reporting Counties/Cities		Thirty-one Counties/Cities
	N	Mean	Mean
1816	56	24.73	24.33
1817	58	31.48	28.65
1818	62	29.01	28.54
1819	63	36.86	28.97
1820	61	39.20	32.88
1821	63	41.66	32.34
1822	66	32.32	30.31
1823	68	34.53	34.42

Year	All Reporting Counties/Cities		Thirty-one Counties/Cities
	N	Mean	Mean
1824	64	36.40	35.89
1825	62	38.28	37.15
1826	66	35.85	34.13
1827	65	35.54	36.31
1828	65	38.66	36.78
Mean			
1816–18		28.41	27.17
1819–21		39.24	31.40
% change		+38.1	+15.6
Mean			
1822–8		35.94	35.00
% change from 1819–21		-8.4	+11.5

Sources: Auditor of Public Records, Overseers of the Poor, Annual Reports, 1829, Virginia State Archives.

Table 6.10: Virginia Mean Real Total Expenditures per Recipient by Region, 1816–28.

Year	Region and Number of Counties/Cities			
	Tidewater	Piedmont	Valley	Trans-Allegheny
	(11)	(12)	(5)	(3)
1816	26.73	22.36	24.82	22.59
1817	26.62	26.28	39.48	27.51
1818	23.37	29.41	37.01	30.00
1819	22.71	27.14	45.59	31.56
1820	27.31	33.65	42.18	34.69
1821	23.17	40.38	40.39	20.36
1822	23.67	28.40	53.82	23.20
1823	29.85	31.55	53.12	31.48
1824	30.80	32.12	55.39	37.16
1825	26.70	41.17	55.22	29.35
1826	24.18	38.67	50.77	24.73
1827	25.23	40.86	58.85	21.20
1828	27.04	35.00	68.81	27.27
Mean				
1816–18	25.57	26.02	33.77	26.70
1819–21	24.40	33.72	42.72	28.87
% change	-4.6	+29.6	+26.5	+8.1
Mean				
1822–8	26.78	35.40	56.57	27.63
% change, 1819–21	+9.8	+5.0	+32.4	-4.3

Sources: Auditor of Public Records, Overseers of the Poor, Annual Reports, 1829, Virginia State Archives.

Table 6.11: Virginia Mean Real Outdoor Expenditures per Recipient, 1816–28.

Year	All Reporting Counties/Cities		Twenty-seven Counties/Cities
	N	Mean	Mean
1816	51	21.45	18.92
1817	53	28.68	23.38

Year	All Reporting Counties/Cities		Twenty-seven Counties/Cities
	N	Mean	Mean
1818	58	26.22	22.45
1819	59	34.58	25.05
1820	56	35.11	25.22
1821	59	36.68	23.46
1822	60	25.41	22.82
1823	62	28.31	25.82
1824	59	32.04	28.46
1825	57	32.96	30.15
1826	61	30.42	26.92
1827	59	30.30	28.40
1828	60	32.26	28.86
Mean			
1816–18		25.45	21.58
1819–21		35.46	24.58
% change		+39.3	+13.9
Mean			
1822–8		30.24	27.35
% change,1819–21		-14.7	+11.3

Sources: Auditor of Public Records, Overseers of the Poor, Annual Reports, 1829, Virginia State Archives.

Table 6.12: Virginia Mean Real Poorhouse Expenditures per Recipient, 1816–28.

Year	All Reporting Counties/Cities		Four Counties/Cities
	N	Mean	Mean
1816	7	41.56	40.37
1817	7	43.69	41.59
1818	7	39.72	41.16
1819	7	40.25	41.49
1820	9	47.21	58.14
1821	8	57.58	46.29
1822	11	55.30	42.79
1823	12	49.39	53.20
1824	13	33.78	45.50
1825	14	35.37	24.34
1826	14	36.49	34.17
1827	15	34.85	38.03
1828	14	41.21	36.35
Mean			
1816–18		41.66	41.04
1819–21		48.35	48.64
% change		+16.1	+18.5
Mean			
1822–8		40.91	39.20
% change from 1819–21		-15.4	-19.4

Sources: Auditor of Public Records, Overseers of the Poor, Annual Reports, 1829, Virginia State Archives.

Table 6.13: Regression Results: Pauper Rates.

Variable	Coefficient	Robust Std Err	t	P>t
popg2030	0.0172463	0.0061635	2.798	0.005
rpied	-4.434587	0.23581	-18.806	0.000
rval	-4.015886	0.2758676	-14.557	0.000
rtran	-5.986911	0.2524821	-23.712	0.000
ph	-2.092625	0.2575086	-8.126	0.000
both	1.668581	0.3378746	4.938	0.000
town	12.10399	3.026586	3.999	0.000
time	0.0816708	0.0296358	2.756	0.006
cons	6.626936	0.2841399	23.323	0.000

Number of observations=830
F(8, 821)=97.98
Prob > F=0.0000
R-squared=0.5308
Root MSE=3.2431

Table 6.14: Regression Results: Real Total Expenditures per Thousand Population.

Variable	Coefficient	Robust Std Err	t	P>t
popg2030	0.0432126	0.1911143	0.219	0.827
rpied	-48.14332	4.996885	-9.635	0.000
rval	-7.353567	8.555255	-0.860	0.390
rtran	-84.79988	4.805312	-17.647	0.000
ph	-34.93341	3.932847	-8.882	0.000
both	76.88837	9.69934	7.921	0.000
town	502.892	50.1936	10.019	0.000
time	1.656388	0.605515	2.736	0.006
cons	113.9454	5.259114	21.666	0.000

Number of observations=943
F(8, 821)=92.33
Prob > F=0.0000
R-squared=0.6608
Root MSE=70.986

Table 6.15: Regression Results: Real Outdoor Expenditures per Thousand Population.

Variable	Coefficient	Robust Std Err	t	P>t
popg2030	-.0381269	0.1859499	-0.205	0.838
rpied	-30.1473	4.16441	-7.239	0.000
rval	7.216217	7.982858	0.904	0.366
rtran	-73.57681	4.371965	-16.829	0.000
ph	-101.2158	3.122342	-32.417	0.000
both	89.7348	7.894453	11.367	0.000
town	277.3011	28.01888	9.897	0.000
time	1.861743	0.4950524	3.761	0.000
cons	102.9193	4.341767	23.704	0.000

Number of observations=923
F(8, 821)=168.64
Prob > F=0.0000
R-squared=0.5139
Root MSE=57.663

Table 6.16: Regression Results: Real Poorhouse Expenditures per Thousand Population.

Variable	Coefficient	Robust Std Err	t	P>t
popg2030	0.0289213	0.0378995	0.763	0.446
rpied	-8.844963	1.650246	-5.360	0.000
rval	-13.78671	2.094395	-6.583	0.000
rtran	-10.07231	1.734756	-5.806	0.000
od	-52.62219	4.216737	-12.479	0.000
both	73.48813	5.133841	14.314	0.000
town	193.3035	26.86131	7.196	0.000
time	0.0785967	0.2218641	0.354	0.723
cons	58.56023	4.613736	12.693	0.000

Number of observations=1024
$F_{(8, 821)}$=107.98
Prob > F=0.0000
R-squared=0.7483
Root MSE=28.291

Table 6.17: Regression Results: Real Total Expenditures per Recipient.

Variable	Coefficient	Robust Std Err	t	P>t
popg2030	-.1340474	.1333649	-1.005	0.315
rpied	7.568113	2.124289	3.563	0.000
rval	29.85876	8.178553	3.651	0.000
rtran	7.433707	2.539182	2.928	0.004
ph	19.87459	5.491759	2.928	0.000
both	-.3828295	6.740922	-0.057	0.955
town	18.6129	6.881932	2.705	0.007
time	2929915	.2385463	1.228	0.220
cons	20.84446	2.761307	7.549	0.000

Number of observations=801
$F_{(8, 821)}$=25.85
Prob > F=0.0000
R-squared=0.1128
Root MSE=35.283

Table 6.18: Regression Results: Real Outdoor Expenditures per Recipient.

Variable	Coefficient	Robust Std Err	t	P>t
popg2030	-.2766043	0.1266289	-2.184	0.029
rpied	9.789542	1.797547	5.446	0.000
rval	31.70157	8.125642	3.901	0.000
rtran	10.38124	2.393422	4.337	0.000
ph	-25.13654	1.028229	-24.446	0.000
both	19.19345	2.991064	6.417	0.000
town	5.871019	6.084912	0.965	0.335
time	0.3289489	0.2222461	1.480	0.139
cons	20.84787	2.587829	8.056	0.000

Number of observations=802
$F_{(8, 821)}$=164.08
Prob > F=0.0000
R-squared=0.1234
Root MSE=33.908

Table 6.19: Regression Results: Real Poorhouse Expenditures per Recipient.

Variable	Coefficient	Robust Std Err	t	P>t
popg2030	.0341467	.0198345	1.722	0.085
rpied	2.109316	.7786115	2.709	0.007
rval	-2.368663	.6614651	-3.581	0.000
rtran	-2.32442	.6628934	-3.506	0.000
ph	-30.42268	4.904481	-6.203	0.000
both	36.40402	2.489008	14.626	0.000
town	12.45026	3.647086	3.414	0.001
time	-.0409247	.0711661	-0.575	0.565
cons	30.56341	5.077895	6.019	0.000

Number of observations=953
$F(8, 821)=73.55$
Prob > F=0.0000
R-squared=0.6960
Root MSE=8.8903

Appendix: Poor Relief Data Sources

Table 6A.1: Poor Relief Data Sources, 1816–30.

	Poor Rates (22)	Pauper Rates (48)	Total Expend. (44)	(31)	Outdoor Expend. (38)	(27)	Poorhouse Expend. (8)	(4)
Counties								
Accomack								
Albemarle		X	X		X			
Alleghany								
Amelia			X		X			
Amherst	X	X						
Augusta			X		X			
Bath	X	X						
Bedford	X							
Berkeley			X		X			
Botetourt		X						
Brooke		X	X					
Brunswick								
Buckingham			X	X				
Cabell	X	X						
Campbell		X	X	X	X	X		
Caroline			X		X			
Charles City								
Charlotte		X	X	X	X	X		
Chesterfield	X							
Culpeper		X	X	X			X	X
Cumberland								
Dinwiddie								
Elizabeth City	X							
Essex		X	X	X	X	X		
Fairfax	X	X	X	X	X	X	X	
Fauquier	X							
Frederick	X		X					
Fluvanna		X						
Franklin		X	X	X	X	X		

	Poor Rates (22)	Pauper Rates (48)	Total Expend.		Outdoor Expend.		Poorhouse Expend.	
			(44)	(31)	(38)	(27)	(8)	(4)
Giles	X	X						
Gloucester								
Goochland								
Grayson	X	X	X	X	X	X		
Greenbrier		X	X	X	X	X		
Greensville								
Hanover		X	X		X			
Halifax			X	X	X	X		
Hampshire								
Hardy			X	X	X	X		
Harrison		X						
Henrico								
Henry		X						
Isle of Wight			X				X	
James City		X	X	X	X	X		
Jefferson								
Kanawha	X							
King and Queen		X						
King George			X		X		X	
King William			X		X			
Lancaster		X	X	X	X	X		
Lee	X							
Lewis								
Logan								
Loudoun	X		X		X			
Louisa	X	X	X	X	X	X		
Lunenburg		X						
Madison		X	X	X	X	X		
Mason		X						
Mathews								
Mecklenburg			X	X	X	X		
Middlesex			X		X	X		
Monongalia	X							
Monroe		X						
Montgomery		X						
Nansemond								
Nelson								
New Kent		X						
Nicholas								
Norfolk		X	X	X				
Northampton								
Northumberland	X	X	X	X	X	X		
Nottoway		X						
Ohio								
Orange								
Patrick		X	X	X	X	X		
Pendleton								
Pittsylvania		X	X	X	X	X		
Pocahontas								
Powhatan								
Preston								
Prince Edward		X	X	X	X	X		
Prince George								
Prince William								

	Poor Rates (22)	Pauper Rates (48)	Total Expend. (44)	(31)	Outdoor Expend. (38)	(27)	Poorhouse Expend. (8)	(4)
Princess Ann		X						
Randolph								
Richmond	X							
Rockbridge		X	X	X	X	X		
Rockingham		X	X	X	X	X		
Russell								
Scott		X						
Shenandoah		X	X	X	X	X	X	X
Southampton								
Spotsylvania	X	X	X				X	
Stafford		X			X			
Suffolk								
Surry		X	X	X	X	X	X	X
Sussex								
Tazewell		X						
Tyler								
Warwick		X	X	X	X	X		
Washington								
Westmoreland	X	X	X	X	X			
Wood		X	X	X	X	X		
Wythe	X							
York		X	X	X	X	X		
Cities								
Lynchburg	X			X				
Norfolk								
Richmond								
Petersburg			X	X	X		X	X
Staunton								

7 THE AFTERMATH OF THE PANIC

Assessing the impact of the Panic of 1819 in Virginia, and even more so across the nation, is complicated by the confluence of events in that critical year. In addition to the economic crisis engendered by the Panic, the debate regarding federalism and states' rights that influenced all political discussions of the day, and particularly those in Virginia, was exacerbated by three other incidents. The first of these 'grew out of John C. Calhoun's attempt to recover through his cabinet position some of the internal improvement ground lost in the Bonus Bill veto'. Facing strong opposition led by Henry Clay, Calhoun's proposal was sharply debated in Congress, and while a compromise gave both sides something, the question of the federal role for internal improvements remained unresolved.[298]

A second event in March of the watershed year 1819 was the Supreme Court's ruling in *McCulloch v. Maryland*. In addition to sustaining the Bank of the United States, Chief Justice John Marshall's decision operated to 'enlarge federal power and enhance its instruments of economic development' by reserving 'almost nothing to the states except what was local and self-contained' and gathering 'under the umbrella of federal supremacy all things not prohibited by the Constitution'.[299]

Finally, the second session of the fifteenth Congress began debate on the issue of admitting the Missouri territory to the Union. The debate actually concerned the sectional balance in Congress, and both sides, slave South and antislavery North, took increasingly hard stands that ended in a deadlock in March 1819. Returning for the sixteenth Congress, northern antislavery forces who had taken their case to the public 'in the first American antislavery political campaign of its kind' evoked strong southern reactions that produced a crisis. With exquisite political skill, compromisers led by Henry Clay found a way through the impasse and achieved the 'immediate goal of pushing aside the slavery issue under a deceptive national truce so Americans could concentrate on even more pressing matters of economic survival'.[300]

The Impact of the Panic

Despite these complicating elements, it is possible to assess the impact of the Panic of 1819 in a number of areas. They include banking, debt relief, poor relief, tariffs and politics. To lesser extent the Panic also impacted internal improvements. For many, however, banking took center stage.

As indicated at the beginning of Chapter 3, Thomas Ritchie, editor of the influential *Richmond Enquirer*, published the following notice on 21 May 1819:

> The times particularly demand information on the subject of political economy. The country is lamentably deficient in important knowledge. – Never did a thicker gloom hang over the monied transactions of this land. The state of the markets, of trade, of the interest of manufactures, the great problems of the banking system, of the precious metals; there is scarce an individual in this country, who does not feel some interest in these questions, – We want light – To multiply the chances of obtaining it, we shall for several months keep open a head in this paper, styled 'Political Economy.' Our object is to excite investigation. ... Things are winding up; but perhaps <u>too fast</u> and in <u>too much panic</u>.

25 and 28 May brought the first response to Ritchie's call from 'Economicus'. The writer took the financial system to task, arguing that 'the multiplication and mismanagement of our banks have caused an enormous speculation and extravagance on the part of individuals'. This 'excess in banking' however, would bring some good: 'Our moral character will be chastened'. Returning to the question of bank management, the writer suggested that the cure to the current problems should be 'effected with as little ruin as possible' and asked of banks, 'are they not winding up too fast, and with too much panic'. The vast majority of letters that followed in the *Enquirer* concerned the banking issue, and typically they affirmed a hard money position and tight state regulation of the necessary evil, banking.[301]

Other issues such as internal improvements and debt relief were addressed in several letters to the newspaper during the remainder of 1819.[302] But, by the end of the year, the Missouri Question, Chief Justice of the Virginia Supreme Court of Appeals Spencer Roane's letters regarding *McCulloch vs Maryland*, and the 1819–20 legislative session had taken over as topics of interest on the editorial page. However, the concentration on banking in the responses to Ritchie's call confirmed Virginians' fear of banks, particularly the Bank of the United States, and the hard money attack on banks continued. One example is Governor Thomas M. Randolph's address to the legislature in December 1820. Banks, according to Randolph, 'beyond all doubt, have a strong tendency to prevent permanent advances by capitalists for the promotion of useful industry, and to facilitate and encourage those employments of money least beneficial to the general interest of society'. Further, the paper currency issued by banks, while 'more convenient than coin as a medium of exchange ... can never be a standard of value by which all property may with certainty and security be measured'. And, 'a still greater evil seems to be inseparably connected with the system of banking. Great fluctuations in the quantity of circulating medium proceeds from their vacillating nature, and such changes are productive of the most distressing consequences in society'. Randolph's hope was that 'some future day' might lead to the transition towards collecting the whole revenue in specie' since it would be 'safe', 'would not be susceptible of a great and sudden increase' and would allow the state to acquire 'a large specie capital'.[303]

While many in Virginia agreed with Randolph, the most pressing economic matter for them and for many other individuals across the nation hurt by the disruptions of the Panic of 1819 and subsequent downturn was money and the access to credit. This meant that banks, and particularly the Bank of the United States, became the focus of attention. Although the depression had multiple causes with the collapse of foreign markets for American commodities leading the list, banks tended to be seen by many as the source of the problem, and it was the banking system that took primary blame at the time for the economic crisis. As a result, hostility toward the Bank of the United States 'intensified', and all banks came under increased suspicion and criticism. The critique of the banking system and the Bank of the United States came in part from long-standing opposition to banks on political and/or constitutional grounds. This was exacerbated by further attacks from two 'diametrically opposed' directions.[304]

One group of bank critics called for increases in the availability of money. These inflationists typically called for some type of inconvertible paper money to be issued either directly by the state or federal government or by the Bank of the United States. The other group, generally fearful of banking, pushed for restrictions on the issue of additional money balances. These hard money advocates, many of whom could be found in Virginia, typically proposed limiting the number of new bank charters, forcing banks to redeem all notes in specie, restricting note issues to the amount of capital, eliminating the limited liability of banking corporations, or some combination of these policies.[305]

In addition to allowing 'non-specie paying banks to continue in operation', those pushing state legislatures to expand the availability of money and credit generally favoured either 'measures to bolster the acceptance of private bank notes' or 'the creation of state-owned banks to issue inconvertible paper notes on a large scale'. An example of the latter occurred in Tennessee, where Felix Grundy, elected to the legislature on a relief platform, pushed the governor to call a special session of the General Assembly to consider the matter of monetary expansion. The governor proposed 'a plan for a state money' issued through 'a loan office under the control of the legislature'. The proposal was expanded upon by Grundy, and despite fierce political battles, including efforts by Andrew Jackson to stop the legislation, an act converting the loan office into the Bank of the State of

Tennessee was passed. The new bank opened in 1820 and was capitalized at $1 million, issued notes that 'were to be eventually redeemed by public funds', was the depository for all public money, 'could not call in more than 10 per cent of a loan when due, except after sixty days notice', and operated under a stay provision that 'held up executions for two years unless the creditor accepted the bank's notes'. Never popular, its notes depreciated rapidly. Ultimately, the Tennessee Supreme Court 'declared the stay provision unconstitutional', and calls for a return to specie convertibility became widespread by mid-1826. These factors all combined to doom the bank, which formally closed in 1831. 'Only staunchly hard money Virginia remained free from expansionist agitation', while Tennessee's and other states' 'monetary ventures began in high hopes to issue large quantities of notes ... all came quickly to grief'.[306]

Although there was some discussion of creating a national inconvertible currency either through suspension of specie payments by the Bank of the United States or through some other mechanism, such proposals 'did not loom large in the Congressional arena during the depression'. Secretary of the Treasury William H. Crawford in his 1820 report to Congress outlined a possible mechanism for issuing paper money but ultimately pulled back from the proposal. And others such as Washington DC's Thomas Law and a variety of writers to newspapers around the nation made proposals, none of which gained any traction. Here as well as with the debates regarding monetary expansion at the state level, there was an 'absence of rigid geographical or class lines in the inflation controversies'.[307]

Notwithstanding that some realized the Second Bank had inflated less than many of the state banks, the early mismanagement and overexpansion of the Bank, combined with a strong tightening of credit under new president Langdon Cheves that continued long past the end of the financial crisis, subjected the Bank to harsh criticism. It was not until after 1823 and the naming of Nicholas Biddle as president that the Bank began to regain public confidence and to begin to establish control over the nation's monetary affairs. However, much damage had been done to the Second Bank, as the Bank War of the early 1830s would confirm.[308]

In Virginia, the apprehension regarding banks expressed by Governor Randolph and felt by many across the Commonwealth in turn helped to ensure the existing level of bank capital in the state would remain virtually constant until the mid-1830s. During that time only a $500,000 increase in capital for the Bank of Virginia, conditional upon its investing that amount in the James River and Kanawha Company, and a $200,000 increase for the Bank of the Valley were allowed.[309] In addition, the Commonwealth's suspicion of banks ensured that no new banks would be chartered in Virginia until 1834, after the decisive battle of the Jacksonian Bank War.[310]

With the onset of hard times in the wake of the Panic of 1819, those in debt were pressed increasingly hard by creditors. As land prices fell and the problems of 'legal judgments accumulating against them for payment of their debts' grew, debtors began to vigorously seek relief. One important group of debtors included those who had acquired federal land through what was a very liberal purchasing system. The boom in western land following the end of the War of 1812 took advantage of the easy terms available, and as the economic crisis worsened, land prices plummeted and more and more land owners found themselves unable to keep their land. In spite of postponement acts by Congress in 1818, 1819 and 1820 that extended forfeiture for an additional year, the problem continued to deepen, and pressure on Congress to resolve the issue intensified.[311]

Following much debate, the final relief legislation for federal land purchasers based on a proposal from Secretary of the Treasury Crawford, passed Congress early in 1821. The act allowed debtors to 'relinquish the unpaid proportion of the land and attain clear title to the remainder', 'discharged interest in arrears', extended payment of the full debt 'for those who did not wish to take advantage of the relinquishment provision' by allowing the remainder of the debt to 'be paid in eight annual installments, without interest charges', and granted 'a special discount of 37 ½ per cent for debtors who would pay promptly'. While Congress had enacted postponement laws frequently in the decade following 1810, this level of federal government intrusion into debtor-creditor relations was unusual for a time when state laws governed such relationships. However, a repeat of the boom-bust cycle in land would reappear in the 1830s, and the severe downturn at the end of that decade would lead to the nation's first federal bankruptcy act in 1841.[312]

Other debtors, facing demands from creditors and cut off from further accommodation by banks, turned to their state legislatures for relief. Debtors typically asked states to intervene in contracts through stay laws that 'postponed execution of property when the debtor signed a pledge to make payment at a certain date in the future' and/or minimum appraisal laws that provided 'no property could be sold for execution below a certain minimum price, the appraised value being generally set by a board of the debtor's neighbors'. While the push for such relief legislation was greater 'in the heavily indebted agricultural states of the West', some form of relief was passed in eleven states, including four eastern states, and passage was close in four additional states, all in the East and including Virginia among them.[313]

A vigorous debate of a minimum appraisal bill took place in Virginia's General Assembly in early 1820. By arguing that a precipitous drop in commodity prices following on the heels of an expansion of bank credit that drove prices up and encouraged debt had left many farmers and others through out the state in dire straits through no fault of their own, those favouring the legislation could combine the strong anti-banking feeling in the Commonwealth with a concern for those in debt. However, the opposition, arguing the sanctity of contracts, personal responsibility for decisions and the role of markets in determining value, ultimately held sway as the bill was defeated on a vote of 113 to 74. The next year two stay laws were proposed but also were defeated.[314]

The national focus on debtors and debt relief that began with the Panic of 1819 meant that 'from the 1820s onward, a growing number of states dramatically curtailed the use of imprisonment for debt'. In addition, many states also 'expanded the range of property that was exempt from execution for debt', including such items as the debtor's 'tools' and 'dwelling house, and forty or fifty acres of surrounding land'.[315]

In addition to concentrating attention on the issue of debt relief, the wake of the Panic of 1819 also brought the issue of poor relief to the forefront of public awareness and marked the beginning of a shift in the way Americans viewed the poor and public responses to poverty. Economic downturns in the 1790s, after the Embargo of 1807 and during the War of 1812 had already created significant hardships for many Americans and put pressure on the mechanisms used to serve the poor. As a result, some efforts to restructure poor relief took place prior to the Panic of 1819. For example, New York City began building the Bellevue complex that included an almshouse in 1811 and opened the institution in 1816, the Pennsylvania Society for the Promotion of Public Economy was established in 1817 to 'stem the rising cost of poor relief in Philadelphia', and the New York Society for the Prevention of Pauperism, formed in 1818, 'led the charge to define poverty as a moral flaw, one best repaired by using community policing and the power of the state to regulate the lives of the poor'. However, it was in the decade following the Panic of 1819 that the most important changes in the way many Americans viewed the poor and the ways in which many states and localities dealt with the poor occurred.[316]

Often the debates regarding poor relief that would be played out across the United States in the 1820s and 1830s reflected the poor law reforms debated in Great Britain during nearly the same period. The increased cost of administering the Poor Laws as a result of the long period of the Napoleonic Wars and economic fluctuations in the decade following 1815 pushed the issue of poor law reform to the fore of political debate. The attack on the Poor Laws coming from Thomas Malthus's *Essay on the Principle of Population* and added to by other political economists of the time, particularly David Ricardo and Nassau Senior, sharpened the debate by advocating gradual abolition of poor relief as it existed. These factors pushing to reconsider the means of providing poor relief were further enhanced by the movement toward moral reform. This crusade generally stressed the importance of individual responsibility and the need to eradicate vice and saw the Poor Laws as a mechanism to enable and encourage the poor in these directions. The result of the combination of forces acting in the decade following 1815 was to create an 'important distinction in future discussion of the poor'. As Parliament debated the issue of poor law reform and appointed a commission to study the administration and operations of the Poor Laws, the poor became increasingly 'categorized in the public mind as the "worthy" and "unworthy" poor. And public outcry against the cost of poor relief became not only acceptable but almost prudent.' The debates of the 1820s and early 1830s concluded with the passage of the Poor Law Amendment Act in 1834. This placed control of poor relief in nationally established, regional boards, thus eliminating local control, and established indoor relief as the only means of public poor relief, erecting workhouses and requiring all those receiving relief to live in the workhouse.[317]

Well-read Americans closely followed the British debates in periodicals and newspapers, both American and British. For example, in February 1819, the *American Monthly Magazine and Critical Review* published an article on the Poor Laws with remarks on the report of a House of Commons select committee. The 'Report of the Committee appointed to inquire into the operation of the Poor Laws' of the Pennsylvania House of Representatives in January 1825 indicated that 'with regard to the question of radical defect in the system itself' the matter had 'been the subject of keen and voluminous discussion in England' and proceeded to summarize the arguments used in the British debates. And the *Albion* published a number of pieces in the early 1830s regarding the British Poor Laws. Finally, for a sense of cross-Atlantic intellectual interaction, Edmond Cocks in his article on the Malthusian population theory provides an extensive list of individuals and publications regarding the validity of that theory.[318]

With the experience of the Panic of 1819 fresh in their minds and with the continuing debates over poor relief in Britain as a constant reminder, a number of state and city governments began to search for ways to reform their approach to poor relief. One of the guiding principles of these various reform efforts was the concept of 'less-eligibility'. 'This meant that the life of someone on relief should not be more desirable [eligible] than that of someone attempting to eke out an existence solely through industrious labor'. To achieve this required that the poor be categorized by the source of their condition – those 'impoverished through no fault of their own' and those 'who only had themselves to blame', temporary versus longer-term, able-bodied versus disabled, etc. Once they had been categorized, control of the poor became an important goal. This, in turn, led to efforts to 'limit access to out-door relief' and to move towards providing relief in almshouses or workhouses that would oversee the poor, ensure their good behaviour and reform the deviant.[319]

The year 1821 saw the beginning of a flurry of actions by cities and states on the question of poor relief. Directed by the previous session of the Massachusetts General Court, a committee chaired by Josiah Quincy issued their report, *Report of the Committee on the Pauper Laws of This Commonwealth*. Having collected information from a number of localities and turned 'their attention to the state of the same subject, in England', the committee concluded 'that the pernicious consequences of the existing system are palpable, that they are increasing, and that they imperiously call for the interference of the Legislature, in some manner, equally prompt and efficacious'. That same year, Boston civic leaders 'proposed a house of industry', the intention being 'to put the able-bodied poor to work for their own support', and the Pennsylvania legislature appointed a commission to collect information on the operation of the poor laws of the state.[320]

The next year, New York City instituted the practice of 'using the stepping mill to extract labor from vagrants and other criminals housed at the Bellevue facility'. In 1823, the city of Baltimore opened a new almshouse facility 'far from the city' and 'forced each inmate to labor in exchange for room and board'. The inmates 'constructed beds and cribs for the facility, laundered sheets and uniforms, and milked cows and grew vegetables on the grounds'. Also in 1823, the New York state legislature instructed the Secretary of State, John Yates, to collect information from across the state 'as would be necessary to give a distinct view of the expenses and operation of the laws, for the relief and settlement of the poor', and 'to gather such information from other states'. This led the next year to the *Report of the Secretary of State in 1824 on the Relief and Settlement of the Poor*, which has come to be called the *Yates Report*.[321]

Analyzing the information on poor relief collected from localities, the *Yates Report* found that the cost of providing relief varied dramatically across the state and that local expenditures on the poor had increased unusually rapidly since 1815. Further, the report found that the cost of administering poor relief was very high, particularly as the result of the cost of settlement, or removing paupers and returning them to their place of origin. Yates's report found fault with almost every aspect of the existing system of poor relief. Outdoor relief was found to be more costly than that provided in almshouses, idleness resulting from lack of work was found to be harmful, and settlement and renting out of paupers resulted in abuse of the poor. As a result, the report recommended a number of reforms, many of which were incorporated in 'An Act to Provide for the Establishment of County Poor-Houses', enacted by the legislature in November 1824. The 1824 law required localities to construct poorhouses, directed them, except in the case of illness, to place those seeking relief in these institutions, established local boards to administer the poorhouses, made all costs of the system the responsibility of the county and abolished the removal of paupers.[322]

In January 1825, the Pennsylvania legislature's committee inquiring into the poor laws submitted its report. Much like the *Yates Report*, the committee found 'that the effect of a public compulsory provision for the poor' was to 'increase the number of paupers', to place an 'oppressive burthen on the country', to 'promote idleness and licentiousness among the laboring class' and to give relief to the 'profligate and abandoned' that should go instead to 'the virtuous and industrious alone'. The committee also indicated that the poor laws 'have not done away with the necessity for private charity, have been onerous to the community, and every way injurious to the morals, comfort, and independence of that class for whose benefit they were intended'. Regarding settlement, the committee objected to the expense involved with removal and to the power it bestowed, which they believed was 'arbitrary, and dangerous, and capable of being used tyrannically and oppressively'. They also objected to the poor rate system and recommended changing the mechanism and limiting increases in future years.[323]

Following on the heels of the legislative committee's report, in 1827, the Philadelphia Board of Guardians of the Poor undertook a study of poor relief in Baltimore, Boston, New York, Providence and Salem and found that 'every system' examined was 'superior to our own'. They found that outdoor relief was the 'most wasteful, the most expensive' and, for the poor, 'the most injurious to their morals, and destructive of their industrious habits'. In addition, they believed 'that in proportion to the means of support, provided for the poor and improvident, they are found to increase and multiply'. The cause of much pauperism, they believed, was intemperance: 'From three-fourths to nine-tenths of the paupers in all parts of our country, may attribute their degradation to the vice of intemperance'. The solution was to require the poor to live and work in almshouses and 'give no money in any case'. But, if outdoor relief was given it should be only in provisions and services. The committee also found 'one of the greatest burthens' they faced was 'the maintenance of the host of worthless foreigners, disgorged upon our shores'. For this problem, they suggested that lists of passengers arriving be provided, and the captain be required to either 'give security they shall not become a public charge, or to commute the cases by the payment of a certain sum per head' as was done in New York.[324]

In response to the legislative committee report and to the Philadelphia report, the state legislature enacted a new law for the relief and employment of the poor in Philadelphia and surrounding areas. The March 1828 act incorporated many of the recommendations of the two reports, including limits on poor rates, erecting almshouses, charging paupers for board, crediting them for work and requiring ship captains to provide a list of immigrants and to make payment for them. As a result, 'the city began phasing out cash payments over seven years, intended to coincide with the construction of a massive new almshouse'. The hope was to move to the point where 'all public relief in Philadelphia would be indoor'.[325]

These and other efforts by state and local governments to reform poor relief in the decade following the Panic of 1819 often generated much discussion and some action but for the most part did not dramatically change the mechanism of poor relief. For example, as Philadelphia moved to eliminate outdoor relief, 'prominent citizens drew attention to the plight of the working poor', making the case that for some, such as seamstresses, the prevailing 'wages were too low for self-support'. Further, the requirement that the poor be provided relief only in workhouses fell by the wayside as 'public officials offered an increasing number of exemptions'. Philadelphia, as was the case in many areas, found that 'less-eligibility proved impossible to enforce if the wages of a full-time job still left working families mired in poverty'. In New York, the 1824 law 'did not impose the system on any county that did not wish to adopt it', and a revision to the law in 1827 'left the choice between outdoor and indoor relief in the hands of local officials'. Thus, 'as economic development across the antebellum period placed an increasing number of working people in the position where they periodically needed temporary and partial relief', the 'perception of the poor as a separate class whose poverty could be attributed to their own personal failures' began to lose relevance and the poorhouse became 'largely an inappropriate response' to the problem of poor relief. These debates did, however, create important changes in the way the public viewed the poor.[326]

Local public support of the poor in Virginia also appears to have shifted significantly in the aftermath of the Panic and the economic doldrums of the 1820s. In Richmond, the 'extraordinary high prices' of food and fuel in 1816–17 led to an extra three-month allowance for distribution to outdoor paupers, and as the downturn developed in 1819 and beyond, the city continued to spend 20 to 25 per cent of its budget on the poor.[327] And, in Petersburg, 'from 1820 to 1823, the bill for poor relief averaged more than five thousand dollars a year, a sum triple or quadruple the normal expense'.[328] The generous support of the poor that occurred as the economic crisis took hold continued across the Commonwealth into the 1820s. As the pauper rate rose, so did both measures of the generosity of poor relief, mean real expenditures per capita and real mean total expenditures per recipient. In Virginia, only in poorhouses did changes occur that matched other areas of the nation. Yet, by the end of the 1820s the public's generosity seems to have begun to disappear as the state moved to reform its welfare system. According to Saunders, it appears that the 'Panic and its aftermath destroyed the sense of community and consensus that had been so prevalent in the 1780s and 1790s among the elite' in Richmond and in other Commonwealth communities. Decreasing levels of assistance from the Overseers of the Poor would become the norm.

The discussions regarding poor relief that played out during the 1820s in Virginia and across the nation were brought on in large measure by the impact the Panic of 1819 had on poor rolls and the cost of administering relief programs. As the United States moved into the 1830s and beyond, increasingly 'upper- and middle-class Americans perceived urban poverty as entrenched rather than eradicable'. This recognition of the evolving market revolution and changing mode of production also meant that 'in most cities, relief programs shrunk as a percentage of municipal budgets, while funding for new police departments rose dramatically'. Finally, as more and more citizens began to see education as 'an antidote to poverty', in state after state across the nation 'taxpayer-funded, compulsory, nonsectarian public schools appeared during the 1830s and 1840s'.[329]

The post-Panic reaction would carry over into other policy areas as well. Although Virginia had, through the Board of Public Works, increased spending on internal improvements in the face of the economic crisis, this would not continue. After 1824, investments in internal improvements declined dramatically and did not recover until the mid-1830s, and did not become significant until the 1850s.[330] Federal funding in the Commonwealth, particularly for a stone dry dock at the Gosport Navy Yard, helped the Norfolk economy as did a break in the British-American trade dispute in 1824–5.[331] However, tensions resumed in 1826 and were not fully resolved until 1830.[332] As a result, the combination of British and American navigation acts continued to deprive Virginia of an important market for its agricultural products through much of the 1820s.

Nationally, many state efforts directed towards internal improvements were temporarily derailed by the Panic of 1819, and it created sufficient concern at the federal level that by the late 1820s much of the national effort had been spoiled and abandoned. While many state programs were restarted with the return of better economic times, 'the widespread failure of state systems in the wake of the panic of 1837' doomed these public efforts and allowed private capital markets to 'step forward and claim the theoretical and practical superiority over public enterprise into the focus on moral choice and private beneficence that were cornerstones of the movement'.[333]

While the debates over banking, debt relief and poor relief occurred at the state and local levels, a long-running debate in Congress was emerging on the issue of protective tariffs. The combination of growth in American manufacturing during the period from the Embargo of 1807 through the War of 1812, with the British dumping of manufactured goods on American markets following the Treaty of Ghent, led to Congress enacting the Tariff of 1816. This was 'a moderate tariff, largely for revenue', but with some measure of protection behind it, largely for cotton textiles. In 1818, tariffs were raised on iron bars to help protect that industry, and a reduction of the tariff on cotton goods scheduled to occur that year was postponed.[334]

With the onset of the economic recession following the Panic of 1819, the protectionist tariff movement was given a tremendous boost. Despite the founding of the American Society for the Promotion of American Industry in 1816 and its subsequent extension into a number of state and local affiliated societies, by 1818 the postwar boom had reduced the movement to being 'more or less dormant'. But, the hard times following the Panic led Mathew Carey of Philadelphia to hold a well-attended Convention of the Friends of National Industry in New York City late in 1819. This and a host of similar meetings, particularly in New England and the Mid-Atlantic states, renewed the vigor of the protectionist movement and created numerous memorials to Congress. As a result, in 1820, Congressman Henry Baldwin of Pennsylvania, Chair of the House Committee on Manufactures, introduced a strongly protectionist tariff bill. With solid support across much of the nation, the bill easily passed the House but fell short in the Senate by one vote. Votes in both houses were along distinctly regional lines. The Mid-Atlantic states were strongly for the tariff, New England and the West for but less overwhelmingly, and the South strongly opposed. From among the Virginia delegation, 'James Barbour, who had voted for the tariff of 1816, led the opposition to the Baldwin bill', and both John Tyler and William Archer made important speeches against increasing duties.[335]

Although failing to secure the protective tariff they sought in 1820, the forces of protectionism were invigorated. Led by Carey, Hezekiah Niles, editor of the influential *Weekly Register*, Daniel Raymond, author of the first American book on economics, and a number of others, the protectionists 'gained a sizable following among the farmers of the middle Atlantic and western states as well as among manufactures of New England'. By 1824, times were ripe for the protective legislation that had failed earlier. The tariff of 1824, 'opposed by twenty-one of the twenty-two Virginians in Congress', increased duties on a number of items as the protectionists 'rejected individualist economic assumptions, already battered by the Panic of 1819, about the beneficence of individual self-interest and unfettered markets'. With the election of John Quincy Adams in 1824, protectionists were further emboldened and in 1828 succeeded in enacting the highest tariff in American history, the so-called 'Tariff of Abominations'. In keeping with their earlier stands, all but three members of Virginia's delegation voted against the new tariff. Rising sectional tensions and the election of Andrew Jackson began to turn the tide of protection and in 1832 a new tariff, 'prompted by the White House's concern about rising southern discontent, cut the average duties of the 1828 tariff by half'. Not satisfied by this action, southerners revolted with South Carolina in the lead. The resulting Nullification Crisis tested the American political system and 'established a crucial democratic precedent'. With tariff acts in 1842 and 1846 the general trend was to further reduce rates, and while tariffs remained an important political issue during the antebellum period, they no longer played the central role they did in the decade following the Panic of 1819.[336]

The final area in which the Panic of 1819 had a significant national impact was politics. The most important political change resulting from the Panic 'was to reinvigorate the city and country democracies, with a renewed focus on economic and financial issues'. In the cities, particularly New York and Philadelphia, the hard times of the recession increased worker unrest. In Philadelphia 'strikes became common, numbering no fewer than ten in the year 1821 alone', and as the decade proceeded workingmen's parties formed 'in response to economic and social changes long evident in all northern cities'. The tensions generated by these changes 'accelerated after the recovery from the Panic of 1819'. Country democrats, particularly in the South and West, 'gained valuable political experience in the battles over debtor relief and related issues'. The economic crisis in the aftermath of the Panic 'also raised fundamental questions about the nationalist economic policies of the new-style Republicans under Madison and Monroe'. These questions focused on the nature of American democracy. Should well-connected private interests 'be permitted to control, to their own benefit, the economic destiny of the entire nation'? Who should be entitled to vote? And should the federal government or citizens of states determine the expansion of slavery? These and other issues dominated the political culture of the 1820s and beyond. And it became clear that 'the Panic of 1819 had galvanized the popular movements that led' directly to the emergence of Andrew Jackson and the transformation of American politics.[337]

In the aftermath of the Panic of 1819, Virginia politics saw 'conservative components' move to 'reassert themselves in a vigorous defense of states' rights, strict construction, and slave property'. This move was led by the Old Virginia center of 'rural, slaveholding tidewater and southeastern piedmont', an area hard hit by the Panic and one that saw its economy continue to stagnate through the decade of the 1820s. Opposition came from a more 'economically dynamic, ethnically and religiously varied, and socially fluid' periphery including areas in an arc from west of the Blue Ridge, along the Potomac to the Eastern Shore combined with the 'Old Dominion's few cities'. The struggle for political control continued through the 1820s as the rapidly growing areas of the periphery's push for 'government aid in the expansion of credit and the construction of internal improvements' was resisted by the political control of the centre. Long-standing criticisms of the Commonwealth's constitution became part of the conflict and in the wake of conflicting results from elections, the General Assembly called for a constitutional convention to meet in Richmond in 1829. The resulting constitution of 1830 was 'a conservative document that brought little change' as 'the eastern slaveholding gentry, jealous of the authority that seemed to be slipping from their grasp, stacked the deck and continued to resist the democratic trend of nineteenth-century America'. It would be several more decades until the 'division between the center and the periphery' in Virginia would give way to modern party politics'.[338]

Summary and Conclusions

For the Commonwealth of Virginia, the Panic of 1819 and ensuing depression was a significant and quite real economic event. It was the state's first awakening to the realities of market-driven boom-bust cycles that would come to dominate the nineteenth century, and it marked the beginning of a change in Virginia's political and economic fortunes.

The Panic's impacts were felt by Virginians in a variety of complex ways. Hard-hit by the depression, Virginia's merchant community faced significantly increased instability with the onset of the Panic. Retail merchants in the capital, Richmond, appear to have been hit hardest, although merchants all across the Commonwealth faced significant problems as the depression deepened. Merchant partnerships had a marginally better chance of survival, but few, whether in partnerships or not, were able to avoid the economic fallout following the Panic of 1819.

Merchants were not alone in suffering the effects of the depression. As the nation's leading producer of tobacco and an important wheat grower, Virginia's agricultural sector was devastated as the real value of the Commonwealth's exports fell 36.8 per cent between 1818 and 1821. Foreign markets for the state's commodities dissolved in part because of British and European recessions and in part as the result of the American Navigation Acts closing US ports to British ships. The resulting agricultural decline meant a collapse of the market for land, significant reductions in rents and rental income, and dramatic falls in wages and in prices for enslaved African Americans.

Because of its origins in contractions by both state banks and the Virginia offices of the new Bank of the United States, the Commonwealth would see no expansion of its banking system for a decade and a half, and those opposed to an expanding federal role would have additional ammunition for their battles over the Constitution. Although the combined banking system played a more neutral role as the Panic developed, the monetary contraction was most often blamed for the devastating deflation.

The combined circumstances of a sharp credit contraction followed by the evaporation of markets for the state's products created hardships for Virginians of all classes as businesses closed, land values plummeted, and farmers were forced to abandon their activities. In addition, the initial generous support Virginians provided for the poor soon turned to a concern for the efficiency of the Overseers of the Poor as funding declined and Virginia moved towards reforming the system in the early 1830s.

Moreover, the hard times left a lasting impact on the political face of the Commonwealth. Opposition to all federal involvement in the economy was strengthened while interest in an interventionist role for state and local government declined. The former would remain a characteristic of Virginia politics through the antebellum period. The latter would be modified for internal improvements, particularly in the 1850s, but not for other areas of activity.[339] Finally, in the turmoil of the Panic and its aftermath, Virginia politics became more factionalized as the Commonwealth attempted and failed to rebuild its political fortunes.[340]

One result of the many changes occurring as the early republic matured was the initiation of a process that by the 1840s would create much of the political, social and economic environment needed for America's economic progress in the second half of the century. This includes in the political arena democratization of the political process, the emergence of national political parties, changes in state and federal roles in the economy and an active series of court decisions strengthening economic relationships.[341] Socially, Americans became more literate as public education and religion's focus on the written word increased demand for published materials at the same time that expansion and decentralization of publishing combined with improved transportation to provide the newspapers, pamphlets, journals and books to meet the surge in demand. Increased literacy combined with other social forces such as abolitionism, women's suffrage and a religious revival focusing on missions to change Americans' perceptions of their role in an increasingly interdependent world.[342] And, economically the integration of transportation networks, financial markets and markets for commodities created a system in which Americans saw clearly their connection to the world economy and the nation's emerging dominant position in that system.[343] While myriad complex factors were at play in the transformation of antebellum America, the first great depression, the Panic of 1819, played a galvanizing role in many of the political, social and economic changes of the time.

NOTES

1. W. Bagehot, 'Essay on Edward Gibbon' as quoted in C. P. Kindleberger, *Manias, Panics, and Crashes: A History of Financial Crises* (New York: Basic Books, 1978), p. vii.
2. Recent works dealing with nineteenth-century business cycles include D. Steeples and D. O. Whitten, *Democracy in Desperation: The Depression of 1893* (Westport, CT: Greenwood, 1998); C. D. Romer, 'Remeasuring Business Cycles', *Journal of Economic History*, 54:3 (1994), pp. 573–609 and D. Glasner (ed.), *Business Cycles and Depression: An Encyclopedia* (Chicago, IL: University of Chicago Press, 1997). J. H. Davis, 'An Annual Index of U.S. Industrial Production, 1790–1915', *Quarterly Journal of Economics*, 119:4 (2004), pp. 1177–215 provides the most detailed analysis of the early-nineteenth-century cycles. His work is discussed in detail in Chapter 2. The vast literature regarding the Great Depression includes M. Freidman and A. J. Schwartz, *The Great Contraction 1929–1933* (Princeton, NJ: Princeton University Press, 1965); J. K. Galbraith, *The Great Crash* (Boston, MA: Houghton Mifflin, 1972); P. Temin, *Did Monetary Forces Cause the Great Depression* (New York: W. W. Norton, 1976) and his *Lessons From the Great Depression* (Cambridge: MIT Press, 1989). Recent contributions include M. D. Bordo, C. Goldin, and E. N. White, *The Defining Moment: The Great Depression and the American Economy in the Twentieth Century* (Chicago, IL: University of Chicago Press, 1998) and T. E. Hall and D. J. Ferguson, *The Great Depression: An International Disaster of Perverse Economic Policies* (Ann Arbor: University of Michigan Press, 1998).
3. Overviews of the Panic of 1819 are provided in M. Rothbard, *The Panic of 1819: Reactions and Policies* (New York: Columbia University Press, 1962); D. C. North, *The Economic Growth of the United States, 1790–1860* (New York: Norton, 1966); S. Rezneck, 'The Depression of 1819–1822, A Social History', *American Historical Review*, 39:1 (1933), pp. 28–47; R. M. Blackson, 'The Panic of 1819 in Pennsylvania' (Phd dissertation, Pennsylvania State University, 1978); C. Sellers, *The Market Revolution: Jacksonian America, 1815–1846* (New York: Oxford University Press, 1991); S. Wilentz, *The Rise of American Democracy: Jefferson to Lincoln* (New York: Norton, 2005) and D. S. Dupre, 'The Panic of 1819 and the Political Economy of Sectionalism', in C. Matson (ed.), *The Economy of Early America: Historical Perspectives and New Directions* (University Park, PA: The Pennsylvania State University Press, 2006), pp. 263–93. C. Matson, 'A House of Many Mansions: Some Thoughts on the Field of Economic History', in Matson (ed.), *Economy of Early America*, pp. 1–70; p.

54. As the subtitle indicates, Rothbard's book focuses primarily on policy reactions in the wake of the Panic. See note 87, below, for a more extensive list.

4. Among the many works dealing with Virginia's political history, see C. H. Ambler, *Thomas Ritchie: A Study in Virginia Politics* (Richmond, VA: Bell, 1913); C. H. Ambler, *Sectionalism in Virginia from 1776 to 1861* (Chicago, IL: University of Chicago Press, 1910); C. S. Sydnor, *The Development of Southern Sectionalism, 1819–1848* (Baton Rouge: Louisiana State University Press, 1946); W. G. Shade, *Democratizing the Old Dominion: Virginia and the Second Party System* (Charlottesville: University Press of Virginia, 1996) and A. G. Freehling, *Drift Toward Dissolution: The Virginia Slavery Debate of 1831–1832* (Baton Rouge: Louisiana State University Press, 1982).

5. C. W. Calomiris and G. Groton, 'The Origins of Banking Panics: Models, Facts, and Bank Regulation', in R. G. Hubbard (ed.), *Financial Markets and Financial Crises* (Chicago, IL: University of Chicago Press, 1991), pp. 109–73; p. 113.

6. See particularly A. F. Burns and W. C. Mitchell, *Measuring Business Cycles* (New York: National Bureau of Economic Research, 1946).

7. Important exceptions include W. E. Folz, 'The Financial Crisis of 1819: A Study in Post-War Readjustment' (Phd dissertation, University of Illinois, 1935); L. M. Schur, 'The Second Bank of the United States and the Inflation after the War of 1812', *Journal of Political Economy*, 68:2 (1960), pp. 118–34; North, *Economic Growth* and W. B. Smith, *Economic Aspects of the Second Bank of the United States* (Cambridge, MA: Harvard University Press, 1953). For a review of many of the earlier studies of the Panic, see Blackson, 'Panic of 1819', Chapter 1.

8. Sellers, *Market Revolution*, p. 136. For details of the Bank's actions see R. D. Womack, *An Analysis of the Credit Controls of the Second Bank of the United States* (New York: Arno Press, 1978).

9. Rothbard, *Panic of 1819*, p. 11.

10. Rezneck, 'The Depression of 1819–1822', p. 29.

11. F. S. Mishkin, 'Asymmetric Information and Financial Crises: A Historical Perspective' in Hubbard (ed.), *Financial Markets*, p. 70. Also see Milton Freidman and Anna J. Schwartz, *A Monetary History of the United States, 1867–1960* (Princeton, NJ: Princeton University Press, 1963).

12. Mishkin, 'Asymmetric Information', pp. 70–1 and p. 72. Also see Calomiris and Groton, 'Banking Panics', pp. 120–9.

13. B. S. Bernanke, 'Nonmonetary Effects of the Financial Crisis in the Propagation of the Great Depression', *American Economic Review*, 73:3 (1983), pp. 257–76; p. 263. Also see B. Bernanke and M. Gertler, 'Agency Cost, Net Worth, and Business Fluctuations', *American Economic Review*, 79:2 (1989), pp. 14–31 and B. Bernanke and M. Gertler, 'Financial Fragility and Economic Performance', *Quarterly Journal of Economics*, 105:1 (1990), pp. 87–114.

14. G. Browne, *Baltimore in the Nation, 1789–1861* (Chapel Hill: University of North Carolina Press, 1980), p. 70.

15. The standard work on the economy of this period is North, *Economic Growth*. Also see Sellers, *Market Revolution* and Wilentz, *American Democracy*.

16. North, *Economic Growth*, p. 53 and p. 46. On an earlier depression see T. Bouton, 'Moneyless in Pennsylvania: Privatization and the Depression of the 1780s' in Madson (ed.), *Economy of Early America*, pp. 218–35.

17. See G. Dangerfield, *The Awakening of American Nationalism, 1815–1828* (New York: Harper and Row, 1965).

18. See Sellers, *Market Revolution*. Also see J. Dorfman, *The Economic Mind in American Civilization* (New York: The Viking Press, 1946) and P. K. Conkin, *Prophets of Prosperity* (Bloomington: Indiana University Press, 1980).

19. North argues for 1818–23 as the appropriate dates for the cycle. He believes earlier studies were in error by identifying the start of the downturn in the years 1816–18 because they involved 'an overweighting of series connected with manufacturing (and to a lesser extent shipping) and reports from newspapers of the Northeast. It was a mixed period for the Northeast, but it was also a booming era in the South and West'. North further makes the case for 1823 and the beginning of the upturn because 'there was a revival in 1821, but was followed by a large gold outflow in 1822 and further sharp fall in prices. Since the United States was geared to the international economy, it seems most likely to me that the real beginning of recovery only took place after this final adjustment had occurred. Again there were important regional differences. The revival of manufacturing in the Northeast occurred in 1821, but the recovery of the South and West did not take place until 1823' (North, *Economic Growth*, pp. 181–2n). As data from this study will show, for much of Virginia the upswing appears to begin in 1821. However, western parts of the state tied to the economy of the Ohio River appear to lag behind the eastern portions of the state, and recovery does not begin until 1822 and 1823. Nevertheless, for this study I will use 1818–21 as the dates for the depression following the Panic of 1819.

20. An important exception is D. S. Dupre, *Transforming the Cotton Frontier: Madison County, Alabama 1800–1840* (Baton Rouge: Louisiana State University Press, 1997).

21. North, *Economic Growth*, pp. 61 and 66.

22. For the economy of the period 1790 to the Embargo see North, *Economic Growth*, Part 1; D. R. Adams, 'American Neutrality and Prosperity, 1793–1808: A Reconsideration', *Journal of Economic History*, 40:4 (1980), pp. 713–38, and C. Goldin and F. Lewis, 'The Role of Exports in American Economic Growth during the Napoleonic Wars, 1793–1807', *Explorations in Economic History*, 17:1 (1980), pp. 6–25.

23. For this period see North, *Economic Growth*, Part 1; L. M. Sears, 'Philadelphia and the Embargo of 1807', *Quarterly Journal of Economics*, 35:2 (1921), pp. 354–9; J. Frankel, 'The 1807–1809 Embargo against Great Britain', *Journal of Economic History*, 42:2 (1982), pp. 291–308 and J. van Fenstermaker, 'The U.S. Embargo Act of 1807: Its Impact on New England Money, Banking, and Economic Activity', *Economic Enquiry*, 28:1 (1990), pp. 163–84.

24. G. H. Evans, *Business Incorporations in the United States, 1800–1943* (New York: National Bureau of Economic Research, 1948).

25. F. Taussig, *Tariff History of the United States* (New York: Kelly, 1967, reprint of 8th edn, 1931), p. 28.

26. Sears, 'Embargo', pp. 33–4. Also see Frankel, 'Embargo', pp. 291–308.

27. B. Hammond, *Banks and Politics in America from the Revolution to the Civil War* (Princeton, NJ: Princeton University Press, 1957); J. van Fenstermaker, *The Development of American Commercial Banking, 1782–1837* (Kent, OH: Kent State University, 1965); H. Bodenhorn, *A History of Banking in Antebellum America: Financial Markets and Economic Development in an Era of Nationbuilding* (Cambridge: Cambridge University Press, 2000); R. E. Wright, *Origins of Commercial Banking in America, 1750–1800* (Lanham, MD: Rowman and Littlefield, 2001) and W. E. Weber, 'Early State Banks in the United States: How Many Were There and When Did They Exist?', *Journal of Economic History*, 66:2 (2006), pp. 433–55. For a discussion of the limitations of Fenstermaker's work, see the Appendix to Chapter 3 below.

28. Sears, 'Embargo', p. 40.

29. North, *Economic Growth*, p. 234.

30. *Historical Statistics of the United States: Colonial Times to 1970* (Washington: Bureau of the Census, 1975), Series E-52.

31. T. S. Berry, *Western Prices Before 1861* (Cambridge, MA: Harvard University Press, 1943), p. 563, Tables 15 and 16.

32. See D. H. Kagin, 'Monetary Aspects of the Treasury Notes of the War of 1812', *Journal of Economic History*, 44:4 (1984), pp. 69–88.

33. See *The Public Statutes at Large of the United States of America*, by authority of Congress (Boston, MA: Charles C. Little and James Brown, 1845–1867), vol. 2, p. 766 and p. 801, vol. 3, p. 100 and p. 161; *Reports on Finances 1812/1814*, vol. 1, p. 529; North, *Economic Growth*, p. 57–8; *Niles' Register*, vol. 8, p. 270 and R. Catterall, *The Second Bank of the United States* (Chicago, IL: University of Chicago Press, 1903), pp. 7–17. For an excellent overview of federal fiscal operations of the time, see E. J. Perkins, *American Public Finance and Financial Services, 1700–1815* (Columbus, OH: Ohio State University Press, 1994).

34. See Evans, *Business Incorporations*, and Table 1.4 below.

35. C. Day, 'The Early Development of the American Cotton Manufacture', *Quarterly Journal of Economics*, 34:3 (1925), pp. 450–68; p. 452.

36. S. Wilentz, *Chants Democratic: New York City and the Rise of the American Working Class, 1788–1850* (New York: Oxford University Press, 1984), p. 23.

37. T. S. Berry, *Production and Population Since 1789: Revised GNP Series in Constant Dollars* (Richmond, VA: Bostwick Press, 1988), Table 3. See Chapter 2 below for a discussion of the limitations of Berry's data.

38. W. B. Smith and A. H. Cole, *Fluctuations in American Business, 1790–1860* (Cambridge, MA: Harvard University Press, 1935), p. 20.

39. On manufacturing see J. Atack and P. Passell, *A New Economic View of American History from Colonial Times to 1940*, 2nd edn (New York: Norton, 1994), Chapter 7, 'The Beginnings of Industrialization'. On re-exports and the West Indies see F. L. Benns, *The American Struggle for the British West India Carrying-Trade, 1815–1830* (Bloomington: Indiana University Studies, Vol. 10, 1923). On ocean freight rates see C. K. Harley, 'Ocean Freight Rates and Productivity, 1740–913: The Primacy of Mechanical Inventions Reaffirmed', *Journal of Economic History*, 48:4 (1988), pp. 851–76, and D. C. North, 'Ocean Freight Rates and Economic Development, 1750–1913', *Journal of Economic History*, 18:4 (1958), pp. 537–55.

40. *American State Papers*, Commerce and Navigation, vol. 2, p. 647.

41. For a discussion of the European agricultural situation and the impact of weather see J. D. Post, *The Last Substance Crisis in the Western World* (Baltimore, MD: Johns Hopkins University Press, 1977).

42. North, *Economic Growth*, p. 244, p. 239 and p. 240. The prices (1830=100) follow:

Year	Export	Import	Cotton
1815	182.98	222.7	213.1
1816	248.22	194.9	297.0
1817	240.35	176.8	266.7
1818	245.46	189.7	342.4

43. North, *Economic Growth*, p. 600.

44. See N. S. Buck, *Development and Organization of Anglo-American Trade, 1800–1850* (New Haven, CT: Yale University Press, 1925); R. W. Hidy, *The House of Baring in American Trade and Finance* (Cambridge, MA: Harvard University Press, 1949) and M. Wilkins, *History of Foreign Investment in the United States to 1914* (Cambridge, MA: Harvard University Press, 1989).

45. On the Tariff of 1816 see E. Stanwood, *American Tariff Controversies in the Nineteenth Century* (Boston, MA: Houghton Mifflin, 1903), pp. 112–13, 138, and Taussig, *Tariff History*, p. 30.

46. W. L. Thorp and W. C. Mitchell, *Business Annals* (New York: National Bureau of Economic Research, 1926), pp. 155–6; A. D. Gayer, W. W. Rostow and A. J. Schwartz, *The Growth and Fluctuation of the British Economy 1790–1830* (Oxford: Clarendon, 1953), ch. 3, and Post, *Substance Crisis*, ch. 3. Europe was America's leading export market at the time accounting for some 70 per cent of all US exports. Britain accounted for about 40 per cent of the total. *Historical Statistics*, Series U-317, 324 and 325.

47. Gayer, Rostow, and Schwartz, *British Economy*, p. 115; Throp and Mitchell, *Business Annals*, p. 156.

48. D. G. Barnes, *A History of the English Corn Laws, from 1660–1846* (New York: A. M. Kelley, 1961), p. 162.

49. Gayer, Rostow and Schwartz, *British Economy*, p. 115; T. Tooke, *A History of Prices and of the Circulation from 1792 to 1856*, reproduced from the original, with an introduction by T. Gregory (New York: Aldephi, 1928), vol. 2, p. 16.

50. Barnes, *Corn Laws*, p. 162.

51. Post, *Substance Crisis*, pp. 44–7.

52. Throp and Mitchell, *Business Annals*, pp. 155–6.

53. *The Works of Thomas Jefferson*, ed. P. L. Ford, 12 vols (New York: Putnam, 1904–5), vol. 12, pp. 34–9. On weather in these years see Post, *Substance Crisis*, ch. 1, and W. R. Baron, 'Retrieving American Climate History: A Bibliographic Essay', *Agricultural History*, 63:2 (1989), pp. 7–35.

54. Benns, *American Struggle*.

55. R. G. Albion, *The Rise of the Port of New York 1815–1860* (New York: Scribner's, 1939), p. 12. Also see R. G. Albion, 'New York and Its Disappointed Rivals', *Journal of Economic and Business History*, 3:4 (1930–1), p. 608; R. F. Dalzell, Jr., *Enterprising Elites: The Boston Associates and the World They Made* (New York: Norton, 1993); W. B. Rothenberg, 'The Invention of New England Capitalism: The Economy of New England in the Federal Period' in P. Temin (ed.), *Engines of Enterprise* (Cambridge,

MA: Harvard University Press, 2000), pp. 96–106, and Buck, *Anglo-American Trade*, pp. 147–8.

56. Buck, *Anglo-American Trade*, p. 147.

57. *American State Papers*, Finance, vol. 3, p. 501 and Buck, *Anglo-American Trade*, pp. 141–5.

58. G. Dangerfield, *The Era of Good Feelings* (New York: Harcourt, Brace, 1952), pp. 176–7.

59. J. Ciment, 'In Light of Failure: Bankruptcy, Insolvency and Financial Failure in New York City 1770–1860' (Phd dissertation, City University of New York, 1992), p. 52. Also see G. Porter and H. Livesay, *Merchants and Manufacturers* (Baltimore, MD: Johns Hopkins University Press, 1971), p. 20.

60. Dangerfield, *Era*, p. 177. Also see V. F. Bonelli, 'The Response of Public and Private Philanthropy to the Panic of 1819 in New York City' (Phd dissertation, Fordham University, 1976), p. 9.

61. Buck, *Anglo-American Trade*, pp. 149–50. For a discussion of the opposition to auctions see L. E. Atherton, 'Auctions as a Threat to American Business in the Eighteen Twenties and Thirties', *Bulletin of the Business Historical Society*, 11:6 (1937), pp. 104–7.

62. Weber, 'Early State Banks', Table 1 and Rothbard, *Panic of 1819*, p. 7. The bank note question will be analyzed in Chapters 2 and 3. Public land sales are considered in more detail below.

63. Catterall, *Second Bank*, ch. 1. Also see Perkins, *Public Finance*.

64. Smith, *Economic Aspects*, ch. 7. For state bank statistics see Fenstermaker, *American Commercial Banking* (data are adjusted for the number of reporting banks). For Bank of the United States data see *Historical Statistics of the United States*, Series X-574–75.

65. North, *Economic Growth*, p. 184.

66. B. H. Hibbard, *A History of the Public Land Policies* (New York: Macmillan, 1924), p. 83.

67. See M. J. Rohrbough, *The Land Office Business: The Settlement and Administration of American Public Lands, 1789–1837* (New York: Oxford University Press, 1968), chs 5 and 6.

68. Hibbard, *Public Land Policies*, p. 94 and R. M. Robbins, *Our Landed Heritage: The Public Domain 1776–1936* (Princeton, NJ: Princeton University Press, 1942), p. 32.

69. *Historical Statistics*, Series Y338. Also see P. Studenski and H. E. Kross, *Financial History of the United States* (New York: McGraw-Hill, 1963).

70. Smith, *Economic Aspects*, ch. 4.

71. Wilentz, *Chants Democratic*, p. 26. Also see R. Mohl, *Poverty in New York* (New York: Oxford University Press, 1970), pp. 14–34.

72. F.-A.-Frederic, duc de La Rochefoucauld-Liancourt, *Travels Through the United States of North America, the Country of the Iroquois, and Upper Canada in the Years 1795, 1796, and 1797; with an Authentic Account of Lower Canada* (London: R. Phillips, 1799), vol. 2, pp. 32–3.

73. Ibid., p. 37.

74. See J. C. Robert, *The Tobacco Kingdom* (Durham, NC: Duke University Press, 1938); Secretary of State of the United States, *Digest of Accounts of Manufacturing Establishments* (Washington: Gales and Seaton, 1823); *Richmond Enquirer*, 20 April 1819 and L. C. Gray, *History of Agriculture in the Southern United States to 1860* (Washington: Carnegie Institution, 1933).

75. 'Report of the Committee on Agriculture and Manufactures', *Journal of the House of Delegates 1831–32*, Document no. 31, p. 215 and T. S. Berry, 'The Rise of Flour Milling in Richmond', *Virginia Magazine of History and Biography*, 78:4 (1970), pp. 387–408.

76. T. Coxe, *A View of the United States of America in a Series of Papers Written at Various Times, in the Years between 1787 and 1794* (Philadelphia, PA: Hall and Wrigley and Berriman, 1794), p. 307.

77. S. P. Adams, *Old Dominion Industrial Commonwealth: Coal, Politics, and Economy in Antebellum America* (Baltimore, MD: Johns Hopkins University Press, 2004) and K. Bruce, *Virginia Iron Manufacture in the Slave Era* (New York: Century, 1931), chs 2 and 3.

78. La Rochefoucauld-Liancourt, *Travels*, vol. 2, p. 7.

79. T. J. Wertenbaker, *Norfolk: Historic Southern Port* (Durham, NC: Duke University Press, 1931), chs 4 and 5.

80. United States, Census Office, *4th Census*, 1820 (Washington: Gales and Seaton, 1821).

81. Shade, *Democratizing the Old Dominion*, pp. 19–20.

82. Ambler, *Sectionalism in Virginia*, p. 98.

83. C. Goodrich, 'The Virginia System of Mixed Enterprise', *Political Science Quarterly*, 62:3 (1949), pp. 355–87; pp. 360–2; J. L. Larson, *Internal Improvement: National Public Works and the Promise of Popular Government in the Early Republic* (Chapel Hill: University of North Carolina Press, 2001), pp. 91–7, and J. Majewski, *A House Dividing: Economic Development in Pennsylvania and Virginia Before the Civil War* (Cambridge: Cambridge University Press, 2000).

84. *Journal of the House of Delegates 1817*, p. 6.

85. Sydnor, *Southern Sectionalism*, p. 134.

86. Ambler, *Sectionalism in Virginia*, p. 101.

87. Some of the more important studies of the Panic of 1819 include H. M. Anderson, 'Frontier Economic Problems in Missouri, 1815–1828', *Missouri Historical Review*, 24:1 (1939), pp. 38–70 and 24:2 (1940), pp. 182–203; R. M. Blackson, 'Pennsylvania Banks and the Panic of 1819: A Reinterpretation', *Journal of the Early Republic*, 9:3 (1989), pp. 335–58; G. L. Browne, 'Baltimore and the Panic of 1819', in A. C. Land, L. G. Carr and E. C. Papenfuse (eds), *Law, Society and Politics in Early Maryland* (Baltimore, MD: Johns Hopkins University Press, 1976), pp. 212–27; A. R. L. Cayton, 'The Fragmentation of "A Great Family": The Panic of 1819 and the Rise of a Middling Interest in Boston, 1818–1822', *Journal of the Early Republic*, 2:2 (1982) pp. 143–67; D. B. Dorsey, 'The Panic of 1819 in Missouri', *Missouri Historical Review*, 29:2 (1935), pp. 79–91; Dupre, 'The Panic of 1819'; T. H. Greer, 'Economic and Social Effects of the Depression of 1819 in the Old Northwest', *Indiana Magazine of History*, 44:3 (1948), pp. 227–43; North, *Economic Growth*; J. H. Parks, 'Felix Grundy and the Depression of 1819 in Tennessee', *Publication of the East Tennessee Historical*

Society, 10 (1938), pp. 19–42; E. J. Perkins, 'Langdon Cheves and the Panic of 1819: A Reassessment', *Journal of Economic History*, 44:2 (1983), pp. 455–61; Rezneck, 'The Depression of 1819–1822'; Rothbard, *Panic of 1819*; Schur, 'Second Bank'; and Smith, *Economic Aspects*. Other works that consider the Panic of 1819 in some detail include Dangerfield, *Era of Good Feelings*; Dupre, *Transforming the Cotton Frontier*; Sellers, *Market Revolution* and Wilentz, *Rise of American Democracy*. The Panic has also been the focus of several unpublished doctoral dissertations. These include, Folz, 'The Financial Crisis of 1819'; Blackson, 'The Panic of 1819 in Pennsylvania'; S. A. Kidd, 'The Search for Moral Order: The Panic of 1819 and the Culture of the Early American Republic' (Phd dissertation, University of Missouri-Columbia, 2002); and D. Lehman, 'Explaining Hard Times: Political Economy and the Panic of 1819 in Philadelphia' (Phd dissertation, University of California, Los Angles, 1992).

88. Rezneck, 'Depression of 1819–1822', p. 29, quoting C. F. Adams, *Memories of John Quincy Adams* (1875), vol. 5, p. 128.

89. Cayton, 'Fragmentation', p. 146 quoting *Columbia Centinal*, 26 June 1819 and 'Commercial Confidence', *Boston Patriot*, 6 September 1819.

90. Rezneck, 'Depression of 1819–1822', p. 31.

91. *Niles' Register*, vol. 18, p. 387.

92. W. M. Gouge, *A Short History of Paper Money and Banking in the United States* (Philadelphia, PA: n.p.,: 1833), part 2, p. 111.

93. J. P. Little, *History of Richmond* (Richmond, VA: Dietz, 1923), p. 143. Also see Rezneck, 'Depression of 1819–1822', p. 32.

94. Sellers, *Market Revolution*, p. 137.

95. See North, *Economic Growth*, pp. 177–88; Smith, *Economic Aspects*, pp. 64–6 and 82–96 and P. Temin, *The Jacksonian Economy* (New York: Norton, 1969), pp. 46–8. Smith and Cole, *Fluctuations in American Business*, suggests, 'The crisis that overtook American business at the close of 1818 was largely due to a shift in the world's demand for American staples' (p. 20).

96. Madison to Rush, April 21, 1821 in *The Writings of James Madison*, ed. G. Hunt, 9 vols (New York, Putnam, 1900–10), vol. 9, part 2, p. 46.

97. The price level is the Warren-Pearson wholesale price index from *Historical Statistics of the United States*, Series E-52 and real GNP is from T. S. Berry, *Production and Population Since 1789*, Table 3. Appendix Chart 2A.1 presents prices and real GNP using the David-Solar consumer price series. See P. A. David and P. Solar, 'A Bicentenary Contribution to the History of the Cost of Living in America', *Research in Economic History*, 2 (1977), pp. 1–80; p. 16.

98. Appendix Chart 2A.2 gives Aggregate Supply-Aggregate Demand equilibria using the David-Solar consumer price series.

99. Davis, 'Annual Index'.

100. T. S. Berry, *Revised Annual Estimates of American Gross National Product: Preliminary Annual Estimates of Four Major Components of Demand 1789–1889* (Richmond, VA: Bostwick Press, 1978), p. 23.

101. Ibid. See Table 23, pp. 35–6 and the formula given in Table 24, p. 37.

102. For some recent efforts to measure GNP in the antebellum period see R. E. Gallman, 'American Economic Growth before the Civil War; the Testimony of the Capital Stock Estimates', and T. Weiss, 'U.S. Labour Force Estimates and Economic Growth,

1800–1840', in R. E. Gallman and T. Weiss (eds), *American Economic Growth and Standards of Living Before the Civil War* (Chicago, IL: University of Chicago Press, National Bureau of Economic Research, 1992), pp. 19–75 and pp. 79–115. Also see the special issue 'The Economy of British North America', *William and Mary Quarterly*, 56:1 (1999). None of these efforts attempts to measure GNP on an annual basis.

103. Davis, 'Annual Index', p. 1179.

104. Ibid., p. 1180.

105. See Chapter 1 above.

106. See Schur, 'Second Bank', p. 122 and A. Frass, 'The Second Bank of the United States: An Instrument for an Integrated Monetary Union', *Journal of Economic History*, 34:2 (1974), pp. 447–67; p. 450. For an alternative explanation of the note flow see Temin, *Jacksonian Economy*, pp. 32–5. This issue will be considered further in Chapter 3.

107. A. Fraas, 'The Second Bank of the United States: An Instrument for an Integrated Monetary Union', *Journal of Economic History*, 34:2 (1974), pp. 447–67, and Womack, *Credit Controls*.

108. See Smith, *Economic Aspects*, ch. 4.

109. I. Fisher, 'The Debt-Deflation Theory of Great Depressions', *Econometrica*, 1:4 (1933), pp. 337–57 and *Booms and Depressions* (New York: Adephia, 1932); M. H. Wolfson, 'Irving Fisher's Debt-Deflation Theory: Its Relevance to Current Conditions', *Cambridge Journal of Economics*, 20:3 (1996), pp. 315–33, and R. W. Dimand, 'Irving Fisher's Debt-Deflation Theory of Great Depressions', *Journal of Social Economy*, 52:1 (1994), pp. 92–107.

110. Fisher, 'Debt-Deflation Theory', p. 341, italics in original, p. 348, italics in original, pp. 341–2.

111. Bernanke, 'Nonmonetary Effects', pp. 257–76, and Bernanke and Gertler, 'Agency Costs', pp. 14–31.

112. Burns and Mitchell, *Measuring Business Cycles*. Also see Rothbard, *Panic of 1819*, pp. 16–19.

113. See J. M. McFaul, *The Politics of Jacksonian Finance* (Ithaca, NY: Cornell University Press, 1972); L. Schweikart, *Banking in the American South from the Age of Jackson to Reconstruction* (Baton Rouge: Louisiana State University Press, 1987) and Temin, *Jacksonian Economy*. Perkins sees a different role for the Second Bank of the United States; see Perkins, 'Langdon Cheves and the Panic of 1819', pp. 455–61.

114. North, *Economic Growth*, p. 189.

115. See J. James, 'Changes in Economic Instability in 19th-Century America', *American Economic Review*, 83:4 (1994), pp. 117–34; M. D. Bordo and A. J. Schwartz (eds), *A Retrospective on the Classical Gold Standard: 1821–1931* (Chicago, IL: University of Chicago Press, 1984); M. D. Bordo, *Financial Crises* (Aldershot: Edward Elgar, 1992) and Calomiris and Hanes, 'Consistent Output Series', pp. 409–22.

116. Davis, 'Annual Index', pp. 1201–4 and Table 7.

117. Downturns in 1860–1, 1869–70, 1887–8 and 1890–1 are not included.

118. The table uses the Warren-Pearson Index for periods before 1890 and the Bureau of Labor Statistics wholesale price index for later periods. See *Historical Statistics*, Series E-40 and E-52. When similar calculations are made using the David-Solar Index of Consumer Prices, the levels of price changes during the various periods change, but

the relative positions remain the same with the 1873–1879 period being more severe then the 1818–21 period (-16.7 per cent vs -11.1 per cent). See Table 2A.1.

119. See Temin, *Jacksonian Economy*, pp. 155–65.

120. The Equation of Exchange, MV=PY (where M=money supply, V=velocity, P=price level, and Y=output), indicates that in the situation where the money supply has increased, prices have fallen, and output has stagnated, velocity must decline.

121. Raguet letter dated Philadelphia, 19 April 1821 in D. Ricardo, J. H. Hollander (ed.), *Minor Papers on the Currency Question, 1809–1823* (Baltimore, MD: Johns Hopkins University Press, 1932), p. 202.

122. J. MacGregor, *Commercial Statistics*, 2nd edn, 5 vols (London: Whittaker and Co., 1850), vol. 3, p. 988.

123. Comparisons of real imports and real exports using the Warren-Pearson and David-Solar price indexes do not change the relative positions of the various time periods although the percentage changes attributable to each do change.

124. *Richmond Enquirer*, 21 May 1819. Italics in original.

125. *Richmond Enquirer*, 25 May 1819. Italics in original.

126. See A. G. Crothers, 'Banks and Economic Development in Post-Revolutionary Northern Virginia, 1790–1812', *Business History Review*, 73:1 (1999), pp. 1–39. The General Assembly also incorporated the Bank of Richmond, but it never opened because of a lack of subscriptions. Also see Wright, *Origins of Commercial Banking*.

127. On banking in Virginia see G. T. Starnes, *Sixty Years of Branch Banking in Virginia* (New York: Macmillan, 1931), pp. 18–25. On Virginia banking also see A. G. Gruchy, *Supervision and Control of Virginia State Banks* (New York: Appleton-Century, 1937); D. R. Dewey, *State Banking before the Civil War* (Washington: Senate Documents, 1909–10); and W. L. Royall, *A History of Virginia Banks and Banking Prior to the Civil War* (New York and Washington: Neale, 1907). On state-issued paper currency see E. J. Ferguson, *The Power of the Purse: A History of American Public Finance, 1776–1790* (Chapel Hill: University of North Carolina Press, 1961) and M. Schweitzer, 'State-Issued Currency and the Ratification of the U.S. Constitution', *Journal of Economic History*, 49:2 (1989), pp. 311–22. On petitions for offices of the Bank of the United States see 'Bank of the United States: Petitions from Virginia Cities and Towns for Establishing Branches, 1791', *Virginia Magazine of History and Biography*, 8:3 (1901), pp. 287–95. For the Bank of Alexandria see Crothers, 'Banks and Economic Development'.

128. Starnes, *Sixty Years*, pp. 25–44.

129. *Journal of the House of Delegates*, 1818, p. 165.

130. Starnes, *Sixty Years*, pp. 12–13 and 59–60. On independent banks see R. Sylla, 'Forgotten Men of Money: Private Bankers in Early U. S. History', and discussion by Lance E. Davis, *Journal of Economic History*, 36:1 (1976), pp. 173–97 and L. Schweikart, 'Private Bankers in the Antebellum South', *Southern Studies*, 25:2, (1986), pp. 125–34. For a study of private banking in Virginia later in the nineteenth century see H. Bodenhorn, 'Private Banking in Antebellum Virginia: Thomas Brand & Sons of Petersburg', *Business History Review*, 71:4 (1997), pp. 513–42.

131. See *Laws of Virginia*, 1816, chs 9 and 10, and *Journal of the House of Delegates*, 1816–17, pp. 27–8. The firms given an extension were The Bank of the South Bank of the

Potomac, The Bank of Winchester in Virginia, The Farmers, and Mechanics, Bank of Harper's Ferry, The Farmers' Mechanics' and Merchants' Bank of Jefferson, The Charleston Manufacturing and Exporting Company, The Leesburg Union Company, The Loudoun Company for the Encouragement of Agriculture and Commerce, The Monongahela Farmers' Company of Virginia, The Ohio Company, The Saline Company, The Virginia Saline Bank, The Warrenton Company, and The Western Bank of Virginia. Also see Starnes, *Sixty Years*, pp. 59–60.

132. *Journal of the House of Delegates*, 1816–17, p. 28.

133. The committee recommended banks be chartered at Abingdon, Charlestown, Clarksburg, Dumfries, in Jefferson County, in Loudoun County, Martinsburg, Morgantown, Parkersburg, Romney, Staunton, Warrenton, West End, Wheeling, and Winchester. See Virginia General Assembly, House of Delegates, Committee to Whom were referred Sundry Petitions for the Establishment of Banks, *Report on Banks (presented to the House of Delegates on the 5th of January, 1815)* (Richmond VA, 1815), p. 15.

134. Starnes, *Sixty Years*, pp. 59–63.

135. *Report on Banks*, p. 10.

136. See Catterall, *The Second Bank*, pp. 17–23, and Smith, *Economic Aspects*, pp. 99–116.

137. See Fenstermaker, *American Commercial Banking*, Table 4, p. 13 and J. van Fenstermaker, J. E. Files and R. S. Herren, 'Monetary Statistics of New England, 1785–1837', *Journal of Economic History*, 44:2 (1984), Table 2B and p. 448.

138. Catterall, *Second Bank*, p. 4.

139. Smith, *Economic Aspects*, p. 101.

140. Smith, *Economic Aspects*, p. 100; Catterall, *Second Bank*, pp. 22, 39–50.

141. See J. P. Boyd, 'John Sergeant's Mission to Europe for the Second Bank of the United States: 1816–1817', *Pennsylvania Magazine of History and Biography*, 58:3 (1934), pp. 213–31; pp. 227–31.

142. *Acts of Congress*, Fourteenth Congress, First Session, vol. 1, p. 1440.

143. *American State Papers, Finance*, vol. 4, pp. 539–40.

144. Smith, *Economic Aspects*, pp. 104, 102.

145. Ibid., pp. 104–6.

146. Schur, 'Second Bank', pp. 118–34. Also see Catterall, *Second Bank*, pp. 33–4.

147. Temin, *Jacksonian Economy*, pp. 31–7 and Fraas, 'Second Bank of the United States', p. 451.

148. Smith, *Economic Aspects*, p. 104 and pp. 106–8; Catterall, *Second Bank*, p. 51 and *American State Papers, Finance*, vol. 3, p. 387.

149. Starnes, *Sixty Years*, p. 55.

150. *Niles' Register*, vol. 12, p. 143 and p. 398.

151. Smith, *Economic Aspects*, pp. 103–4. Also see *American State Papers*, vol. 4, pp. 539–40.

152. *Niles' Register*, vol. 11, p. 196

153. See Chapter 4 below for a detailed discussion of the state's exports and the Richmond commodity price index.

154. *Niles' Register*, vol. 12, p. 143 and p. 398.

155. For details of the issues regarding specie see Starnes, *Sixty Years*, pp. 65–6.

156. Perkins, 'Langdon Cheves', pp. 456–7.

157. *Historical Statistics*, Series Y-493.

158. Smith, *Economic Aspects*, p. 65.

159. See *Journal of the House of Delegates, 1824–1825*, Second Auditor's Report on Canal and Turnpike Companies.

160. For a discussion of the American navigation acts see chapter 4 below.

161. See R. Arthur, *History of Fort Monroe* (Fort Monroe, VA: The Coast Artillery School, 1930) and *American State Papers*, part 6, vol. 1, pp. 434–43, 480, 582.

162. For a discussion of Norfolk during the War of 1812 see Wertenbaker, *Norfolk*, pp. 120–6.

163. Starnes, *Sixty Years*, pp. 71–86. For a detailed discussion of reactions to the Panic of 1819, see Rothbard, *Panic of 1819*. Rothbard's chapters 3 and 5 provide information about banking. For reactions in Virginia, see pp. 66–7 and pp. 137–40.

164. For examples, see *Richmond Enquirer*, 25 May, 1 June, 4 June, 15 June, 16 November, and 18 December 1819 and 21 March, 28 March, and 18 April 1820.

165. *Journal of the House of Delegates, 1820–1821*, pp. 11–12.

166. *Richmond Enquirer*, 21 March 1820.

167. Rothbard, *Panic of 1819*, p. 140.

168. Starnes, *Sixty Years*, p. 70.

169. *Virginia Herald*, 16 February 1820 and *Richmond Enquirer*, 10 February 1820.

170. For a history of the American Navigation Acts see Benns, *American Struggle*.

171. *American State Papers, Commerce and Navigation*, vol. 2 (Washington: Gales and Seaton, 1834), p. 522.

172. *Norfolk Gazette and Public Ledger*, 15 February and 18 February 1815.

173. M. N. Stanard, *Richmond: Its People and Its Story* (Philadelphia, PA: Lippincott, 1923), p. 112.

174. *Norfolk Gazette and Public Ledger*, 16 March and 25 February 1815.

175. Benns, *American Struggle*, p. 29.

176. *Norfolk Gazette and Ledger*, 16 March 1815.

177. See Benns, *American Struggle*, pp. 29–86.

178. T. Weiss, 'U.S. Labour Force Estimates and Economic Growth, 1800–1860', in R. E. Gallman and J. J. Wallis (eds), *American Economic Growth and Standards of Living Before the Civil War* (Chicago, IL: University of Chicago Press for NBER, 1992), p. 22 and *1820 Census*.

179. I have been unable to locate complete state data for the period of this study. However, in 1817 and 1818 Virginia was the nation's leading tobacco producer, and exported 29.2 per cent (1817) and 29.3 per cent (1818) of US tobacco exports. *Richmond Enquirer*, 20 April 1819. In 1839, Virginia was still the leading tobacco producer, accounting for 34 percent of output, and the fourth leading wheat producer (after Ohio, Pennsylvania, and New York), contributing 12 percent of the crop. See J. MacGregor, *A Dictionary of Commerce and Commercial Navigation*, ed. H. Vethake, 2 vols. (Philadelphia, PA: Thomas Wardle, 1841).

180. *Richmond Enquirer*, 20 April 1819. Later data suggests that this ratio likely held for the period of this study. In the years 1835–6, 'inspections averaged 46,482 hogsheads and exports about 28,000' or about 60 percent of American exports. See Gray, *History of Agriculture*, vol. 2, pp. 753–4.

181. The index of British business activity declined from 91.1 in 1818 to 79.8 in 1819 (-12.4 per cent). The index then stayed almost level through 1821. Gayer, Rostow and Schwartz, *British Economy*, p. 354.

British imports of grain from the United States in thousands of Winchester quarters were:

1817	316.4
1818	187.6
1819	47.7
1820	91.9
1821	38.5
1822	6.2
1823	4.2

MacGregor, *Dictionary of Commerce*, vol. 1, p. 507.

182. See Benns, *American Struggle*. Also see Wertenbaker, *Norfolk*, ch. 7.

183. In addition to the Warren-Pearson and David-Solar price indexes utilized in Chapter 2, other examples of price indexes for this period include D. R. Adams, Jr., 'Prices and Wages in Maryland, 1750–1850', *Journal of Economic History*, 46:3 (1986), pp. 625–45; D. R. Adams, Jr., 'Prices and Wages in Antebellum America: The West Virginia Experience', *Journal of Economic History*, 52:1 (1992), pp. 206–16; Berry, *Western Prices*; A. Bezanson, R. Gray and M. Hussey, *Wholesale Prices in Philadelphia 1784–1861* (Philadelphia: University of Pennsylvania Press, 1937); A. H. Cole, *Wholesale Commodity Prices in the United States 1700–1861* (Cambridge, MA: Harvard University Press, 1935); P. G. M. Harris, 'Inflation and Deflation in Early America, 1634–1860', *Social Science History*, 20:4 (1996), pp. 469–505; W. B. Rothenberg, 'A Price Index for Rural Massachusetts, 1750–1855', *Journal of Economic History*, 39:4 (1979), pp. 975–1001, and G. R. Taylor, 'Wholesale Commodity Prices at Charleston, South Carolina, 1796–1861', *Journal of Economic and Business History*, 4:4 (1932), pp. 848–76.

184. Cole, *Wholesale Commodity Prices*, pp. 109–10.

185. See Table 2.2.

186. North, *Economic Growth*, p. 187.

187. For American and Virginia exports, see Table 4.1 and Chart 4.1. For US export prices see North, *Economic Growth*, pp. 273–91. For Virginia prices, see Chart 4.2. Berry, 'Rise of Flour Milling', p. 401.

188. Gray, *History of Agriculture*, p. 820.

189. A. O. Craven, *Soil Exhaustion as a Factor in the Agricultural History of Virginia and Maryland, 1606–1860* (Urbana: University of Illinois Studies in the Social Sciences, vol. 13, no. 1, 1925), p. 120.

190. C. F. Mercer in *Proceedings and Debates of the Virginia State Convention of 1829–30* (Richmond, VA: Thomas Ritchie, 1830), p. 178.

191. Berry, 'Rise of Flour Milling', p. 401, and Ambler, *Sectionalism in Virginia*, p. 112.

192. 'This law would prevent any sale of property under execution unless the property sold for at least three-fourths of its "value" as appraised by a governmentally appointed commission' (Rothbard, *Panic of 1819*, p. 36).

193. During this period, minimum appraisal laws were approved in Indiana, Kentucky, Missouri, Ohio and Pennsylvania. Stay laws were passed in Illinois, Indiana, Kentucky,

Louisiana, Maryland, Missouri, Ohio, Tennessee and Vermont. See Rothbard, *Panic of 1819*, ch. 2.

194. Rothbard, *Panic of 1819*, pp. 24–30, 35–8.

195. U. B. Phillips, *American Negro Slavery: A Survey of the Supply, Employment and Control of Negro Labor as Determined by the Plantation Regime* (Baton Rouge: Louisiana State University Press, 1966), p. 370.

196. Shade, *Democratizing the Old Dominion*, p. 19, and S. Deyle, *Carry Me Back: The Domestic Slave Trade in American Life* (New York: Oxford University Press, 2005), p. 42.

197. For the impact of western development on prices of enslaved African Americans, see P. Passell and G. Wright, 'The Effects of Pre-Civil War Territorial Expansion on the Prices of Slaves', *Journal of Political Economy*, 80:6 (1972), pp. 1188–202, and L. Kotlikoff and S. Pinera, 'The Old South's Stake in the Inter-Regional Movement of Slaves, 1850–1860', *Journal of Economic History*, 37:2 (1977), pp. 434–50. Also see L. J. Kotlikoff, 'The Structure of Slave Prices in New Orleans, 1804–1862', *Economic Inquiry*, 17:4 (1979), pp. 496–518; H. Freudenberger and J. B. Pritchett, 'The Domestic United States Slave Trade: New Evidence', *Journal of Interdisciplinary History*, 21:3 (1991), pp. 447–77; J. B. Pritchett and H. Freudenberger, 'A Peculiar Sample: The Selection of Slaves for the New Orleans Market', *Journal of Economic History*, 52:1 (1992), pp. 109–27; J. B. Pritchett and R. M. Chamberlain, 'Selection in the Market for Slaves, New Orleans, 1830–1860', *Quarterly Journal of Economics*, 108:2 (1993), pp. 461–73; J. B. Pritchett, 'Quantitative Estimates of the United States Interregional Slave Trade, 1820–1860', *Journal of Economic History*, 61:2 (2001), pp. 467–75; B. T. Ewing, 'Price Transmission in the Antebellum Slave Markets: A Time Series Analysis', *Review of Regional Studies*, 32:2 (2002), pp. 275–92, and A. N. Coleman and W. K. Hutchinson, 'Trade Restrictions and Factor Prices: Slave Prices in Early Nineteenth Century US', Department of Economics, Vanderbilt University, Working Paper no. 05–W21 (2005).

198. Passell and Wright, 'Prices of Slaves', p. 1199, and Kotlikoff and Pinera, 'Movement of Slaves', p. 447.

199. Benjamin Brand Papers Virginia Historical Society (MSS B7332a 18–19). Caskaden purchased a Richmond retail license in the years 1814–17. He may have purchased a license in earlier years; however, the earlier records are not available.

200. Letter dated 27 March 1819, Marshall Papers, College of William and Mary.

201. Letter dated 24 June 1819, Haxall Family Papers, Virginia Historical Society (Mss H3203d 3203).

202. The actual impact on merchant activity of the decline in merchant license revenue depends upon the composition of firms that drop from the market. If they are mostly small, marginal retailers, the overall impact might not be as dramatic as the figures suggest. Evidence from the 1930s suggests small firms in fact are hit disproportionally by the debt-deflation mechanism. See Bernanke, 'Nonmonetary Effects', pp. 260–1.

203. *Acts Passed at a General Assembly of the Commonwealth of Virginia, 1815–1816*, p. 4; *1816–17*, p. 3; *1817–1818*, p. 4; *1818–1819*, p. 4; *1819–1820*, p. 4; *1820–1821*, p. 4, *1821–1822*, p. 4.

204. *Acts Passed at a General Assembly of the Commonwealth of Virginia, 1822–1823*, p. 4; *1823–1824*, p. 4.

205. Retail licenses rose slightly from 233 in 1822 to 235 in 1823 while wholesale licenses fell from twenty-nine in 1822 to twenty-two in 1823.

206. See Table 5.6 below. During the same period only two purchasers of wholesale licenses in Richmond had been issued retail licenses in the city in any prior year for which data are available (two of forty-three or 4.6 percent).

207. For some insights regarding data sources for the antebellum period see P. R. Knights, 'City Directories as Aids to Antebellum Urban Studies: A Research Note', *Historical Methods Newsletter*, 2:4 (1969), pp. 1–10. Also see R. H. Steckel, 'Census Manuscript Schedules Matched with Property Tax Lists: A Source of Information on Long-term Trends in Wealth Inequality', *Historical Methods*, 27 (1994), pp. 71–85, and P. R. Knights, *The Plain People of Boston, 1820–1860: A Study in City Growth* (New York: Oxford University Press, 1971).

208. The following notation is derived from T. Dunne, Mark J. Roberts and Larry Samuelson, 'Patterns of Firm Entry and Exit in U. S. Manufacturing Industries', *RAND Journal of Economics*, 19:4 (1988), pp. 257–77; p. 502.

209. It is possible that variations in spelling could lead to license holders being linked where no link existed. This would lead to an understating of turnover. To avoid such a problem, a very conservative approach was taken to linking names when spelling variations were present. Names were linked only when one or two letters in the last name were different and the first name (or initial) and middle initial, if given, were the same. Likewise, names were linked when the last name was spelled the same way but there was a one- or two-letter variation in the first name or if an initial or initials were given one year and a first name that matched the first initial the other.

210. For an analysis of partnerships later in this study, in each of these cases a partnership is considered to have dissolved.

211. *City Directories of the United States, 1860–1901* (Woodbridge, CT: Research Publications, 1983), which includes entries before 1860, and D. N. Spears, *Biography of American Directories Through 1860* (Worcester: American Antiquarian Society, 1961) were checked for Virginia directories of the period studied. No others were found.

212. The fifteen include one each of the following: china merchant, clothing store, fancy glass store, hardware, hatter, high constable, lumber house, manufacturer of tobacco, miller, milliner, rope maker, shoemaker, shop, tanner and courier, and tailor.

213. A good summary of the vast literature and many issues concerning the entry and exit of firms is J. R. Baldwin, *The Dynamics of Industrial Competition: A North American Perspective* (Cambridge: Cambridge University Press, 1995), chs 1–3. Much of the literature concerns manufacturing firms.

214. Information regarding various aspects of how merchants of this period operated is found in S. W. Bruchy, *Robert Oliver, Merchant of Baltimore* (Baltimore, MD: Johns Hopkins Press, 1956) and E. Tooker, *Nathan Trotter: Philadelphia Merchant, 1787–1853* (Cambridge, MA: Harvard University Press, 1955). For a discussion of the role of the country store in providing merchandise, marketing farm crops, and providing credit and exchange see L. E. Atherton, *The Southern Country Store, 1800–1860* (Baton Rouge: Louisiana State University Press, 1949), particularly chs 3, 5, and 6. A discussion of the operation of a Pittsylvania County, Virginia merchant family named Grasty is found on pp. 72–3, 110–11 and 177, and details of credit terms on

which they obtained goods on p. 118. The impact of the Panic of 1819 on the inter-dependent network of debt and obligation in frontier Alabama is discussed in Dupre, *Transforming the Cotton Frontier*, pp. 49–57. Insights regarding bank credit at this time are provided in Virginia, General Assembly, *Report on Banks*. The report indicates, 'If the accounts of any American bank be examined, it will be seen that more than one half of its outstanding debts are found on what is called *standing accommodations*; that is the discounted notes which the Banks may, but it is understood, will not call in at the end of sixty days. Much of that debt will be found to have arisen from assurances, on the part of the bank, that the actual payment of it, will not be required for many months, and some part of it, for several years.' The report goes on to indicate, 'The capital adventured, is usually insured against accidents of the voyage in which it is invested; the payment of the note or bond, on which it is obtained, is endorsed by approved security, and new endorsers may be required, every sixty days, should a change of fortune be discovered or suspected by the bank in the circumstances of the drawer or endorser' (p. 10).

215. The following model is a simplification of the model developed in T. J. Holmes and J. A. Schmitz, Jr., 'On the Turnover of Business Firms and Business Managers', *Journal of Political Economy*, 103:5 (1995), pp. 1005–38. See pp. 1010–24 in particular.

216. Individuals managing businesses may also decide to sell. However, the data for this study does not allow the determination of when a business is sold or the identity of the purchaser. Thus, if a business is sold the seller is considered to have exited and the purchaser appears as a new entrant. Because this study deals with licenses, this situation presents no problems. However, as discussed earlier, to the extent licenses serve as a proxy for firms, this will lead to an overstating of the exit and entry of firms in any one period.

217. Bernanke, 'Nonmonetary Effects', p. 261.

218. Data for the years in which records are available from the combined counties are provided below:

Number of Counties	Year and Number of Licenses					
	1817	1818	1819	1820	1821	1822
5	141	137	136			
4	134	128	129	122		
2	92	91	89	92	95	103

219. In this case a license holder is considered to have continued from 1817 through 1819. Between 1819 and 1820 an exit occurs and between 1820 and 1821 a re-entry. The license holder then continues through the end of the study.

220. In this case a wholesale license holder exits between 1818 and 1819, re-enters in 1820, and continues through the end of the study.

221. As discussed earlier, adjusting for the possible underreporting of licenses during the period may be accomplished by assuming that any license holders that drop out and then return have in reality remained in business each year in between. Thus, a license holder who failed to purchase a license in any year but did so in a subsequent year is considered to have continued operating and simply been missed by the commissioner of the revenue.

222. Identifying partnerships from the tax list is a problem. For this study a partnership is defined as a license issued to at least two distinct individuals. Their last names may be

different or the same, but it must be clear that at least two individuals are associated with the license being issued. Thus, the more common x and company or the occasional x and son(s) which might be partnerships are not included.

223. N. R. Lamoreaux, 'The Partnership Form of Organization: Its Popularity in Early-Nineteenth-Century Boston' in C. E. Wright and K. P. Viens (eds), *Entrepreneurs: The Boston Business Community, 1700–1850* (Boston: Massachusetts Historical Society distributed by Northeastern University Press, 1997), pp. 269–95.

224. Ibid., pp. 293, 270–80.

225. The partnership continuity rate PCR(t-1) = PNC(t-1) / PNT(t-1) where PNC(t-1) is the number of partnerships that continue between years t-1 and t and PNT(t-1) is the total number of partnerships in year t-1.

226. The continuity rates for individual (non-partnership) wholesale license holders are 0.500 (1817/18), 0.462 (1818/19), 0.625 (1819/20), 0.636 (1820/21), 0.667 (1821/22), and 0.571 (1822/23).

227. The continuity rates for individual (non-partnership) retail license holders are 0.773 (1817/18), 0.683 (1818/19), 0.655 (1819/20), 0.656 (1820/21), 0.611 (1821/22), and 0.531 (1822/23).

228. Following Lamoreaux, Richmond partnerships were considered to have survived if most or all of their 1818 partners were listed as members of the same firm in 1822. Firms were considered to have dissolved if they were not listed in 1822 but at least one of their members was. If none of the 1818 partners could be located in the 1822 list, the partnership was considered to have disappeared. See Lamoreaux, 'Partnership', p. 282.

229. The wholesale partnerships that survived are: Brockenbrough and Harvie, Ellis and Allen, Lucke and Sizer, Morris and Jones, Otis and Dunlap, and Ralston and Pleasants. The retail partnerships are: Charter and Williams, J. and S. Cosby, Thomas and Robert Crouch, Galt and Johnson, Hayes and Lormer, Jude and Meure, David and William Kyle, H. and R. Kyle, J. and O. Williams, and Wortham and McGruder.

230. The wholesale partnerships that dissolved (and surviving partner) are: Ludham and Allen (Ludham); Pulling and Palmer (Palmer); Sheppard and Webb (Webb); and Smith and Riddle (Smith). The retail partnerships are: Colton and Reed (Colton); French and Alann (French); B. and J. Hollings (B. Hollings); F. and M. Lacy (Fleming Lacy); Mitchell and Vail (Mitchell); A. and D. Nisbet (David Nisbet); J. and S. Parkhill (Samuel Parkhill); and Rehine and Judah (Zalma Rehine).

231. There were no major economic downturns in the period 1845–50, a period that witnessed the war with Mexico. A mild slowdown occurred after the war, but strong prosperity was the case by the beginning of the next decade. See W. L. Thorp, *Business Annals* (New York: National Bureau of Economic Research, 1926), pp. 124–5.

232. Partnerships as a percentage of retail license holders for Spotsylvania and Richmond are:

	1817	1818	1819	1820	1821	1822	1823
Spotsylvania	8.6	7.2	12.9	10.8	4.7	9.5	6.3
Richmond	17.6	15.0	17.3	18.0	15.8	11.6	9.4

233. However, keep in mind that retail merchants were generally financed by wholesalers who in turn used their own capital and/or bank loans. In addition, private banks operated in Virginia, particularly in areas not served by the state-chartered banks, but

their operations were being constrained at this time. See Chapter 3 above. For later in the antebellum period, see Bodenhorn, 'Private Banking', pp. 513–42.

234. See Gayer, Rostow and Schwartz, *British Economy,* and Post, *Subsistence Crisis.*

235. L. Marco, 'Faillites et Crisis Economiques en France au XIXe Siecle', *Annales ESC,* 2:2 (1989), pp. 355–78.

236. I. P. H. Duffy, *Bankruptcy and Insolvency in London during the Industrial Revolution* (New York: Garland, 1985), p. 378.

237. *Historical Statistics,* Business Failure Rate, Series V23.

238. A. D. H. Kaplan, *Small Business: Its Place and Problems* (New York: McGraw-Hill, 1948), pp. 55–7.

239. G. W. Starr and G. A. Steiner, 'Births and Deaths of Retail Stores in Indiana, 1929–1937', *Dun's Review,* 48 (January 1940), p. 27.

240. R. G. Hutchinson, A. R. Hutchinson and M. Newcomer, 'A Study in Business Mortality – Length of Life of Business Enterprises in Poughkeepsie, N.Y. 1843–1936', *American Economic Review,* 28:3 (September 1938), pp. 497–514 and R. G. Hutchinson, A. R. Hutchinson and M. Newcomer, 'Business Life and Death in a Hudson River Town', *Dun's Review,* 47 (June 1939), pp. 12–18.

241. J. Popkin and Company, 'Business Survival Rates by Age Cohorts of Business' (United States Small Business Administration, RS Number 122, 1989), Tables 1 and 2.

242. Holmes and Schmitz, 'Turnover', pp. 1008–9 and Table 1.

243. J. W. Tyler, 'Persistence and Change within the Boston Business Community', in C. E. Wright and K. P. Viens (eds), *Entrepreneurs: The Boston Business Community, 1700–1850* (Boston: Massachusetts Historical Society distributed by Northeastern University Press, 1997), pp. 97–119.

244. T. M. Doerflinger, *A Vigorous Spirit of Enterprise: Merchants and Economic Development in Revolutionary Philadelphia* (Chapel Hill: Published for the Institute of Early American History and Culture by the University of North Carolina Press, 1986), pp. 248–9.

245. E. C. Papenfuse, *In Pursuit of Profit: The Annapolis Merchants in the Era of the American Revolution, 1763–1805* (Baltimore, MD: Johns Hopkins University Press, 1975), p. 175.

246. See Office of Advocacy, U.S. Small Business Administration, http://app1.sba.gov/faqs/faqindex.cfm?areaID=24. Source, US Bureau of the Census.

247. *Journal of the House of Delegates 1819,* p. 6. For more about the emphasis on character and morality in response to the hard times generated by the depression see S. A. Kidd, 'The Search for Moral Order: The Panic of 1819 and the Culture of the Early American Republic' (Phd dissertation, University of Missouri-Columbia, 2002).

248. R. M. Saunders, 'Modernization and the Political Process: Governmental Principles and Practices in Richmond, Virginia, from the Revolution to the Civil War', *Southern Studies,* 24 (1985), pp. 117–42; p. 124.

249. S. Lebsock, *The Free Women of Petersburg: Status and Culture in a Southern Town, 1784–1860* (New York: Norton, 1984), p. 213.

250. Ibid.

251. See Saunders, 'Modernization'. Also see E. Irish, '"Neglect, Delay, and Tightfistedness:" Poor Relief in Antebellum Richmond', unpublished paper. Irish points out that in Richmond 'Overseer of the Poor funding represented an increasingly smaller percent-

age of the city's expenditures during the last thirty years of the antebellum period.' (p. 6). Suzanne Lebsock indicates that in Petersburg, 'even as late as the middle 1850s, despite substantial population growth, annual spending for the poor did not come close to the amounts spent in the crisis years of the early 1820s'. Lebsock, *Free Women*, p. 214.

252. Saunders, 'Modernization', p. 125.

253. W. W. Hening, *Statutes at Large; Being a Collection of All the Laws of Virginia from the First Session of the Legislature in the Year 1619*, 13 vols (New York: Published for the author, 1819–23), vol. 1, p. 159 and pp. 183–4, vol. 2, p. 269. On the colonial Poor Laws see H. Mackey, 'The Operation of the English Old Poor Law in Colonial Virginia', *Virginia Magazine of History and Biography*, 73:1 (1965), pp. 29–40 and M. W. McCartney, 'Virginia's Workhouses for the Poor: Care for "Divers Idle and Disorderly Persons"', *North American Archaelogist*, 8:4 (1987), pp. 287–303.

254. Mackey, 'Operation', pp. 30 and pp. 33–4.

255. Hening, *Statutes*, vol. 6, p. 477. Also see Mackey, 'Operation', p. 39. McCartney, 'Virginia's Workhouses' describes these colonial poorhouses.

256. Mackey, 'Operation', p. 40; Hening, *Statutes*, vol. 9, p. 527 and vol. 10, pp. 288–90.

257. J. Yates, *Report of the Secretary of State in 1824 on the Relief and Settlement of the Poor*, app. B, pt. 2, sec. 1, Virginia, reprinted in D. Rothman (ed.), *The Almshouse Experience* (New York: Arno Press and the *New York Times*, 1971), p. 1102.

258. *The Revised Code of the Laws of Virginia* (Richmond, VA: Ritchie, 1819), C. 239, pp. 264–79. For a general discussion of the administration of the poor laws in six antebellum southern states see J. W. Ely, Jr., '"There are Few Subjects in Political Economy of Greater Difficulty": The Poor Laws of the Antebellum South', *American Bar Foundation Research Journal*, 10:4 (1985), pp. 849–79.

259. *Revised Code*, pp. 264–79.

260. Ibid.

261. *Supplement to the Revised Code of the Laws of Virginia* (Richmond: Shepherd, 1833), pp. 496–7. Records of the Auditor of Public Accounts, Archives and Manuscripts, Library of Virginia.

262. Because annual population for each city and county is not available, annual population was interpolated from the 1810, 1820 and 1830 censuses. Population was assumed to increase at a constant rate between each census. The number of persons receiving relief each year, either indoor or outdoor, was obtained from the reports by Overseers of the Poor to the Auditor of Public Records discussed above.

263. See R. M. Usry, 'The Overseers of the Poor in Accomack, Pittsylvania, and Rockingham Counties, 1787–1802' (MA thesis, Department of Economics, College of William and Mary, 1960).

264. Fauquier County, Minutes, Overseers of the Poor, Virginia State Archives. J. D. Watkinson, '"Fit Objects of Charity": Community, Race, Faith, and Welfare in Antebellum Lancaster County, Virginia, 1817–1860', *Journal of the Early Republic*, 21:1 (2001), pp. 41–70. Table 2, and data provided by Watkinson.

265. The year 1817 is used to begin the sample of eighteen because beginning with the year 1816 would mean one-third of the sample would be lost. Keeping the sample size as large as possible is important when dealing with relatively small numbers of units.

266. The Appendix to this chapter provides details regarding the data available by county and city.

267. Free blacks were 3.5 percent of the total population in 1820 and 5.8 percent of the free (nonenslaved) population (see Table 1.8). The mean number of free blacks receiving outdoor relief as a percentage of the mean total receiving outdoor relief was 7.2 per cent for 1816–18, 8.6 per cent for 1819–21, and 6.8 per cent for 1822–8. Thus, free blacks appear to have been overrepresented relative to their proportion of the population among those receiving outdoor relief. This is not surprising given the limited opportunities available to many free blacks.

268. J. U. Hannon, 'The Generosity of Antebellum Poor Relief', *Journal of Economic History*, 44:3 (September 1984), pp. 810–21; p. 810. As Hannon suggests, this measure is 'influenced by trends in both expenditures per recipient and the number of recipients.'

269. Expenditures per recipient should be standardized for the length of time relief was provided. However, information regarding the duration individuals received poor relief is not available. Thus, for this study, expenditures per recipient is simply the appropriate expenditure measure in each city or county divided by the number of individuals receiving relief.

270. J. U. Hannon, 'Explaining Nineteenth Century Dependency Rates: Interplay of Life Cycles and Labor Markets', unpublished paper, Department of Economics, St. Mary's College, 1996. Also see L. L. Kiesling and R. A. Margo, 'Explaining the Rise in Antebellum Pauperism: New Evidence' (National Bureau of Economic Research Working Papers Series on Historical Factors in Long Run Growth, Historical Paper 92, 1996) and their 'Explaining the Rise in Antebellum Pauperism, 1850–1860: New Evidence', *Quarterly Review of Economics and Finance*, 37:2 (1997), pp. 405–17.

271. R. E. Cray, Jr. *Paupers and Poor Relief in New York and its Rural Environs, 1700–1830* (Philadelphia, PA: Temple University Press, 1988), p. 4.

272. Kiesling and Margo, 'Explaining', working paper, p. 11.

273. In addition to private benevolence organizations, the poor could turn to kinship networks and neighbors or could move looking for better opportunities. See G. S. Murray, 'Poverty and its Relief in the Antebellum South: Perceptions and Realities in Three Selected Cities Charleston, Nashville and New Orleans' (Phd dissertation, Memphis State University, 1991), pp. 260–4.

274. P. F. Clement, *Welfare and the Poor in the Nineteenth-Century City: Philadelphia, 1800–1854* (Rutherford, NJ: Fairleigh Dickinson University Press, 1985), p. 52.

275. Ibid., p. 49.

276. Mohl, *Poverty in New York*, pp. 89–90.

277. Hannon, 'Generosity', p. 812 and J. U. Hannon, 'Poor Relief Policy in Antebellum New York State: The Rise and Decline of the Poor House', *Explorations in Economic History*, 22:3 (1885), pp. 244–56; pp. 238–9.

278. Mohl, *Poverty*, p. 92.

279. Hannon, 'Poor Relief', pp. 237.

280. D. J. Rothman, *The Discovery of the Asylum: Social Order and Disorder in the New Republic* (Boston, MA: Little, Brown and Company, 1971), p.159, and Cray, *Paupers and Poor Relief*, p. 138.

281. M. Creech. *Three Centuries of Poor Law Administration: A Study of Legislation in Rhode Island* (New York: Columbia University Press, 1936), pp. 185–6.

282. L. J. Piccarello, 'Social Structures and Public Welfare Policy in Danvers, MA 1750–1850', *Essex Institute Historical Collection*, 118:4 (1982), pp. 248–63; pp. 254–5.

283. Mohl, *Poverty* p. 159.

284. D. C. Vogt, 'Poor Relief in Frontier Mississippi', *Journal of Mississippi History*, 51:2 (1989), pp. 181–99; p. 191.

285. Dupre, *Transforming the Cotton Frontier*, p. 158.

286. Murray, 'Poverty and its Relief', pp. 166–8.

287. B. L. Bellows. *Benevolence among Slaveholders: Assisting the Poor in Charleston 1670–1860* (Baton Rouge: Louisiana State University Press, 1993), p. 126.

288. See Clement, *Welfare and the Poor*, ch. 6, particularly p. 142. Also see Bellows, *Benevolence* and V. F. Bonelli, *The Response of Public and Private Philanthropy to the Panic of 1819 in New York City* (Pittsburgh, PA: Dorrance Publishing, 2003).

289. Murray, 'Poverty and its Relief', p. 170.

290. J. C. Dann, 'Humanitarian Reform and Organized Benevolence in the Southern United States, 1780–1830' (Phd dissertation, College of William and Mary, 1975), Appendix B.

291. Dann, 'Humanitarian Reform', Appendix B and Lebsock, *Free Women*, p. 217.

292. Rothman, *Discovery of the Asylum*, pp. 155–6.

293. B. J. Klebaner, *Public Poor Relief in America, 1790–1860* (New York: Arno, 1976), p. 5.

294. Mohl, *Poverty*, chs 15 and 16.

295. *Journal of the House of Delegates, 1830–1831*, Doc. No. 9, 'Report or abstract of various returns, made to the auditor of public accounts, by the clerks or agents of the overseers of the poor; prepared in compliance with resolutions of the house of delegates, of the 18th and 30th December, 1829.'

296. Ibid.

297. Ely, 'Poor Laws of the Antebellum South', note 54; *The Laws Now in Force Which Relate to the Duties of the Overseers of the Poor*, app. 34 (Richmond: Ritchie, 1832) and *Code of Virginia*, 2nd edn (Richmond, VA: Ritchie, Dunnavant, and Co., 1860), p. 294.

298. Larson, *Internal Improvement*, p. 127, and pp. 126–9.

299. Wilentz, *American Democracy*, p. 213 and Larson, *Internal Improvement*, p. 131.

300. Wilentz, *American Democracy*, p. 230 and p. 240. Also see G. Moore, *The Missouri Controversy, 1819–1821* (Lexington: University of Kentucky Press, 1953).

301. See *Richmond Enquirer*, June–November 1819. Also see Rothbard, *Panic of 1819*, pp. 137–40.

302. *Richmond Enquirer*, 25 June 1819, 20 July 1819 and 19 November 1819.

303. *Journal of the House of Delegates*, 1820–1, pp. 10–12.

304. Rothbard, *Panic of 1819*, p. 158.

305. Ibid., chs 3, 4, 5, p. 141 and p. 158.

306. Ibid., pp. 59, 91–7 and 110. Also see Parks, 'Felix Grundy', pp. 20–32.

307. Rothbard, *Panic of 1819*, p. 129, p. 135 and Ch. 4.

308. Wilentz, *American Democracy*, pp. 215–16, Rothbard, *Panic of 1819*, p. 59, and Bodenhorn, *History of Banking*, pp. 168–77.

309. Starnes, *Sixty Years*, pp. 73–6.
310. Fenstermaker, *American Commercial Banking*, p. 183. On the Bank War, see Temin, *Jacksonian Economy*, and R. V. Remini, *Andrew Jackson and the Bank War* (New York: Norton, 1967).
311. Rothbard, *Panic of 1819*, p, 32. See Rohrbough, *Land Office Business*.
312. Rothbard, *Panic of 1819*, p. 26. For the Federal Bankruptcy Act of 1841, see E. J. Balleisen, *Navigating Failure: Bankruptcy and Commercial Society in Antebellum America* (Chapel Hill: University of North Carolina Press, 2001).
313. Rothbard, *Panic of 1819*, pp. 32, 40, and Wilentz, *American Democracy*, p. 209. The eastern states passing relief legislation were Maryland, New York, Rhode Island and Vermont. Those close to passage included Delaware, New Jersey, North Carolina and Virginia.
314. Rothbard, *Panic of 1819*, pp. 35–8.
315. Balleisen, *Navigating Failure*, p. 12.
316. S. Rockman, *Welfare Reform in the Early Republic: A Brief History with Documents* (Boston, MA: Bedford/St. Martins, 2003), pp. 10, 167 and 49.
317. See G. Himmelfarb, *The Idea of Poverty: England in the Early Industrial Age* (New York: Vintage, 1983); J. R. Poynter, *Society and Pauperism: English Ideas on Poor Relief, 1795–1834* (London: Routledge and Kagan Paul, 1969); G. R. Boyer, *An Economic History of the English Poor Law, 1750–1850* (Cambridge: Cambridge University Press, 1990); Murray, 'Poverty and its Relief', p. 21, and Rockman, *Welfare Reform*, pp. 169–70.
318. See [Anon.], 'Considerations on the Impolicy and Pernicious Tendency of the Poor Laws; with Remarks on the Report, of the Select Committee of the House of Commons upon them. And Suggestions for Improving the Condition of the Poor', *American Monthly Magazine and Critical Review*, 4:4 (1818), pp. 251–5; [Anon.], 'Annals of Pauperism', *Register of Pennsylvania*, 2:4 (9 August 1828), pp. 49–55; [Anon.], 'The English Poor Laws', *Albion, A Journal of News, Politics and Literature*, 2:4 (8 February 1832), p. 47 and E. Cocks, 'The Malthusian Theory in Pre-Civil War America: The Original Relation to the Universe', *Population Studies*, 20:3 (1967), p. 350.
319. Rockman, *Welfare Reform*, pp. 20–21.
320. J. Quincy, *Report of the Committee on the Pauper Laws of This Commonwealth* (1821), reprinted in Rothman (ed.), *Almshouse Experience*, pp. 2 and 3; Rockman, *Welfare Reform*, pp. 23 and 168 and [Anon.], 'Annals of Pauperism', p. 49.
321. Rockman, *Welfare Reform*, pp. 168 and 22; J. Yates, *Report of the Secretary of State in 1824 on the Relief and Settlement of the Poor*, reprinted in Rothman (ed.), *Almshouse Experience*, p. 1.
322. Yates, *Report*, pp. 939–63; 'An Act to Provide for the Establishment of County Poor-Houses', *Laws of the State of New York* (Albany, 1824), ch. 331, p. 382.
323. [Anon.], 'Annals of Pauperism', pp. 68–9.
324. *Report of the Committee Appointed by the Board of Guardians of the Poor of the City and Districts of Philadelphia, to Visit the Cities of Baltimore, New-York, Providence, Boston, and Salem* (Philadelphia, PA: Samuel Parker, 1827), reprinted in part in Rockman, *Welfare Reform*, pp. 126–30.

325. [Anon.], 'Poor Law', *Register of Pennsylvania*, 1 (24 May 1828), p. 326, and Rockman, *Welfare Reform*, p. 22.
326. Rockman, *Welfare Reform*, p. 22 and Hannon, 'Poor Relief Policy', pp. 233–56, 254.
327. Saunders, 'Modernization and the Political Process', p. 124.
328. Lebsock, *Free Women of Petersburg*, p. 213.
329. Rockman, *Welfare Reform*, pp. 26–7.
330. See Goodrich, 'Virginia System', pp. 355–87, Table 2. Also see Larson, *Internal Improvement*, pp. 91–6; J. Majewski, 'The Social Origins of the Market Revolution: Markets and Politics in Pennsylvania and Virginia, 1790–1860' (Phd dissertation University of California, Los Angles, 1998) and Majewski, *House Dividing*.
331. See Wertenbaker, *Norfolk*, p. 164.
332. See Benns, *American Struggle*, chs 4–6.
333. Larson, *Internal Improvement*, pp. 193, 6.
334. Rothbard, *Panic of 1819*, p. 159 and Stanwood, *Tariff Controversies*, pp. 160–78.
335. Rothbard, *Panic of 1819*, pp. 160–4; Stanwood, *Tariff Controversies*, pp. 180–93, and Shade, *Democratizing the Old Dominion*, p. 234. Also see J. L. Huston, 'Virtue Besieged: Virtue, Equality and the General Welfare in the Tariff Debates of the 1820s', *Journal of the Early Republic*, 14:4 (1994), pp. 523–47.
336. Wilentz, *American Democracy*, pp. 297, 298, 374, 388; Stanwood, *Tariff Controversies*, chs 8–12, Shade, *Democratizing the Old Dominion*, p. 234; Dupre, 'Panic of 1819', pp. 282–93 and Huston, 'Virtue Besieged'.
337. Wilentz, pp. 209, 252, 282, 293.
338. Shade, *Democratizing the Old Dominion*, pp. 55, 59, 63, 76, 77.
339. Brent Tarter raises the question of what role state ownership of significant shares of the Commonwealth's internal improvement companies and political leaders' personal interest in such companies played in Virginia's opposition to federal internal improvements. B. Tarter, 'The New Virginia Bookshelf', *Virginia Magazine of History and Biography*, 104:1 (1996), p. 42.
340. For example, see F. T. Miller, 'The Richmond Junto: The Secret All-Powerful Club – or Myth', *Virginia Magazine of History and Biography*, 99:1 (1991), pp. 63–80.
341. See for example, L. R. Gunn, *The Decline of Authority: Public Economic Policy and Political Development in New York State, 1800–1860* (Ithaca, NY: Cornell University Press, 1988) and T. A. Freyer, *Producers Versus Capitalists: Constitutional Conflict in Antebellum America* (Charlottesville: University Press of Virginia, 1994).
342. See W. J. Gilmore, *Reading Becomes a Necessity of Life: Material and Cultural Life in Rural New England, 1780–1835* (Knoxville: University of Tennessee Press, 1989) and J. V. Matthews, *Toward A New Society: American Thought and Culture 1800–1830* (Boston, MA: Twayne, 1991).
343. See G. R. Taylor, *The Transportation Revolution, 1815–1860* (New York: Holt, Rinehart and Winston, 1951); C. Goodrich, *Canals and American Economic Development* (New York: Columbia University Press, 1961); H. Bodenhorn, 'Capital Mobility and Financial Integration in Antebellum America', *Journal of Economic History*, 53:2 (1992), pp. 585–610 and G. Bjork, 'The Weaning of the American Economy', *Journal of Economic History*, 24:4 (1964), pp. 541–60.

BIBLIOGRAPHY

Manuscripts

Benjamin Brand Papers, Virginia Historical Society.

Faquier County, Minutes, Overseers of the Poor, Archives and Manuscripts, Library of Virginia.

Haxall Family Papers, Virginia Historical Society.

Marshall Papers, College of William and Mary.

Records of the Auditor of Public Accounts, Archives and Manuscripts, Library of Virginia.

Newspapers and Journals

Albion, A Journal of News, Politics and Literature (New York).

American Monthly Magazine and Critical Review (New York).

Niles' Register (Baltimore).

Norfolk Gazette and Ledger.

Register of Pennsylvania.

Richmond Enquirer.

Virginia Herald (Fredericksburg).

Primary Sources

Acts Passed at a General Assembly of the Commonwealth of Virginia, various years.

[Anon.], 'Considerations on the Impolicy and Pernicious Tendency of the Poor Laws; with Remarks on the Report, of the Select Committee of the House of Commons upon them. And Suggestions for Improving the Condition of the Poor', *American Monthly Magazine and Critical Review,* 4:4 (1818), pp. 251–5.

—, 'Poor Law', *Register of Pennsylvania*, 1 (24 May 1828), p. 326

—, 'Annals of Pauperism', *Register of Pennsylvania*, 2:4 (9 August 1828), pp. 49–55.

—, 'The English Poor Laws', *Albion, A Journal of News, Politics and Literature*, 2:4 (8 February 1832), p. 47.

American State Papers, United States, Congress (Washington: Gales and Seaton, 1832–1861).

Census for 1820, United States, Department of State (Washington: Gales and Seaton, 1821).

Code of Virginia, 2nd edn (Richmond, VA: Ritchie, Dunnavant, and Co., 1860).

Coxe, T., *A View of the United States of America in a Series of Papers Written at Various Times, in the Years between 1787 and 1794* (Philadelphia, PA: Hall and Wrigley and Berriman, 1794).

Gouge, W. M., *A Short History of Paper Money and Banking in the United States* (Philadelphia, PA: n.p., 1833).

Hening, W. W., *Statutes at Large; Being a Collection of All the Laws of Virginia from the First Session of the Legislature in the Year 1619*, 13 vols (New York: Published for the author, 1819–23).

Historical Statistics of the United States: Colonial Times to 1970 (Washington: Bureau of the Census, 1975).

Jefferson, T., *The Works of Thomas Jefferson*, ed. P. L. Ford, 12 vols (New York: Putnam, 1904–5).

Journal of the House of Delegates (Richmond, VA: Thomas Ritchie, various dates).

Laws of the State of New York (Albany, 1824).

The Laws Now in Force Which Relate to the Duties of the Overseers of the Poor (Richmond, VA: Thomas Ritchie, 1832).

Madison, J., *The Writings of James Madison*, ed. G. Hunt, 9 vols (New York: Putnam, 1900–10).

Proceedings and Debates of the Virginia State Convention of 1829–30 (Richmond, VA: Thomas Ritchie, 1830).

The Public Statutes at Large of the United States of America, by authority of Congress (Boston, MA: Charles C. Little and James Brown, 1845–67).

'Report or abstract of various returns, made to the auditor of public accounts, by the clerks or agents of the overseers of the poor; prepared in compliance with resolutions of the house of delegates, of the 18th and 30th December, 1829', *Journal of the House of Delegates, 1830–1831*, Document no. 9.

'Report of the Committee on Agriculture and Manufactures', *Journal of the House of Delegates 1831–32*, Document no. 31.

The Revised Code of the Laws of Virginia (Richmond, VA: Ritchie, 1819).

Rochefoucauld-Liancourt, F-A-Frederic, duc de la, *Travels Through the United States of North America, the Country of the Iroquois, and Upper Canada in the Years 1795, 1796, and 1797; with an Authentic Account of Lower Canada* (London: R. Phillips, 1799).

Secretary of State of the United States. *Digest of Accounts of Manufacturing Establishments* (Washington: Gales and Seaton, 1823).

Supplement to the Revised Code of the Laws of Virginia (Richmond, VA: Shepherd, 1833).

United States, Census Office, *4th Census*, 1820 (Washington: Gales and Seaton, 1821).

United States Congress, House, *Bank of the United States*, House Executive Document 147, Twenty-Second Congress, First session, 1835.

—, *Condition of State Banks*, House Document 79, January 8, 1838, Twenty-Fifth Congress, Second Session.

United States Congress, Senate, *Statement of the Appropriations and Expenditures for Public Buildings, Rivers and Harbors, Forts, Arsenals, Armories and Other Public Works from 1789–1882*, Senate Document 196, Forty-Seventh Congress, First Session, 1883.

Virginia General Assembly, House of Delegates, Committee to Whom were referred Sundry Petitions for the Establishment of Banks, *Report on Banks (Presented to the House of Delegates on the 5th of January, 1815)* (Richmond, VA, 1815).

Yates, J., *Report of the Secretary of State in 1824 on the Relief and Settlement of the Poor*, app. B, pt.2, sec. 1, Virginia reprinted in D. J. Rothman (ed.), *The Almshouse Experience* (New York: Arno Press and the *New York Times*, 1971).

Secondary Sources

Adams, D. R., 'American Neutrality and Prosperity, 1793–1808: A Reconsideration', *Journal of Economic History*, 40:1 (1980), pp. 713–38.

—, 'Prices and Wages in Maryland, 1750–1850', *Journal of Economic History*, 46:3 (1986), pp. 625–45.

—, 'Prices and Wages in Antebellum America: The West Virginia Experience', *Journal of Economic History*, 52:1 (1992), pp. 206–16.

Adams, S. P., *Old Dominion Industrial Commonwealth: Coal, Politics, and Economy in Antebellum America* (Baltimore, MD: Johns Hopkins University Press, 2004).

Albion, R. G., 'New York and its Disappointed Rivals', *Journal of Economic and Business History*, 3:4 (1930–1), pp. 602–29.

—, *The Rise of the Port of New York 1815–1860* (New York: Scribner's, 1939).

Ambler, C. H., *Sectionalism in Virginia from 1776 to 1861* (Chicago, IL: University of Chicago Press, 1910).

—, *Thomas Ritchie: A Study in Virginia Politics* (Richmond, VA: Bell, 1913).

Anderson, H. M., 'Frontier Economic Problems in Missouri, 1815–1828', *Missouri Historical Review*, 24:1 (1939), pp. 38–70 and 24:2 (1940), pp. 182–203.

Arthur, R., *History of Fort Monroe* (Fort Monroe, VA: The Coast Artillery School, 1930).

Atack, J., and P. Passell, *A New Economic View of American History from Colonial Times to 1940*, 2nd edn (New York: Norton, 1994).

Atherton, L. E., 'Auctions as a Threat to American Business in the Eighteen Twenties and Thirties', *Bulletin of the Business Historical Society*, 11:6 (1937), pp. 104–7.

—, *The Southern Country Store, 1800–1860* (Baton Rouge: Louisiana State University Press, 1949).

Baldwin, J. R., *The Dynamics of Industrial Competition: A North American Perspective* (Cambridge: Cambridge University Press, 1995).

Balleisen, E. J., *Navigating Failure: Bankruptcy and Commercial Society in Antebellum America* (Chapel Hill: University of North Carolina Press, 2001).

'Bank of the United States: Petitions from Virginia Cities and Towns for Establishing Branches, 1791', *Virginia Magazine of History and Biography*, 8:3 (1901), pp. 287–95.

Barnes, D. G., *A History of the English Corn Laws, from 1660–1846* (New York: A. M. Kelley, 1961).

Baron, W. R., 'Retrieving American Climate History: A Bibliographic Essay', *Agricultural History*, 63:2 (1989), pp. 7–35.

Bellows, B. L., *Benevolence among Slaveholders: Assisting the Poor in Charleston 1670–1860* (Baton Rouge: Louisiana State University Press, 1993).

Benns, F. L., *The American Struggle for the British West India Carrying-Trade, 1815–1830* (Bloomington: Indiana University Studies, Vol. 10, 1923).

Bernanke, B. S., 'Nonmonetary Effects of the Financial Crisis in Propagation of the Great Depression', *American Economic Review*, 73:3 (1983), pp. 257–76.

Bernanke, B. S, and M. Gertler, 'Agency Costs, Net Worth, and Business Fluctuations', *American Economic Review*, 79:1 (1989), pp. 14–31.

—, 'Financial Fragility and Economic Performance', *Quarterly Journal of Economics*, 105:1 (1990), pp. 87–114.

Berry, T. S., *Western Prices Before 1861* (Cambridge, MA: Harvard University Press, 1943).

—, 'The Rise of Flour Milling in Richmond', *Virginia Magazine of History and Biography*, 78:4 (1970), pp. 387–408.

—, *Revised Annual Estimates of American Gross National Product: Preliminary Annual Estimates of Four Major Components of Demand 1789–1889* (Richmond, VA: Bostwick Press, 1978).

—, *Production and Population Since 1789: Revised GNP Series in Constant Dollars* (Richmond, VA: Bostwick Press, 1988).

Bezanson, A, R. Gray and M. Hussey, *Wholesale Prices in Philadelphia 1784–1861* (Philadelphia: University of Pennsylvania Press, 1937).

Bjork, G., 'The Weaning of the American Economy', *Journal of Economic History*, 24:4 (1964), pp. 541–60.

Blackson, R. M., 'The Panic of 1819 in Pennsylvania' (Phd dissertation, Pennsylvania State University, 1978).

—, 'Pennsylvania Banks and the Panic of 1819: A Reinterpretation', *Journal of the Early Republic*, 9:3 (1989), pp. 335–58.

Bodenhorn, H., 'Capital Mobility and Financial Integration in Antebellum America', *Journal of Economic History*, 52:3 (September 1992), pp. 585–610.

—, 'Private Banking in Antebellum Virginia: Thomas Branch and Sons of Petersburg', *Business History Review*, 71:4 (1997), pp. 513–42.

—, *A History of Banking in Antebellum America: Financial Markets and Economic Development in an Era of Nationbuilding* (Cambridge: Cambridge University Press, 2000).

Bonelli, V. F., 'The Response of Public and Private Philanthropy to the Panic of 1819 in New York City' (Phd dissertation, Fordham University, 1976).

—, *The Response of Public and Private Philanthropy to the Panic of 1819 in New York City* (Pittsburgh, PA: Dorrance Publishing, 2003).

Bordo, M. D., *Financial Crises* (Aldershot: Edward Elgar, 1992).

Bordo, M., and A. J. Schwartz (eds), *A Retrospective on the Classical Gold Standard: 1821–1931* (Chicago, IL: University of Chicago Press, 1984).

Bordo, M., C. Goldin and E. N. White, *The Defining Moment: The Great Depression and the American Economy in the Twentieth Century* (Chicago, IL: University of Chicago Press, 1998)

Bouton, T., 'Moneyless in Pennsylvania: Privatization and the Depression of the 1780s' in C. Matson (ed.), *The Economy of Early America: Historical Perspectives and New Directions* (University Park, PA: The Pennsylvania State University Press, 2006), pp. 218–35.

Boyd, J. P., 'John Sergeant's Mission to Europe for the Second Bank of the United States: 1816–1817', *Pennsylvania Magazine of History and Biography*, 58:3 (1934), pp. 213–31.

Boyer, G. R., *An Economic History of the English Poor Law, 1750–1850* (Cambridge: Cambridge University Press, 1990).

Browne, G. L., 'Baltimore and the Panic of 1819' in A. C. Land, L. G. Carr and E. C. Papenfuse (eds), *Law, Society and Politics in Early Maryland* (Baltimore, MD: Johns Hopkins University Press, 1976), pp. 212–27.

—, *Baltimore in the Nation, 1789–1861* (Chapel Hill: University of North Carolina Press, 1980).

Bruce, K., *Virginia Iron Manufacture in the Slave Era* (New York: Century, 1931).

Bruchy, S. W., *Robert Oliver, Merchant of Baltimore* (Baltimore, MD: Johns Hopkins Press, 1956).

Buck, N. S. *Development and Organization of Anglo-American Trade, 1800–1850* (New Haven, CT: Yale University Press, 1925).

Burns, A. F., and W. C. Mitchell, *Measuring Business Cycles* (New York: National Bureau of Economic Research, 1946).

Calomiris, C. W., and G. Groton, 'The Origins of Banking Panics: Models, Facts, and Bank Regulation', in R. G. Hubbard (ed.), *Financial Markets and Financial Crises* (Chicago, IL: University of Chicago Press, 1991), pp. 109–73.

Calomiris, C. W., and C. Hanes, 'Consistent Output Series for the Antebellum and Postbellum Periods: Issues and Preliminary Results', *Journal of Economic History* 54:2 (1993), pp. 409–22.

Catterall, R., *The Second Bank of the United States* (Chicago, IL: University of Chicago Press, 1903).

Cayton, A. R. L., 'The Fragmentation of "A Great Family": The Panic of 1819 and the Rise of a Middling Interest in Boston, 1818–1822', *Journal of the Early Republic*, 2:2 (1982), pp. 143–67.

Ciment, J., 'In Light of Failure: Bankruptcy, Insolvency and Financial Failure in New York City 1770–1860' (Phd dissertation, City University of New York, 1992).

City Directories of the United States, 1860–1901 (Woodbridge, CT: Research Publications, 1983).

Clement, P. F., *Welfare and the Poor in the Nineteenth-Century City: Philadelphia, 1800–1854* (Rutherford, NJ: Fairleigh Dickinson University Press, 1985).

Cocks, E., 'The Malthusian Theory in Pre-Civil War America: The Original Relation to the Universe', *Population Studies*, 20:3 (1967), pp. 343–63.

Cole, A. H., *Wholesale Commodity Prices in the United States 1700–1861* (Cambridge, MA: Harvard University Press, 1935).

Coleman, A. N., and W. K. Hutchinson, 'Trade Restrictions and Factor Prices: Slave Prices in Early Nineteenth Century US', Department of Economics, Vanderbilt University, Working Paper no. 05–W21 (2005).

Conkin, P. K., *Prophets of Prosperity* (Bloomington: Indiana University Press, 1980).

Craven, A. O., *Soil Exhaustion as a Factor in the Agricultural History of Virginia and Maryland, 1606–1860* (Urbana: University of Illinois Studies in the Social Sciences, vol. 13, no, 1, 1925).

Cray, R. E., Jr, *Paupers and Poor Relief in New York and its Rural Environs, 1700–1830* (Philadelphia, PA: Temple University Press, 1988).

Creech, M., *Three Centuries of Poor Law Administration: A Study of Legislation in Rhode Island* (New York: Columbia University Press, 1936).

Crothers, A. G., 'Banks and Economic Development in Post-Revolutionary Northern Virginia, 1790–1812', *Business History Review*, 73:1 (1999), pp. 1–39.

Dalzell, R. F., Jr., *Enterprising Elites: The Boston Associates and the World They Made* (New York: Norton, 1993).

Dangerfield, G., *The Awakening of American Nationalism, 1815–1828* (New York: Harper and Row, 1965).

—, *The Era of Good Feelings* (New York: Harcourt, Brace, 1952).

Dann, J. C., 'Humanitarian Reform and Organized Benevolence in the Southern United States, 1780–1830' (Phd dissertation, College of William and Mary, 1975).

David, P. A., and P. Solar, 'A Bicentenary Contribution to the History of the Cost of Living in America', *Research in Economic History*, 2 (1977), pp. 1–80.

Davis, J. H., 'An Annual Index of U.S. Industrial Production, 1790–1915', *Quarterly Journal of Economics*, 119:4 (2004), pp. 1177–215.

Day, C., 'The Early Development of the American Cotton Manufacture', *Quarterly Journal of Economics*, 34:3 (1925), pp. 450–68.

DeBow, J. D. B., *Statistical View of the United States ... Being a Compendium of the Seventh Census* (Washington: A. D. P. Nicholson, 1854).

Dewey, D. R., *State Banking Before the Civil War* (Washington: Senate Documents, 1909–10).

Deyle, S., *Carry Me Back: The Domestic Slave Trade in American Life* (New York: Oxford University Press, 2005).

Dimand, R. W., 'Irving Fisher's Debt-Deflation Theory of Great Depressions', *Journal of Social Economy*, 52:1 (1994), pp. 92–107.

Doerflinger, T. M., *A Vigorous Spirit of Enterprise: Merchants and Economic Development in Revolutionary Philadelphia* (Chapel Hill: Published for the Institute of Early American History and Culture by the University of North Carolina Press, 1986).

Dorfman, J., *The Economic Mind in American Civilization* (New York: The Viking Press, 1946).

Dorsey, D. B., 'The Panic of 1819 in Missouri', *Missouri Historical Review* 29:2 (1935), pp. 79–91.

Duffy, I. P. H., *Bankruptcy and Insolvency in London during the Industrial Revolution* (New York: Garland, 1985).

Dunne, T., M. J. Roberts, and L. Samuelson, 'Patterns of Firm Entry and Exit in U. S. Manufacturing Industries', *RAND Journal of Economics*,19:4 (1988), pp. 257–77.

Dupre, D. S., 'The Panic of 1819 and the Political Economy of Sectionalism', in C. Matson (ed.), *The Economy of Early America: Historical Perspectives and New Directions* (University Park, PA: The Pennsylvania State University Press, 2006), pp. 263–93.

—, *Transforming the Cotton Frontier: Madison County, Alabama 1800–1840* (Baton Rouge: Louisiana State University Press, 1997).

'The Economy of British North America', *William and Mary Quarterly*, 56:1 (1999).

Ely, J. W. Jr, '"There are Few Subjects in Political Economy of Greater Difficulty": The Poor Laws of the Antebellum South', *American Bar Foundation Research Journal*, 10:4 (1985), pp. 849–79.

Evans, G.H., *Business Incorporations in the United States, 1800–1943* (New York: National Bureau of Economic Research, 1948).

Ewing, B. T., 'Price Transmission in the Antebellum Slave Markets: A Time Series Analysis', *Review of Regional Studies*, 32:2 (2002), pp. 275–92.

Fenstermaker, J. van, *The Development of American Commercial Banking, 1782–1837* (Kent, OH: Kent State University, 1965).

—, *A Statistical Summary of the Commercial Banks Incorporated in the United States Prior to 1819* (Kent, OH: Kent State University Press, 1965).

Fenstermaker, J. van, J. E. Files and R. S. Herren, 'Monetary Statistics of New England, 1785–1837', *Journal of Economic History*, 44:4 (1984), pp. 441–54.

—, 'The U.S. Embargo Act of 1807: Its Impact on New England Money, Banking, and Economic Activity', *Economic Enquiry*, 28:1 (1990), pp. 163–84.

Ferguson, E. J., *The Power of the Purse: A History of American Public Finance, 1776–1790* (Chapel Hill: University of North Carolina Press, 1961).

Fisher, I., *Booms and Depressions* (New York: Adephia, 1932).

—, 'The Debt-Deflation Theory of Great Depressions', *Econometrica*, 1:4 (1933), pp. 337–57.

Folz, W. E., 'The Financial Crisis of 1819: A Study in Post-War Economic Readjustment' (Phd dissertation, University of Illinois, 1935).

Frankel, J., 'The 1807–1809 Embargo Against Great Britain', *Journal of Economic History*, 42:2 (1982), pp. 291–308.

Fraas, A., 'The Second Bank of the United States: An Instrument for an Integrated Monetary Union', *Journal of Economic History*, 34:2 (1974), pp. 447–67.

Freehling, A. G., *Drift Toward Dissolution: The Virginia Slavery Debate of 1831–1832* (Baton Rouge: Louisiana State University Press, 1982).

Freyer, T. A., *Producers Verses Capitalist: Constitutional Conflict in Antebellum America* (Charlottesville: University Press of Virginia, 1994).

Freidman, M., and A. J. Schwartz, *A Monetary History of the United States, 1867–1960* (Princeton, NJ: Princeton University Press, 1963).

—, *The Great Contraction 1929–1933* (Princeton, NJ: Princeton University Press, 1965).

Freudenberger, H., and J. B. Pritchett, 'The Domestic United States Slave Trade: New Evidence', *Journal of Interdisciplinary History*, 21:3 (1991), pp. 447–77.

Galbraith, J. K., *The Great Crash* (Boston, MA: Houghton Mifflin, 1972).

Gallman, R. E., 'American Economic Growth before the Civil War; the Testimony of the Capital Stock Estimates', in R. E. Gallman and T. Weiss (eds), *American Economic Growth and Standards of Living Before the Civil War* (Chicago IL: University of Chicago Press, National Bureau of Economic Research, 1992), pp. 19–75.

Gayer, A. D., W. W. Rostow, and A. J. Schwartz, *The Growth and Fluctuation of the British Economy 1790–1830* (Oxford: Clarendon, 1953).

Gilmore, W. J., *Reading Becomes a Necessity of Life: Material and Cultural Life in Rural New England, 1780–1835* (Knoxville: University of Tennessee Press, 1989).

Glasner, D. (ed.), *Business Cycles and Depression: An Encyclopedia* (Chicago, IL: University of Chicago Press, 1997).

Goldin, C., and F. Lewis, 'The Role of Exports in American Economic Growth during the Napoleonic Wars, 1793–1807', *Explorations in Economic History*, 17:1 (1980), pp. 6–25.

Goodrich, C., 'The Virginia System of Mixed Enterprise', *Political Science Quarterly*, 64:3 (1949), pp. 355–87.

—, *Canals and American Economic Development* (New York: Columbia University Press, 1961).

Gray, L. C., *History of Agriculture in the Southern United States to 1860* (Washington: Carnegie Institution, 1933).

Greer, T. H., 'Economic and Social Effects of the Depression of 1819 in the Old Northwest', *Indiana Magazine of History*, 44:3 (1948), pp. 227–43.

Gruchy, A. G., *Supervision and Control of Virginia State Banks* (New York: Appleton-Century, 1937).

Gunn, L. R., *The Decline of Authority: Public Economic Policy and Political Development in New York State, 1800–1860* (Ithaca, NY: Cornell University Press, 1988).

Hall, T. E., and D. J. Ferguson, *The Great Depression: An International Disaster of Perverse Economic Policies* (Ann Arbor: University of Michigan Press, 1998).

Hammond, B., *Banks and Politics in America from the Revolution to the Civil War* (Princeton, NJ: Princeton University Press, 1957).

Hannon, J. U., 'Explaining Nineteenth Century Dependency Rates: Interplay of Life Cycles and Labor Markets', unpublished paper, Department of Economics, St Mary's College, 1996.

—, 'The Generosity of Antebellum Poor Relief', *Journal of Economic History*, 44:3 (1984), pp. 810–21.

—, 'Poor Relief Policy in Antebellum New York State: The Rise and Decline of the Poorhouse', *Explorations in Economic History*, 22:3 (1985), pp. 233–56.

Harley, C K., 'Ocean Freight Rates and Productivity, 1740–1913: The Primacy of Mechanical Inventions Reaffirmed', *Journal of Economic History*, 48:4 (1988), pp. 851–76.

Harris, P. G. M., 'Inflation and Deflation in Early America, 1634–1860', *Social Science History*, 20:4 (1996), pp. 469–505.

Hibbard, B. H., *A History of the Public Land Policies* (New York: Macmillan, 1924).

Hibbard, W. (comp), *Statistical History of Virginia Coalmining: 241 Years of Data from 1748 to 1988* (Blacksburg, VA: VPI & SU, 1989).

Hidy, R. W., *The House of Baring in American Trade and Finance* (Cambridge, MA: Harvard University Press, 1949).

Himmelfarb, G., *The Idea of Poverty: England in the Early Industrial Age* (New York: Vintage, 1983).

Holmes, T. J., and J. A. Schmitz, Jr., 'On the Turnover of Business Firms and Business Managers', *Journal of Political Economy*, 103:5 (1995), pp. 1005–38.

Huston, J. L., 'Virtue Besieged: Virtue, Equality and the General Welfare in the Tariff Debates of the 1820s', *Journal of the Early Republic*, 14:4 (1994), pp. 523–47.

Hutchinson, R. G., A. R. Hutchinson and M. Newcomer, 'A Study in Business Mortality – Length of Life of Business Enterprises in Poughkeepsie, N.Y. 1843–1936', *American Economic Review*, 28:3 (September 1938), pp. 497–514.

—, 'Business Life and Death in a Hudson River Town', *Dun's Review* (June 1939), pp. 12–18.

Irish, E., '"Neglect, Delay, and Tightfistedness:" Poor Relief in Antebellum Richmond', unpublished.

James, J., 'Changes in Economic Instability in 19th-Century America', *American Economic Review* 83:4 (1994), pp. 117–34.

Kagin, D. H., 'Monetary Aspects of the Treasury Notes of the War of 1812', *Journal of Economic History*, 44:4 (1984), pp. 69–88.

Kaplan, A. D. H., *Small Business: Its Place and Problems* (New York: McGraw-Hill, 1948).

Karmel, J. R., 'Banking on the People: Banks, Politics, and Market Evolution in Early National Pennsylvania, 1781–1824' (Phd dissertation, State University of New York at Buffalo, 1999).

Kidd, S. A., 'The Search for Moral Order: The Panic of 1819 and the Culture of the Early American Republic' (Phd dissertation, University of Missouri-Columbia, 2002).

Kiesling, L. L., and R. A. Margo, 'Explaining the Rise in Antebellum Pauperism: New Evidence' (National Bureau of Economic Research Working Papers Series on Historical Factors in Long Run Growth, Historical Paper 92, 1996).

—, 'Explaining the Rise in Antebellum Pauperism, 1850–1860: New Evidence', *Quarterly Review of Economics and Finance*, 37:2 (1997), pp. 405–17.

Kindleberger, C. P., *Manias, Panics, and Crashes: A History of Financial Crises* (New York: Basic Books, 1978).

Klebaner, B. J., *Public Poor Relief in America, 1790–1860* (New York: Arno, 1976).

Knights, P. R., 'City Directories as Aids to Antebellum Urban Studies: A Research Note', *Historical Methods Newsletter*, 2:4 (1969), pp. 1–10.

—, *The Plain People of Boston, 1820–1860: A Study in City Growth* (New York: Oxford University Press, 1971).

Komlos, J., *The Hapsburg Monarchy as a Customs Union: Economic Development in Austria-Hungary in the Nineteenth Century* (Princeton, NJ: Princeton University Press, 1983).

Kotlikoff, L., 'The Structure of Slave Prices in New Orleans, 1804–1862', *Economic Inquiry*, 17:4 (1979), pp. 496–518.

Kotlikoff, L., and S. Pinera, 'The Old South's Stake in the Inter-Regional Movement of Slaves, 1850–1860', *Journal of Economic History*, 37:2 (1977), pp. 434–50.

Lamoreaux, N. R., 'The Partnership Form of Organization: Its Popularity in Early-Nineteenth-Century Boston', in C. E. Wright and K. P. Viens (eds), *Entrepreneurs: The Boston Business Community, 1700–1850* (Boston: Massachusetts Historical Society distributed by Northeastern University Press, 1997), pp. 269–95.

Larson, J. L., *Internal Improvement: National Public Works and the Promise of Popular Government in the Early Republic* (Chapel Hill: University of North Carolina Press, 2001).

Lebsock, S., *The Free Women of Petersburg: Status and Culture in a Southern Town, 1784–1860* (New York: Norton: 1984).

Lehman, D., 'Explaining Hard Times: Political Economy and the Panic of 1819 in Philadelphia' (Phd Dissertation, University of California, Los Angles, 1992).

Little, J. P., *History of Richmond* (Richmond, VA: Dietz, 1923).

Luckett, T. M., 'Credit and Commercial Society in France, 1740–1789' (Phd dissertation, Princeton University, 1992).

McCartney, M. W., 'Virginia's Workhouses for the Poor: Care for "Divers Idle and Disorderly Persons"', *North American Archaeologist*, 8:4 (1987), pp. 287–303.

McCulloch, J. R., *A Dictionary of Commerce and Commerical Navigation*, ed. Henry Vathake, 2 vols (Philadelphia, PA: Thomas Wardle, 1841).

McFaul, J. M., *The Politics of Jacksonian Finance* (Ithaca, NY: Cornell University Press, 1972).

MacGregor, J., *A Dictionary of Commerce and Commercial Navigation*, ed. H. Vethake, 2 vols (Philadelphia, PA: Thomas Wardle, 1841).

—, *Commercial Statistics*, 2nd edn, 5 vols (London: Whittaker and Co., 1850).

Mackey, H., 'The Operation of the English Old Poor Law in Colonial Virginia', *Virginia Magazine of History and Biography*, 73:1 (1965), pp. 29–40.

Majewski, J., 'The Social Origins of the Market Revolution: Markets and Politics in Pennsylvania and Virginia, 1790–1860' (Phd dissertation, University of California, Los Angles, 1998).

—, *A House Dividing: Economic Development in Pennsylvania and Virginia Before the Civil War* (Cambridge: Cambridge University Press, 2000).

Marco, L., 'Faillites et Crisis Economiques en France au XIXe Siecle', *Annels E.S.C.*, 2:2 (1989), pp. 355–78.

Matson, C., 'A House of Many Mansions: Some Thoughts on the Field of Economic History', in C. Matson (ed.), *The Economy of Early America: Historical Perspectives and New Directions* (University Park, PA: The Pennsylvania State University Press, 2006), pp. 1–70.

Matthews, J. V., *Toward A New Society: American Thought and Culture 1800–1830* (Boston, MA: Twayne, 1991).

Miller, F. T., 'The Richmond Junto: The Secret All-Powerful Club – or Myth', *Virginia Magazine of History and Biography*, 99:1 (1991), pp. 63–80.

Mishkin, F. S., 'Asymmetric Information and Financial Crises: A Historical Perspective' in R. G. Hubbard (ed.), *Financial Markets and Financial Crises* (Chicago, IL: University of Chicago Press, 1991), pp. 69–108.

Mitchell, B. R., *Abstract of British Historical Statistics* (Cambridge: Cambridge University Press, 1971).

—, *European Historical Statistics, 1750–1970* (London: Macmillan, 1975).

Mohl, R., *Poverty in New York* (New York: Oxford University Press, 1970).

Moore, G., *The Missouri Controversy, 1819–1821* (Lexington: University of Kentucky Press, 1953).

Murray, G. S., 'Poverty and its Relief in the Antebellum South: Perceptions and Realities in Three Selected Cities Charleston, Nashville, and New Orleans' (Phd dissertation, Memphis State University, 1991).

North, D. C, *The Economic Growth of the United States, 1790–1860* (New York: Norton, 1966).

—, 'Ocean Freight Rates and Economic Development, 1750–1913', *Journal of Economic History*, 18:4 (1958), pp. 537–55.

Papenfuse, E. C., *In Pursuit of Profit: The Annapolis Merchants in the Era of the American Revolution, 1763–1805* (Baltimore, MD: Johns Hopkins University Press, 1975).

Parks, J. H., 'Felix Grundy and the Depression of 1819 in Tennessee', *Publication of the East Tennessee Historical Society*, 10 (1938), pp. 19–42.

Passell, P., and G. Wright, 'The Effects of Pre-Civil War Territorial Expansion on the Prices of Slaves', *Journal of Political Economy*, 80:6 (1972), pp. 1188–202.

Perkins, E. J., *American Public Finance and Financial Services, 1700–1815* (Columbus, OH: Ohio State University Press, 1994).

—, 'Langdon Cheves and the Panic of 1819: A Reassessment', *Journal of Economic History*, 44:2 (1983), pp. 455–61.

Phillips, U. B., *American Negro Slavery: A Survey of the Supply, Employment and Control of Negro Labor as Determined by the Plantation Regime* (Baton Rouge: Louisiana State University Press, 1966).

Piccarello, L. J., 'Social Structures and Public Welfare Policy in Danvers, MA 1750–1850', *Essex Institute Historical Collection*, 118:4 (1982), pp. 248–63.

Pitkin, T., *A Statistical View of the Commerce of the United States of America* (New Haven, CT: Durrie and Peck, 1835).

Popkin, J., and Company, 'Business Survival Rates by Age Cohorts of Business' (United States Small Business Administration, RS Number 122, 1989).

Porter, G., and H. Livesay, *Merchants and Manufacturers* (Baltimore, MD: Johns Hopkins University Press, 1971).

Post, J. D. *The Last Substance Crisis in the Western World* (Baltimore, MD: Johns Hopkins University Press, 1977).

Poynter, J. R. *Society and Pauperism: English Ideas on Poor Relief, 1795–1834* (London: Routledge and Kagan Paul, 1969).

Pritchett, J. B., 'Quantitative Estimates of the United States Interregional Slave Trade, 1820–1860', *Journal of Economic History*, 61:2 (2001), pp. 467–75.

Pritchett, J. B, and R. M. Chamberlain, 'Selection in the Market for Slaves, New Orleans, 1830–1860', *Quarterly Journal of Economics*, 108:2 (1993), pp. 461–73.

Pritchett, J. B, and H. Freudenberger, 'A Peculiar Sample: The Selection of Slaves for the New Orleans Market', *Journal of Economic History*, 52:1 (1992), pp. 109–27.

Remini, R. V., *Andrew Jackson and the Bank War* (New York: Norton, 1967).

Rezneck, S., 'The Depression of 1819–1822, A Social History', *American Historical Review*, 39:1 (1933), pp. 28–47.

Ricardo, D., *Minor Papers on the Currency Question, 1809–1823*, ed. J. H. Hollander, (Baltimore, MD: Johns Hopkins Press, 1932).

Robert, J. C., *The Tobacco Kingdom* (Durham, NC: Duke University Press, 1938).

Robbins, R. M., *Our Landed Heritage: The Public Domain 1776–1936* (Princeton, NJ: Princeton University Press, 1942).

Rockman, S., *Welfare Reform in the Early Republic: A Brief History with Documents* (Boston, MA: Bedford/St Martins, 2003).

Rohrbough, M. J., *The Land Office Business: The Settlement and Administration of American Public Lands, 1789–1837* (New York: Oxford University Press, 1968).

Romer, C. D., 'The Prewar Business Cycle Reconsidered: New Estimates of GNP 1869–1908', *Journal of Political Economy*, 97:1 (1989), pp. 1–37.

—, 'Remeasuring Business Cycles', *Journal of Economic History*, 54:3 (1994), pp. 573–609.

Rothbard, M., *The Panic of 1819: Reactions and Policies* (New York: Columbia University Press, 1962).

—, 'A Price Index for Rural Massachusetts, 1750–1855', *Journal of Economic History*, 39:4 (1979), pp. 975–1001.

—, 'The Invention of New England Capitalism: The Economy of New England in the Federal Period', in P. Temin (ed.), *Engines of Enterprise* (Cambridge, MA: Harvard University Press, 2000), pp. 96–106.

Rothman, D. J. (ed.), *The Almshouse Experience: Collected Reports* (New York: Arno Press, 1971).

—, *The Discovery of the Asylum: Social Order and Disorder in the New Republic* (Boston, MA: Little, Brown and Company, 1971).

Royall, W. L., *A History of Virginia Banks and Banking Prior to the Civil War* (New York and Washington: Neale, 1907).

Saunders, R. M., 'Modernization and the Political Process: Governmental Principles and Practices in Richmond, Virginia, from the Revolution to the Civil War', *Southern Studies*, 24 (1985), pp. 117–42.

Schur, L. M., 'The Second Bank of the United States and the Inflation after the War of 1812', *Journal of Political Economy*, 68:2 (1960), pp. 118–34.

Schweikart, L., *Banking in the American South from the Age of Jackson to Reconstruction* (Baton Rouge: Louisiana State University Press, 1987).

—, 'Private Bankers in the Antebellum South', *Southern Studies*, 25:2 (1986), pp. 125–34.

Schweitzer, M., 'State-Issued Currency and the Ratification of the U.S. Constitution', *Journal of Economic History*, 49:2 (1989), pp. 311–22.

Sears, L. M., 'Philadelphia and the Embargo of 1807', *Quarterly Journal of Economics*, 35:2 (1921), pp. 354–9.

Sellers, C., *The Market Revolution: Jacksonian America, 1815–1846* (New York: Oxford University Press, 1991).

Shade, W. D., *Democratizing the Old Dominion: Virginia and the Second Party System* (Charlottesville: University Press of Virginia, 1996).

Smith, W. B., *Economic Aspects of the Second Bank of the United States* (Cambridge, MA: Harvard University Press, 1953).

Smith, W. B., and A. H. Cole, *Fluctuations in American Business, 1790–1860* (Cambridge, MA: Harvard University Press, 1935).

Spears, D. N., *Biography of American Directories through 1860* (Worcester, MA: American Antiquarian Society, 1961).

Stanard, M. N., *Richmond: Its People and Its Story* (Philadelphia, PA: Lippincott, 1923).

Stanwood, E., *American Tariff Controversies in the Nineteenth Century* (Boston, MA: Houghton Mifflin, 1903).

Starnes, G. T., *Sixty Years of Branch Banking In Virginia* (New York: Macmillan, 1931).

Starr, G. W., and G. A. Steiner, 'Births and Deaths of Retail Stores in Indiana, 1929–1937', *Dun's Review*, 48 (January 1940), p. 27.

Steckel, R. H., 'Census Manuscript Schedules Matched with Property Tax Lists: A Source of Information on Long-Term Trends in Wealth Inequality', *Historical Methods*, 27 (1994), pp. 71–85.

Steeples, D., and D. O. Whitten, *Democracy in Desperation: The Depression of 1893* (Westport, CT: Greenwood, 1998).

Studenski, P., and H. E. Kross, *Financial History of the United States* (New York: McGraw-Hill, 1963).

Sydnor, C. S., *The Development of Southern Sectionalism, 1819–1848* (Baton Rouge: Louisiana State University Press, 1946).

Sylla, R., 'Forgotten Men of Money: Private Bankers in Early U. S. History', and discussion by Lance E. Davis, *Journal of Economic History*, 36:1 (1976), pp. 173–97.

Tarter, B., 'The New Virginia Bookshelf', *Virginia Magazine of History and Biography*, 104:1 (1996), p. 42.

Taussig, F., *Tariff History of the United States* (New York: Kelly, 1967, reprint of 8th edn, 1931).

Taylor, G. R., *The Transportation Revolution, 1815–1860* (New York: Holt, Rinehart and Winston, 1951).

—, 'Wholesale Commodity Prices at Charleston, South Carolina, 1796–1861', *Journal of Economic and Business History*, 4:4 (1932), pp. 848–76.

Temin, P., *Did Monetary Forces Cause the Great Depression* (New York: W. W. Norton, 1976).

— (ed.), *Engines of Enterprise* (Cambridge, MA: Harvard University Press, 2000).

—, *The Jacksonian Economy* (New York: Norton, 1969).

—, *Lessons From the Great Depression* (Cambridge: MIT Press, 1989).

Thorp, W. L., *Business Annals* (New York: National Bureau of Economic Research, 1926).

Thorp, W. L., and W C. Mitchell. *Business Annals* (New York: National Bureau of Economic Research, 1926).

Tooke, T., *A History of Prices and of the Circulation from 1792 to 1856*, reproduced from the original, with an introduction by T. Gregory (New York: Aldephi, 1928).

Tooker, E., *Nathan Trotter: Philadelphia Merchant, 1787–1853* (Cambridge, MA: Harvard University Press, 1955).

Tucker, G., *Progress of the United States in Population and Wealth in Fifty Years* (Boston, MA: Little and Brown, 1843).

Tyler, J. W., 'Persistence and Change within the Boston Business Community', in C. E. Wright and K. P. Viens (eds), *Entrepreneurs: The Boston Business Community, 1700–1850* (Boston, MA: Massachusetts Historical Society distributed by Northeastern University Press, 1997), pp. 97–119.

Usry, R. M., 'The Overseers of the Poor in Accomac, Pittsylvania, and Rockingham Counties, 1787–1802' (MA thesis, Department of Economics, College of William and Mary, 1960).

Vogt, D. C., 'Poor Relief in Frontier Mississippi', *Journal of Mississippi History*, 51:2 (1989), pp. 181–99.

Watkinson, J. D., '"Fit Objects of Charity": Community, Race, Faith, and Welfare in Antebellum Lancaster County, Virginia, 1817–1860', *Journal of the Early Republic*, 21:1 (2001), pp. 41–70.

Weber, W. E., 'Early State Banks in the United States: How Many Were There and When Did They Exist?', *Journal of Economic History*, 66:2 (2006), pp. 433–55.

Weiss, T., 'U.S. Labour Force Estimates and Economic Growth, 1800–1840', in R. E. Gallman and T. Weiss (eds), *American Economic Growth and Standards of Living*

Before the Civil War (Chicago, IL: University of Chicago Press, National Bureau of Economic Research, 1992), pp. 79–115.

Wertenbaker, T. J., *Norfolk: Historic Southern Port* (Durham, NC: Duke University Press, 1931).

Wilentz, S., *Chants Democratic: New York City and the Rise of the American Working Class, 1788–1850* (New York: Oxford University Press, 1984).

—, *The Rise of American Democracy: Jefferson to Lincoln* (New York: Norton, 2005).

Wilkins, M., *History of Foreign Investment in the United States to 1914* (Cambridge, MA: Harvard University Press, 1989).

Wolfson, M. H., 'Irving Fisher's Debt-Deflation Theory: Its Relevance to Current Conditions', *Cambridge Journal of Economics*, 20:3 (1996), pp. 315–33.

Womack, R. D., *An Analysis of the Credit Controls of the Second Bank of the United States* (New York: Arno Press, 1978).

Wright, R. E., *Origins of Commercial Banking in America, 1750–1800* (Lanham, MD: Rowman and Littlefield, 2001).

INDEX

For Product Safety Concerns and Information please contact our EU
representative GPSR@taylorandfrancis.com
Taylor & Francis Verlag GmbH, Kaufingerstraße 24, 80331 München, Germany

www.ingramcontent.com/pod-product-compliance
Ingram Content Group UK Ltd.
Pitfield, Milton Keynes, MK11 3LW, UK
UKHW021633240425

457818UK00018BA/378